Y0-DKL-902

SUPER HOROSCOPE

VIRGO

20 00

August 22 - September 22

BERKLEY BOOKS, NEW YORK

The publishers regret that they cannot answer
individual letters requesting personal horoscope information.

2000 SUPER HOROSCOPE VIRGO

PRINTING HISTORY
Berkley Trade Edition / August 1999

The Penguin Putnam Inc. World Wide Web site address is
http://www.penguinputnam.com

ISBN: 0-425-16883-2

BERKLEY®
Berkley Books are published by The Berkley Publishing Group,
a division of Penguin Putnam Inc.,
375 Hudson Street, New York, New York 10014.
"BERKLEY" and the "B" logo
are trademarks belonging to Penguin Putnam Inc.

PRINTED IN THE UNITED STATES OF AMERICA

10 9 8 7 6 5 4 3 2 1

CONTENTS

THE CUSP-BORN VIRGO

Are you *really* a Virgo? If your birthday falls during the fourth week of August, at the beginning of Virgo, will you still retain the traits of Leo, the sign of the Zodiac before Virgo? And what if you were born late in September—are you more Libra than Virgo? Many people born at the edge, or cusp, of a sign have great difficulty determining exactly what sign they are. If you are one of these people, here's how you can figure it out, once and for all.

Consult the cusp table on the facing page, then locate the year of your birth. The table will tell you the precise days on which the Sun entered and left your sign for the year of your birth. In that way you can determine if you are a true Virgo—or whether you are a Leo or Libra—according to the variations in cusp dates from year to year (see also page 17).

If you were born either at the beginning or the end of Virgo, yours is a lifetime reflecting a process of subtle transformation. Your life on earth will symbolize a significant change in consciousness, for you are either about to enter a whole new way of living or are leaving one behind.

If you were born at the beginning of Virgo, you may want to read the horoscope book for Leo as well as Virgo, for Leo holds the key to much of your complexity of spirit, reflects certain hidden weaknesses and compulsions, and your unspoken wishes. Your tie to Leo symbolizes your romantic dilemma and your unusual—often timid—approach to love. You are afraid of taking a gamble and letting everything ride on your emotions. You may resist giving up the rational, logical, clear-minded approach to life, but you can never really flee from your need for love.

You symbolize the warmth and fullness of a late summer day, a natural ripeness and maturity that is mellow and comfortable to be near.

If you were born sometime after the third week of September, you may want to read the horoscope book for Libra as well as Virgo, for Libra is possibly your greatest asset. Though you are eager to get involved with another person and you crave warmth and companionship, you may hover between stiff mental analyzing and poetic romanticism. You have that Garboesque desire to be secluded, untouched—yet you want to share your life with another. You are a blend of monastic, spartan simplicity with grace,

4

harmony, and gentle beauty. You combine a profound power to sift, purify, and analyze with the sensibilities of recognizing what is right, beautiful, and just. You can be picky and faultfinding, inconsistent and small, needing someone desperately but rejecting the one you love most. Yet you are fundamentally a thoughtful, loving person with the sincere wish to serve and make someone happy.

Developing your capacity to share will aid you in joint financial ventures, bring your values into harmony, and create a balance in your life.

THE CUSPS OF VIRGO

DATES SUN ENTERS VIRGO (LEAVES LEO)

August 23 every year from 1900 to 2000, except for the following:

August 22				August 24
1960	1980	1992	1903	1919
64	84	93	07	23
68	88	96	11	27
72	89	97	15	
76			2000	

DATES SUN LEAVES VIRGO (ENTERS LIBRA)

September 23 every year from 1900 to 2000, except for the following:

September 22				September 24
1948	1968	1981	1992	1903
52	72	84	93	07
56	76	85	96	
60	77	88	97	
64	80	89	2000	

THE ASCENDANT: VIRGO RISING

Could you be a "double" Virgo? That is, could you have Virgo as your Rising sign as well as your Sun sign? The tables on pages 8–9 will tell you Virgos what your Rising sign happens to be. Just find the hour of your birth, then find the day of your birth, and you will see which sign of the Zodiac is your Ascendant, as the Rising sign is called. The Ascendant is called that because it is the sign rising on the eastern horizon at the time of your birth. For a more detailed discussion of the Rising sign and the twelve houses of the Zodiac, see pages 17–20.

The Ascendant, or Rising sign, is placed on the 1st house in a horoscope, of which there are twelve houses. The first house represents your response to the environment—your unique response. Call it identity, personality, ego, self-image, facade, come-on, body-mind-spirit—whatever term best conveys to you the meaning of the you that acts and reacts in the world. It is a you that is always changing, discovering a new you. Your identity started with birth and early environment, over which you had little conscious control, and continues to experience, to adjust, to express itself. The 1st house also represents how others see you. Has anyone ever guessed your sign to be your Rising sign? People may respond to that personality, that facade, that body type governed by your Rising sign.

Your Ascendant, or Rising sign, modifies your basic Sun sign personality, and it affects the way you act out the daily predictions for your Sun sign. If your Rising sign is indeed Virgo, what follows is a description of its effects on your horoscope. If your Rising sign is not Virgo, but some other sign of the Zodiac, you may wish to read the horoscope book for that sign as well.

With Virgo on the Ascendant, that is, in the 1st house, your ruling planet Mercury is therefore in the 1st house. You are known for your inquiring mind, sharp verbal skills, love of learning. Your very appearance—fastidious, lean, efficient—gives the impression of a great openness to the environment; you seem to pick up clues from the most cursory observations, filing them away for future use. Mercury in the 1st house, however, can make you too self-absorbed with your own interests and thus lacking in sympathy for other people. And your quick wit and loquaciousness, if put into the service of petty gossip, could make you a tattletale who gets in trouble with people.

Your striving for perfection and your liking for details make many of you with Virgo Rising master craftspeople. That talent is not restricted to the arts of fashioning jewelry, fabric, metals, food, and other materials of the earth, though you are an earth sign. Mercury, your ruler, gives you a quicksilver mind, and you excel in the mathematical and scientific arts. Your memory is splendid, too. If you are not actually working in complex systems such as computer science or engineering, your talent for organizing details and structuring information certainly benefits your work life, as well as your social life.

Your love of learning has few boundaries, and no limits if you with Virgo Rising consistently apply yourself. You are equally attracted to medicine, art, science, literature. Your analytical mind, scalpel-sharp, can cut through a mass of confused information, selecting the wheat from the chaff, so to speak. Certainly you can distinguish theory from practice, and you know when and how to use the practice. Many of you, for that reason, and also because you like to help people, find yourselves in health and medical service careers.

Personally you are interested in the perfection of the body and the purity of the mind. Translated into everyday activities, you could be very fussy about your diet, your clothes, your living quarters, your spiritual beliefs, your exercise programs. It is not unlikely that you experiment often in these areas, and sometimes you're accused of being a faddist. If you cannot change where you live frequently, you'll be satisfied to take a few long trips and many short ones during your lifetime.

Basically you are patient, methodical, ambitious sometimes in a secretive way. Your caustic wit, which strips the facade from people, hides your true feelings and melancholy of spirit. As much as you like to quip in bright dialogue with others, you like to be alone. Even your travels can be solitary adventures; you commune with the nature around you. Some of these experiences may motivate an in-depth study of art and literature at some point in your lifetime. And you may well become a writer, merging a myriad of facts with personal data you are loathe to talk about.

For you with Virgo Rising, two key words are self-mastery and service. But while you are perfecting your knowledge and skills in serving others, don't forget your own needs. Develop compassion for yourself.

RISING SIGNS FOR VIRGO

Hour of Birth*	Day of Birth		
	August 22–26	**August 27–31**	**September 1–5**
Midnight	Gemini	Gemini	Cancer
1 AM	Cancer	Cancer	Cancer
2 AM	Cancer	Cancer	Cancer
3 AM	Leo	Leo	Leo
4 AM	Leo	Leo	Leo
5 AM	Leo	Leo; Virgo 8/31	Virgo
6 AM	Virgo	Virgo	Virgo
7 AM	Virgo	Virgo	Virgo
8 AM	Libra	Libra	Libra
9 AM	Libra	Libra	Libra
10 AM	Libra	Libra; Scorpio 8/29	Scorpio
11 AM	Scorpio	Scorpio	Scorpio
Noon	Scorpio	Scorpio	Scorpio
1 PM	Sagittarius	Sagittarius	Sagittarius
2 PM	Sagittarius	Sagittarius	Sagittarius
3 PM	Sagittarius	Capricorn	Capricorn
4 PM	Capricorn	Capricorn	Capricorn
5 PM	Capricorn; Aquarius 8/26	Aquarius	Aquarius
6 PM	Aquarius	Aquarius	Aquarius; Pisces 9/3
7 PM	Pisces	Pisces	Pisces
8 PM	Aries	Aries	Aries
9 PM	Aries; Taurus 8/26	Taurus	Taurus
10 PM	Taurus	Taurus	Taurus; Gemini 9/3
11 PM	Gemini	Gemini	Gemini

*Hour of birth given here is for Standard Time in any time zone. If your hour of birth was recorded in Daylight Saving Time, subtract one hour from it and consult that hour in the table above. For example, if you were born at 7 PM D.S.T., see 6 PM above.

Hour of Birth*	Day of Birth		
	September 6–10	September 11–15	September 16–24
Midnight	Cancer	Cancer	Cancer
1 AM	Cancer	Cancer	Cancer; Leo 9/21
2 AM	Leo	Leo	Leo
3 AM	Leo	Leo	Leo
4 AM	Leo	Leo; Virgo 9/14	Virgo
5 AM	Virgo	Virgo	Virgo
6 AM	Virgo	Virgo	Virgo; Libra 9/21
7 AM	Libra	Libra	Libra
8 AM	Libra	Libra	Libra
9 AM	Libra	Scorpio	Scorpio
10 AM	Scorpio	Scorpio	Scorpio
11 AM	Scorpio	Scorpio	Scorpio; Sagittarius 9/21
Noon	Sagittarius	Sagittarius	Sagittarius
1 PM	Sagittarius	Sagittarius	Sagittarius
2 PM	Sagittarius	Capricorn	Capricorn
3 PM	Capricorn	Capricorn	Capricorn
4 PM	Capricorn; Aquarius 9/10	Aquarius	Aquarius
5 PM	Aquarius	Aquarius	Pisces
6 PM	Pisces	Pisces	Pisces; Aries 9/21
7 PM	Aries	Aries	Aries
8 PM	Aries; Taurus 9/10	Taurus	Taurus
9 PM	Taurus	Taurus	Gemini
10 PM	Gemini	Gemini	Gemini
11 PM	Gemini	Gemini	Cancer

*See note on facing page.

THE PLACE OF ASTROLOGY IN TODAY'S WORLD

Does astrology have a place in the fast-moving, ultra-scientific world we live in today? Can it be justified in a sophisticated society whose outriders are already preparing to step off the moon into the deep space of the planets themselves? Or is it just a hangover of ancient superstition, a psychological dummy for neurotics and dreamers of every historical age?

These are the kind of questions that any inquiring person can be expected to ask when they approach a subject like astrology which goes beyond, but never excludes, the materialistic side of life.

The simple, single answer is that astrology works. It works for many millions of people in the western world alone. In the United States there are 10 million followers and in Europe, an estimated 25 million. America has more than 4000 practicing astrologers, Europe nearly three times as many. Even down-under Australia has its hundreds of thousands of adherents. In the eastern countries, astrology has enormous followings, again, because it has been proved to work. In India, for example, brides and grooms for centuries have been chosen on the basis of their astrological compatibility.

Astrology today is more vital than ever before, more practicable because all over the world the media devotes much space and time to it, more valid because science itself is confirming the precepts of astrological knowledge with every new exciting step. The ordinary person who daily applies astrology intelligently does not have to wonder whether it is true nor believe in it blindly. He can see it working for himself. And, if he can use it—and this book is designed to help the reader to do just that—he can make living a far richer experience, and become a more developed personality and a better person.

Astrology and Relationships

Astrology is the science of relationships. It is not just a study of planetary influences on man and his environment. It is the study of man himself.

We are at the center of our personal universe, of all our relationships. And our happiness or sadness depends on how we act, how we relate to the people and things that surround us. The emotions that we generate have a distinct effect—for better or worse—on the world around us. Our friends and our enemies will confirm this. Just look in the mirror the next time you are angry. In other words, each of us is a kind of sun or planet or star radiating our feelings on the environment around us. Our influence on our personal universe, whether loving, helpful, or destructive, varies with our changing moods, expressed through our individual character.

Our personal "radiations" are potent in the way they affect our moods and our ability to control them. But we usually are able to throw off our emotion in some sort of action—we have a good cry, walk it off, or tell someone our troubles—before it can build up too far and make us physically ill. Astrology helps us to understand the universal forces working on us, and through this understanding, we can become more properly adjusted to our surroundings so that we find ourselves coping where others may flounder.

The Challenge of Love

The challenge of love lies in recognizing the difference between infatuation, emotion, sex, and, sometimes, the intentional deceit of the other person. Mankind, with its record of broken marriages, despair, and disillusionment, is obviously not very good at making these distinctions.

Can astrology help?

Yes. In the same way that advance knowledge can usually help in any human situation. And there is probably no situation as human, as poignant, as pathetic and universal, as the failure of man's love.

Love, of course, is not just between man and woman. It involves love of children, parents, home, and friends. But the big problems usually involve the choice of partner.

Astrology has established degrees of compatibility that exist between people born under the various signs of the Zodiac. Because people are individuals, there are numerous variations and modifications. So the astrologer, when approached on mate and marriage matters, makes allowances for them. But the fact remains that some groups of people are suited for each other and some are not, and astrology has expressed this in terms of characteristics we all can study and use as a personal guide.

No matter how much enjoyment and pleasure we find in the different aspects of each other's character, if it is not an overall compatibility, the chances of our finding fulfillment or enduring happiness in each other are pretty hopeless. And astrology can help us to find someone compatible.

Astrology and Science

Closely related to our emotions is the "other side" of our personal universe, our physical welfare. Our body, of course, is largely influenced by things around us over which we have very little control. The phone rings, we hear it. The train runs late. We snag our stocking or cut our face shaving. Our body is under a constant bombardment of events that influence our daily lives to varying degrees.

The question that arises from all this is, what makes each of us act so that we have to involve other people and keep the ball of activity and evolution rolling? This is the question that both science and astrology are involved with. The scientists have attacked it from different angles: anthropology, the study of human evolution as body, mind and response to environment; anatomy, the study of bodily structure; psychology, the science of the human mind; and so on. These studies have produced very impressive classifications and valuable information, but because the approach to the problem is fragmented, so is the result. They remain "branches" of science. Science generally studies effects. It keeps turning up wonderful answers but no lasting solutions. Astrology, on the other hand, approaches the question from the broader viewpoint. Astrology began its inquiry with the totality of human experience and saw it as an effect. It then looked to find the cause, or at least the prime movers, and during thousands of years of observation of man and his *universal* environment came up with the extraordinary principle of planetary influence—or astrology, which, from the Greek, means the science of the stars.

Modern science, as we shall see, has confirmed much of astrology's foundations—most of it unintentionally, some of it reluctantly, but still, indisputably.

It is not difficult to imagine that there must be a connection between outer space and Earth. Even today, scientists are not too sure how our Earth was created, but it is generally agreed that it is only a tiny part of the universe. And as a part of the universe, people on Earth see and feel the influence of heavenly bodies in almost every aspect of our existence. There is no doubt that the Sun has the greatest influence on life on this planet. Without it there would be no life, for without it there would be no warmth, no division into day and night, no cycles of time or season at all. This is clear and easy to see. The influence of the Moon, on the other hand, is more subtle, though no less definite.

There are many ways in which the influence of the Moon manifests itself here on Earth, both on human and animal life. It is a well-known fact, for instance, that the large movements of water on our planet—that is the ebb and flow of the tides—are caused by the Moon's gravitational pull. Since this is so, it follows that these water movements do not occur only in the oceans, but that all bodies of water are affected, even down to the tiniest puddle.

The human body, too, which consists of about 70 percent water, falls within the scope of this lunar influence. For example the menstrual cycle of most women corresponds to the 28-day lunar month; the period of pregnancy in humans is 273 days, or equal to nine lunar months. Similarly, many illnesses reach a crisis at the change of the Moon, and statistics in many countries have shown that the crime rate is highest at the time of the Full Moon. Even human sexual desire has been associated with the phases of the Moon. But it is in the movement of the tides that we get the clearest demonstration of planetary influence, which leads to the irresistible correspondence between the so-called metaphysical and the physical.

Tide tables are prepared years in advance by calculating the future positions of the Moon. Science has known for a long time that the Moon is the main cause of tidal action. But only in the last few years has it begun to realize the possible extent of this influence on mankind. To begin with, the ocean tides do not rise and fall as we might imagine from our personal observations of them. The Moon as it orbits around Earth sets up a circular wave of attraction which pulls the oceans of the world after it, broadly in an east to west direction. This influence is like a phantom wave crest, a loop of power stretching from pole to pole which passes over and around the Earth like an invisible shadow. It travels with equal effect across the land masses and, as scientists were recently amazed to observe, caused oysters placed in the dark in the middle of the United States where there is no sea to open their shells to receive the nonexistent tide. If the land-locked oysters react to this invisible signal, what effect does it have on us who not so long ago in evolutionary time came out of the sea and still have its salt in our blood and sweat?

Less well known is the fact that the Moon is also the primary force behind the circulation of blood in human beings and animals, and the movement of sap in trees and plants. Agriculturists have established that the Moon has a distinct influence on crops, which explains why for centuries people have planted according to Moon cycles. The habits of many animals, too, are directed by the movement of the Moon. Migratory birds, for instance, depart only at or near the time of the Full Moon. And certain sea creatures, eels in particular, move only in accordance with certain phases of the Moon.

Know Thyself—Why?

In today's fast-changing world, everyone still longs to know what the future holds. It is the one thing that everyone has in common: rich and poor, famous and infamous, all are deeply concerned about tomorrow.

But the key to the future, as every historian knows, lies in the past. This is as true of individual people as it is of nations. You cannot understand your future without first understanding your past, which is simply another way of saying that you must first of all know yourself.

The motto "know thyself" seems obvious enough nowadays, but it was originally put forward as the foundation of wisdom by the ancient Greek philosophers. It was then adopted by the "mystery religions" of the ancient Middle East, Greece, Rome, and is still used in all genuine schools of mind training or mystical discipline, both in those of the East, based on yoga, and those of the West. So it is universally accepted now, and has been through the ages.

But how do you go about discovering what sort of person you are? The first step is usually classification into some sort of system of types. Astrology did this long before the birth of Christ. Psychology has also done it. So has modern medicine, in its way.

One system classifies people according to the source of the impulses they respond to most readily: the muscles, leading to direct bodily action; the digestive organs, resulting in emotion; or the brain and nerves, giving rise to thinking. Another such system says that character is determined by the endocrine glands, and gives us such labels as "pituitary," "thyroid," and "hyperthyroid" types. These different systems are neither contradictory nor mutually exclusive. In fact, they are very often different ways of saying the same thing.

Very popular, useful classifications were devised by Carl Jung, the eminent disciple of Freud. Jung observed among the different faculties of the mind, four which have a predominant influence on character. These four faculties exist in all of us without exception, but not in perfect balance. So when we say, for instance, that someone is a "thinking type," it means that in any situation he or she tries to be rational. Emotion, which may be the opposite of thinking, will be his or her weakest function. This thinking type can be sensible and reasonable, or calculating and unsympathetic. The emotional type, on the other hand, can often be recognized by exaggerated language—everything is either marvelous or terrible—and in extreme cases they even invent dramas and quarrels out of nothing just to make life more interesting.

The other two faculties are intuition and physical sensation. The sensation type does not only care for food and drink, nice clothes and furniture; he or she is also interested in all forms of physical experience. Many scientists are sensation types as are athletes and nature-lovers. Like sensation, intuition is a form of perception and we all possess it. But it works through that part of the mind which is not under conscious control—consequently it sees meanings and connections which are not obvious to thought or emotion. Inventors and original thinkers are always intuitive, but so, too, are superstitious people who see meanings where none exist.

Thus, sensation tells us what is going on in the world, feeling (that is, emotion) tells us how important it is to ourselves, thinking enables us to interpret it and work out what we should do about it, and intuition tells us what it means to ourselves and others. All four faculties are essential, and all are present in every one of us. But some people are guided chiefly by one, others by another. In addition, Jung also observed a division of the human personality into the extrovert and the introvert, which cuts across these four types.

A disadvantage of all these systems of classification is that one cannot tell very easily where to place oneself. Some people are reluctant to admit that they act to please their emotions. So they deceive themselves for years by trying to belong to whichever type they think is the "best." Of course, there is no best; each has its faults and each has its good points.

The advantage of the signs of the Zodiac is that they simplify classification. Not only that, but your date of birth is personal— it is unarguably yours. What better way to know yourself than by going back as far as possible to the very moment of your birth? And this is precisely what your horoscope is all about, as we shall see in the next section.

WHAT IS A HOROSCOPE?

If you had been able to take a picture of the skies at the moment of your birth, that photograph would be your horoscope. Lacking such a snapshot, it is still possible to recreate the picture—and this is at the basis of the astrologer's art. In other words, your horoscope is a representation of the skies with the planets in the exact positions they occupied at the time you were born.

The year of birth tells an astrologer the positions of the distant, slow-moving planets Jupiter, Saturn, Uranus, Neptune, and Pluto. The month of birth indicates the Sun sign, or birth sign as it is commonly called, as well as indicating the positions of the rapidly moving planets Venus, Mercury, and Mars. The day and time of birth will locate the position of our Moon. And the moment—the exact hour and minute—of birth determines the houses through what is called the Ascendant, or Rising sign.

With this information the astrologer consults various tables to calculate the specific positions of the Sun, Moon, and other planets relative to your birthplace at the moment you were born. Then he or she locates them by means of the Zodiac.

The Zodiac

The Zodiac is a band of stars (constellations) in the skies, centered on the Sun's apparent path around the Earth, and is divided into twelve equal segments, or signs. What we are actually dividing up is the Earth's path around the Sun. But from our point of view here on Earth, it seems as if the Sun is making a great circle around our planet in the sky, so we say it is the Sun's apparent path. This twelvefold division, the Zodiac, is a reference system for the astrologer. At any given moment the planets—and in astrology both the Sun and Moon are considered to be planets—can all be located at a specific point along this path.

Now where in all this are you, the subject of the horoscope? Your character is largely determined by the sign the Sun is in. So that is where the astrologer looks first in your horoscope, at your Sun sign.

The Sun Sign and the Cusp

There are twelve signs in the Zodiac, and the Sun spends approximately one month in each sign. But because of the motion of the Earth around the Sun—the Sun's apparent motion—the dates when the Sun enters and leaves each sign may change from year to year. Some people born near the cusp, or edge, of a sign have difficulty determining which is their Sun sign. But in this book a Table of Cusps is provided for the years 1900 to 2000 (page 5) so you can find out what your true Sun sign is.

Here are the twelve signs of the Zodiac, their ancient zodiacal symbol, and the dates when the Sun enters and leaves each sign for the year 2000. Remember, these dates may change from year to year.

ARIES	Ram	March 20–April 19
TAURUS	Bull	April 19–May 20
GEMINI	Twins	May 20–June 20
CANCER	Crab	June 20–July 22
LEO	Lion	July 22–August 22
VIRGO	Virgin	August 22–September 22
LIBRA	Scales	September 22–October 22
SCORPIO	Scorpion	October 22–November 21
SAGITTARIUS	Archer	November 21–December 21
CAPRICORN	Sea Goat	December 21–January 20
AQUARIUS	Water Bearer	January 20–February 19
PISCES	Fish	February 19–March 20

It is possible to draw significant conclusions and make meaningful predictions based simply on the Sun sign of a person. There are many people who have been amazed at the accuracy of the description of their own character based only on the Sun sign. But an astrologer needs more information than just your Sun sign to interpret the photograph that is your horoscope.

The Rising Sign and the Zodiacal Houses

An astrologer needs the exact time and place of your birth in order to construct and interpret your horoscope. The illustration on the next page shows the flat chart, or natural wheel, an astrologer uses. Note the inner circle of the wheel labeled 1 through 12. These 12 divisions are known as the houses of the Zodiac.

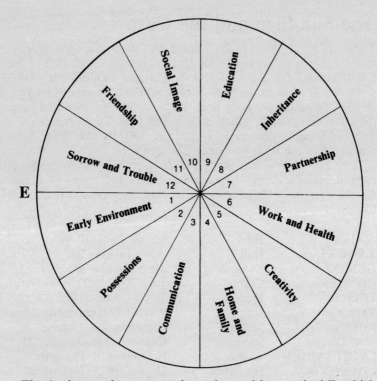

The 1st house always starts from the position marked E, which corresponds to the eastern horizon. The rest of the houses 2 through 12 follow around in a "counterclockwise" direction. The point where each house starts is known as a cusp, or edge.

The cusp, or edge, of the 1st house (point E) is where an astrologer would place your Rising sign, the Ascendant. And, as already noted, the exact time of your birth determines your Rising sign. Let's see how this works.

As the Earth rotates on its axis once every 24 hours, each one of the twelve signs of the Zodiac appears to be "rising" on the horizon, with a new one appearing about every 2 hours. Actually it is the turning of the Earth that exposes each sign to view, but in our astrological work we are discussing apparent motion. This Rising sign marks the Ascendant, and it colors the whole orientation of a horoscope. It indicates the sign governing the 1st house of the chart, and will thus determine which signs will govern all the other houses.

To visualize this idea, imagine two color wheels with twelve divisions superimposed upon each other. For just as the Zodiac is divided into twelve constellations that we identify as the signs, another twelvefold division is used to denote the houses. Now imagine one wheel (the signs) moving slowly while the other wheel (the houses) remains still. This analogy may help you see how the signs keep shifting the "color" of the houses as the Rising sign continues to change every two hours. To simplify things, a Table of Rising Signs has been provided (pages 8–9) for your specific Sun sign.

Once your Rising sign has been placed on the cusp of the 1st house, the signs that govern the rest of the 11 houses can be placed on the chart. In any individual's horoscope the signs do not necessarily correspond with the houses. For example, it could be that a sign covers part of two adjacent houses. It is the interpretation of such variations in an individual's horoscope that marks the professional astrologer.

But to gain a workable understanding of astrology, it is not necessary to go into great detail. In fact, we just need a description of the houses and their meanings, as is shown in the illustration above and in the table below.

THE 12 HOUSES OF THE ZODIAC

1st	Individuality, body appearance, general outlook on life	Personality house
2nd	Finance, possessions, ethical principles, gain or loss	Money house
3rd	Relatives, communication, short journeys, writing, education	Relatives house
4th	Family and home, parental ties, land and property, security	Home house
5th	Pleasure, children, creativity, entertainment, risk	Pleasure house
6th	Health, harvest, hygiene, work and service, employees	Health house
7th	Marriage and divorce, the law, partnerships and alliances	Marriage house
8th	Inheritance, secret deals, sex, death, regeneration	Inheritance house
9th	Travel, sports, study, philosophy and religion	Travel house
10th	Career, social standing, success and honor	Business house
11th	Friendship, social life, hopes and wishes	Friends house
12th	Troubles, illness, secret enemies, hidden agendas	Trouble house

The Planets in the Houses

An astrologer, knowing the exact time and place of your birth, will use tables of planetary motion in order to locate the planets in your horoscope chart. He or she will determine which planet or planets are in which sign and in which house. It is not uncommon, in an individual's horoscope, for there to be two or more planets in the same sign and in the same house.

The characteristics of the planets modify the influence of the Sun according to their natures and strengths.

Sun: Source of life. Basic temperament according to the Sun sign. The conscious will. Human potential.

Moon: Emotions. Moods. Customs. Habits. Changeable. Adaptive. Nurturing.

Mercury: Communication. Intellect. Reasoning power. Curiosity. Short travels.

Venus: Love. Delight. Charm. Harmony. Balance. Art. Beautiful possessions.

Mars: Energy. Initiative. War. Anger. Adventure. Courage. Daring. Impulse.

Jupiter: Luck. Optimism. Generous. Expansive. Opportunities. Protection.

Saturn: Pessimism. Privation. Obstacles. Delay. Hard work. Research. Lasting rewards after long struggle.

Uranus: Fashion. Electricity. Revolution. Independence. Freedom. Sudden changes. Modern science.

Neptune: Sensationalism. Theater. Dreams. Inspiration. Illusion. Deception.

Pluto: Creation and destruction. Total transformation. Lust for power. Strong obsessions.

Superimpose the characteristics of the planets on the functions of the house in which they appear. Express the result through the character of the Sun sign, and you will get the basic idea.

Of course, many other considerations have been taken into account in producing the carefully worked out predictions in this book: the aspects of the planets to each other; their strength according to position and sign; whether they are in a house of exaltation or decline; whether they are natural enemies or not; whether a planet occupies its own sign; the position of a planet in relation to its own house or sign; whether the sign is male or female; whether the sign is a fire, earth, water, or air sign. These are only a few of the colors on the astrologer's pallet which he or she must mix with the inspiration of the artist and the accuracy of the mathematician.

How To Use These Predictions

A person reading the predictions in this book should understand that they are produced from the daily position of the planets for a group of people and are not, of course, individually specialized. To get the full benefit of them our readers should relate the predictions to their own character and circumstances, coordinate them, and draw their own conclusions from them.

If you are a serious observer of your own life, you should find a definite pattern emerging that will be a helpful and reliable guide.

The point is that we always retain our free will. The stars indicate certain directional tendencies but we are not compelled to follow. We can do or not do, and wisdom must make the choice.

We all have our good and bad days. Sometimes they extend into cycles of weeks. It is therefore advisable to study daily predictions in a span ranging from the day before to several days ahead.

Daily predictions should be taken very generally. The word "difficult" does not necessarily indicate a whole day of obstruction or inconvenience. It is a warning to you to be cautious. Your caution will often see you around the difficulty before you are involved. This is the correct use of astrology.

In another section (pages 78–84), detailed information is given about the influence of the Moon as it passes through each of the twelve signs of the Zodiac. There are instructions on how to use the Moon Tables (pages 85–92), which provide Moon Sign Dates throughout the year as well as the Moon's role in health and daily affairs. This information should be used in conjunction with the daily forecasts to give a fuller picture of the astrological trends.

HISTORY OF ASTROLOGY

The origins of astrology have been lost far back in history, but we do know that reference is made to it as far back as the first written records of the human race. It is not hard to see why. Even in primitive times, people must have looked for an explanation for the various happenings in their lives. They must have wanted to know why people were different from one another. And in their search they turned to the regular movements of the Sun, Moon, and stars to see if they could provide an answer.

It is interesting to note that as soon as man learned to use his tools in any type of design, or his mind in any kind of calculation, he turned his attention to the heavens. Ancient cave dwellings reveal dim crescents and circles representative of the Sun and Moon, rulers of day and night. Mesopotamia and the civilization of Chaldea, in itself the foundation of those of Babylonia and Assyria, show a complete picture of astronomical observation and well-developed astrological interpretation.

Humanity has a natural instinct for order. The study of anthropology reveals that primitive people—even as far back as prehistoric times—were striving to achieve a certain order in their lives. They tried to organize the apparent chaos of the universe. They had the desire to attach meaning to things. This demand for order has persisted throughout the history of man. So that observing the regularity of the heavenly bodies made it logical that primitive peoples should turn heavenward in their search for an understanding of the world in which they found themselves so random and alone.

And they did find a significance in the movements of the stars. Shepherds tending their flocks, for instance, observed that when the cluster of stars now known as the constellation Aries was in sight, it was the time of fertility and they associated it with the Ram. And they noticed that the growth of plants and plant life corresponded with different phases of the Moon, so that certain times were favorable for the planting of crops, and other times were not. In this way, there grew up a tradition of seasons and causes connected with the passage of the Sun through the twelve signs of the Zodiac.

Astrology was valued so highly that the king was kept informed of the daily and monthly changes in the heavenly bodies, and the results of astrological studies regarding events of the future. Head astrologers were clearly men of great rank and position, and the office was said to be a hereditary one.

Omens were taken, not only from eclipses and conjunctions of the Moon or Sun with one of the planets, but also from storms and earthquakes. In the eastern civilizations, particularly, the reverence inspired by astrology appears to have remained unbroken since the very earliest days. In ancient China, astrology, astronomy, and religion went hand in hand. The astrologer, who was also an astronomer, was part of the official government service and had his own corner in the Imperial Palace. The duties of the Imperial astrologer, whose office was one of the most important in the land, were clearly defined, as this extract from early records shows:

This exalted gentleman must concern himself with the stars in the heavens, keeping a record of the changes and movements of the Planets, the Sun and the Moon, in order to examine the movements of the terrestrial world with the object of prognosticating good and bad fortune. He divides the territories of the nine regions of the empire in accordance with their dependence on particular celestial bodies. All the fiefs and principalities are connected with the stars and from this their prosperity or misfortune should be ascertained. He makes prognostications according to the twelve years of the Jupiter cycle of good and evil of the terrestrial world. From the colors of the five kinds of clouds, he determines the coming of floods or droughts, abundance or famine. From the twelve winds, he draws conclusions about the state of harmony of heaven and earth, and takes note of good and bad signs that result from their accord or disaccord. In general, he concerns himself with five kinds of phenomena so as to warn the Emperor to come to the aid of the government and to allow for variations in the ceremonies according to their circumstances.

The Chinese were also keen observers of the fixed stars, giving them such unusual names as Ghost Vehicle, Sun of Imperial Concubine, Imperial Prince, Pivot of Heaven, Twinkling Brilliance, Weaving Girl. But, great astrologers though they may have been, the Chinese lacked one aspect of mathematics that the Greeks applied to astrology—deductive geometry. Deductive geometry was the basis of much classical astrology in and after the time of the Greeks, and this explains the different methods of prognostication used in the East and West.

Down through the ages the astrologer's art has depended, not so much on the uncovering of new facts, though this is important, as on the interpretation of the facts already known. This is the essence of the astrologer's skill.

But why should the signs of the Zodiac have any effect at all on the formation of human character? It is easy to see why people thought they did, and even now we constantly use astrological expressions in our everyday speech. The thoughts of "lucky star," "ill-fated," "star-crossed," "mooning around," are interwoven into the very structure of our language.

Wherever the concept of the Zodiac is understood and used, it could well appear to have an influence on the human character. Does this mean, then, that the human race, in whose civilization the idea of the twelve signs of the Zodiac has long been embedded, is divided into only twelve types? Can we honestly believe that it is really as simple as that? If so, there must be pretty wide ranges of variation within each type. And if, to explain the variation, we call in heredity and environment, experiences in early childhood, the thyroid and other glands, and also the four functions of the mind together with extroversion and introversion, then one begins to wonder if the original classification was worth making at all. No sensible person believes that his favorite system explains everything. But even so, he will not find the system much use at all if it does not even save him the trouble of bothering with the others.

In the same way, if we were to put every person under only one sign of the Zodiac, the system becomes too rigid and unlike life. Besides, it was never intended to be used like that. It may be convenient to have only twelve types, but we know that in practice there is every possible gradation between aggressiveness and timidity, or between conscientiousness and laziness. How, then, do we account for this?

A person born under any given Sun sign can be mainly influenced by one or two of the other signs that appear in their individual horoscope. For instance, famous persons born under the sign of Gemini include Henry VIII, whom nothing and no one could have induced to abdicate, and Edward VIII, who did just that. Obviously, then, the sign Gemini does not fully explain the complete character of either of them.

Again, under the opposite sign, Sagittarius, were both Stalin, who was totally consumed with the notion of power, and Charles V, who freely gave up an empire because he preferred to go into a monastery. And we find under Scorpio many uncompromising characters such as Luther, de Gaulle, Indira Gandhi, and Montgomery, but also Petain, a successful commander whose name later became synonymous with collaboration.

A single sign is therefore obviously inadequate to explain the differences between people; it can only explain resemblances, such as the combativeness of the Scorpio group, or the far-reaching devotion of Charles V and Stalin to their respective ideals—the Christian heaven and the Communist utopia.

But very few people have only one sign in their horoscope chart. In addition to the month of birth, the day and, even more, the hour to the nearest minute if possible, ought to be considered. Without this, it is impossible to have an actual horoscope, for the word horoscope literally means "a consideration of the hour."

The month of birth tells you only which sign of the Zodiac was occupied by the Sun. The day and hour tell you what sign was occupied by the Moon. And the minute tells you which sign was rising on the eastern horizon. This is called the Ascendant, and, as some astrologers believe, it is supposed to be the most important thing in the whole horoscope.

The Sun is said to signify one's heart, that is to say, one's deepest desires and inmost nature. This is quite different from the Moon, which signifies one's superficial way of behaving. When the ancient Romans referred to the Emperor Augustus as a Capricorn, they meant that he had the Moon in Capricorn. Or, to take another example, a modern astrologer would call Disraeli a Scorpion because he had Scorpio Rising, but most people would call him Sagittarius because he had the Sun there. The Romans would have called him Leo because his Moon was in Leo.

So if one does not seem to fit one's birth month, it is always worthwhile reading the other signs, for one may have been born at a time when any of them were rising or occupied by the Moon. It also seems to be the case that the influence of the Sun develops as life goes on, so that the month of birth is easier to guess in people over the age of forty. The young are supposed to be influenced mainly by their Ascendant, the Rising sign, which characterizes the body and physical personality as a whole.

It is nonsense to assume that all people born at a certain time will exhibit the same characteristics, or that they will even behave in the same manner. It is quite obvious that, from the very moment of its birth, a child is subject to the effects of its environment, and that this in turn will influence its character and heritage to a decisive extent. Also to be taken into account are education and economic conditions, which play a very important part in the formation of one's character as well.

People have, in general, certain character traits and qualities which, according to their environment, develop in either a positive or a negative manner. Therefore, selfishness (inherent selfishness, that is) might emerge as unselfishness; kindness and consideration as cruelty and lack of consideration toward others. In the same way, a naturally constructive person may, through frustration, become destructive, and so on. The latent characteristics with which people are born can, therefore, through environment and good or bad training, become something that would appear to be its opposite, and so give the lie to the astrologer's description of their character. But this is not the case. The true character is still there, but it is buried deep beneath these external superficialities.

Careful study of the character traits of various signs of the Zodiac are of immeasurable help, and can render beneficial service to the intelligent person. Undoubtedly, the reader will already have discovered that, while he is able to get on very well with some people, he just "cannot stand" others. The causes sometimes seem inexplicable. At times there is intense dislike, at other times immediate sympathy. And there is, too, the phenomenon of love at first sight, which is also apparently inexplicable. People appear to be either sympathetic or unsympathetic toward each other for no apparent reason.

Now if we look at this in the light of the Zodiac, we find that people born under different signs are either compatible or incompatible with each other. In other words, there are good and bad interrelating factors among the various signs. This does not, of course, mean that humanity can be divided into groups of hostile camps. It would be quite wrong to be hostile or indifferent toward people who happen to be born under an incompatible sign. There is no reason why everybody should not, or cannot, learn to control and adjust their feelings and actions, especially after they are aware of the positive qualities of other people by studying their character analyses, among other things.

Every person born under a certain sign has both positive and negative qualities, which are developed more or less according to our free will. Nobody is entirely good or entirely bad, and it is up to each of us to learn to control ourselves on the one hand and at the same time to endeavor to learn about ourselves and others.

It cannot be emphasized often enough that it is free will that determines whether we will make really good use of our talents and abilities. Using our free will, we can either overcome our failings or allow them to rule us. Our free will enables us to exert sufficient willpower to control our failings so that they do not harm ourselves or others.

Astrology can reveal our inclinations and tendencies. Astrology can tell us about ourselves so that we are able to use our free will to overcome our shortcomings. In this way astrology helps us do our best to become needed and valuable members of society as well as helpmates to our family and our friends. Astrology also can save us a great deal of unhappiness and remorse.

Yet it may seem absurd that an ancient philosophy could be a prop to modern men and women. But below the materialistic surface of modern life, there are hidden streams of feeling and thought. Symbology is reappearing as a study worthy of the scholar; the psychosomatic factor in illness has passed from the writings of the crank to those of the specialist; spiritual healing in all its forms is no longer a pious hope but an accepted phenomenon. And it is into this context that we consider astrology, in the sense that it is an analysis of human types.

Astrology and medicine had a long journey together, and only parted company a couple of centuries ago. There still remain in medical language such astrological terms as "saturnine," "choleric," and "mercurial," used in the diagnosis of physical tendencies. The herbalist, for long the handyman of the medical profession, has been dominated by astrology since the days of the Greeks. Certain herbs traditionally respond to certain planetary influences, and diseases must therefore be treated to ensure harmony between the medicine and the disease.

But the stars are expected to foretell and not only to diagnose.

Astrological forecasting has been remarkably accurate, but often it is wide of the mark. The brave person who cares to predict world events takes dangerous chances. Individual forecasting is less clear cut; it can be a help or a disillusionment. Then we come to the nagging question: if it is possible to foreknow, is it right to foretell? This is a point of ethics on which it is hard to pronounce judgment. The doctor faces the same dilemma if he finds that symptoms of a mortal disease are present in his patient and that he can only prognosticate a steady decline. How much to tell an individual in a crisis is a problem that has perplexed many distinguished scholars. Honest and conscientious astrologers in this modern world, where so many people are seeking guidance, face the same problem.

Five hundred years ago it was customary to call in a learned man who was an astrologer who was probably also a doctor and a philosopher. By his knowledge of astrology, his study of planetary influences, he felt himself qualified to guide those in distress. The world has moved forward at a fantastic rate since then, and yet people are still uncertain of themselves. At first sight it seems fantastic in the light of modern thinking that they turn to the most ancient of all studies, and get someone to calculate a horoscope for them. But is it *really* so fantastic if you take a second look? For astrology is concerned with tomorrow, with survival. And in a world such as ours, tomorrow and survival are the keywords for the twenty-first century.

ASTROLOGICAL BRIDGE TO THE 21st CENTURY

As the last decade of the twentieth century comes to a close, planetary aspects for its final years connect you with the future. Major changes completed in 1995 and 1996 give rise to new planetary cycles that form the bridge to the twenty-first century and new horizons. The years 1996 through 1999 and into the year 2000 reveal hidden paths and personal hints for achieving your potential, for making the most of your message from the planets.

All the major planets begin new cycles in the late 1990s. Jupiter, planet of good fortune, transits four zodiacal signs from 1996 through 1999 and goes through a complete cycle in each of the elements earth, air, fire, and water. Jupiter is in Capricorn, then in Aquarius, next in Pisces, and finally in Aries as the century turns. With the dawning of the twenty-first century, each new yearly Jupiter cycle follows the natural progression of the Zodiac, from Aries in 2000, then Taurus in 2001, next Gemini in 2002, and so on through Pisces in 2011. The beneficent planet Jupiter promotes your professional and educational goals while urging informed choice and deliberation. Jupiter sharpens your focus and hones your skills. And while safeguarding good luck, Jupiter can turn unusual risks into achievable aims.

Saturn, planet of reason and responsibility, has begun a new cycle in the spring of 1996 when it entered fiery Aries. Saturn in Aries through March 1999 heightens a longing for independence. Your movements are freed from everyday restrictions, allowing you to travel, to explore, to act on a variety of choices. With Saturn in Aries you get set to blaze a new trail. Saturn enters earthy Taurus in March 1999 for a three-year stay over the turn of the century into the year 2002. Saturn in Taurus inspires industry and affection. Practicality, perseverance, and planning can reverse setbacks and minimize risk. Saturn in Taurus lends beauty, order, and structure to your life. In order to take advantage of opportunity through responsibility, to persevere against adversity, look to beautiful planet Saturn.

Uranus, planet of innovation and surprise, started an important new cycle in January of 1996. At that time Uranus entered its natural home in airy Aquarius. Uranus in Aquarius into the year 2003 has a profound effect on your personality and the lens through which you see the world. A basic change in the way you project yourself is just one impact of Uranus in Aquarius. More significantly, a whole new consciousness is evolving. Winds of change blowing your way emphasize movement and freedom. Uranus in Aquarius poses involvement in the larger community beyond self, family, friends, lovers, associates. Radical ideas and progressive thought signal a journey of liberation. As the century turns, follow Uranus on the path of humanitarianism. While you carve a prestigious niche in public life, while you preach social reform and justice, you will be striving to make the world a better place for all people.

Neptune, planet of vision and mystery, is in earthy Capricorn until late 1998. Neptune in Capricorn excites creativity while restraining fanciful thinking. Wise use of resources helps you build persona and prestige. Then Neptune enters airy Aquarius during November 1998 and is there into the year 2011. Neptune in Aquarius, the sign of the Water Bearer, represents two sides of the coin of wisdom: inspiration and reason. Here Neptune stirs powerful currents bearing a rich and varied harvest, the fertile breeding ground for idealistic aims and practical considerations. Neptune's fine intuition tunes in to your dreams, your imagination, your spirituality. You can never turn your back on the mysteries of life. Uranus and Neptune, the planets of enlightenment and renewed idealism both in the sign of Aquarius, give you glimpses into the future, letting you peek through secret doorways into the twenty-first century.

Pluto, planet of beginnings and endings, has completed one cycle of growth November 1995 in the sign of Scorpio. Pluto in Scorpio marked a long period of experimentation and rejuvenation. Then Pluto entered the fiery sign of Sagittarius on November 10, 1995 and is there into the year 2007. Pluto in Sagittarius during its long stay of twelve years can create significant change. The great power of Pluto in Sagittarius may already be starting its transformation of your character and lifestyle. Pluto in Sagittarius takes you on a new journey of exploration and learning. The awakening you experience on intellectual and artistic levels heralds a new cycle of growth. Uncompromising Pluto, seeker of truth, challenges your identity, persona, and self-expression. Uncovering the real you, Pluto holds the key to understanding and meaningful communication. Pluto in Sagittarius can be the guiding light illuminating the first decade of the twenty-first century. Good luck is riding on the waves of change.

THE SIGNS OF THE ZODIAC

Dominant Characteristics

Aries: March 21–April 20

The Positive Side of Aries

The Aries has many positive points to his character. People born under this first sign of the Zodiac are often quite strong and enthusiastic. On the whole, they are forward-looking people who are not easily discouraged by temporary setbacks. They know what they want out of life and they go out after it. Their personalities are strong. Others are usually quite impressed by the Ram's way of doing things. Quite often they are sources of inspiration for others traveling the same route. Aries men and women have a special zest for life that can be contagious; for others, they are a fine example of how life should be lived.

The Aries person usually has a quick and active mind. He is imaginative and inventive. He enjoys keeping busy and active. He generally gets along well with all kinds of people. He is interested in mankind, as a whole. He likes to be challenged. Some would say he thrives on opposition, for it is when he is set against that he often does his best. Getting over or around obstacles is a challenge he generally enjoys. All in all, Aries is quite positive and young-thinking. He likes to keep abreast of new things that are happening in the world. Aries are often fond of speed. They like things to be done quickly, and this sometimes aggravates their slower colleagues and associates.

The Aries man or woman always seems to remain young. Their whole approach to life is youthful and optimistic. They never say die, no matter what the odds. They may have an occasional setback, but it is not long before they are back on their feet again.

The Negative Side of Aries

Everybody has his less positive qualities—and Aries is no exception. Sometimes the Aries man or woman is not very tactful in communicating with others; in his hurry to get things done he is apt to be a little callous or inconsiderate. Sensitive people are likely to find him somewhat sharp-tongued in some situations. Often in his eagerness to get the show on the road, he misses the mark altogether and cannot achieve his aims.

At times Aries can be too impulsive. He can occasionally be stubborn and refuse to listen to reason. If things do not move quickly enough to suit the Aries man or woman, he or she is apt to become rather nervous or irritable. The uncultivated Aries is not unfamiliar with moments of doubt and fear. He is capable of being destructive if he does not get his way. He can overcome some of his emotional problems by steadily trying to express himself as he really is, but this requires effort.

Taurus: April 21–May 20

The Positive Side of Taurus

The Taurus person is known for his ability to concentrate and for his tenacity. These are perhaps his strongest qualities. The Taurus man or woman generally has very little trouble in getting along with others; it's his nature to be helpful toward people in need. He can always be depended on by his friends, especially those in trouble.

Taurus generally achieves what he wants through his ability to persevere. He never leaves anything unfinished but works on something until it has been completed. People can usually take him at his word; he is honest and forthright in most of his dealings. The Taurus person has a good chance to make a success of his life because of his many positive qualities. The Taurus who aims high seldom falls short of his mark. He learns well by experience. He is thorough and does not believe in shortcuts of any kind. The Bull's thoroughness pays off in the end, for through his deliberateness he learns how to rely on himself and what he has learned. The Taurus person tries to get along with others, as a rule. He is not overly critical and likes people to be themselves. He is a tolerant person and enjoys peace and harmony—especially in his home life.

Taurus is usually cautious in all that he does. He is not a person who believes in taking unnecessary risks. Before adopting any one line of action, he will weigh all of the pros and cons. The Taurus person is steadfast. Once his mind is made up it seldom changes. The person born under this sign usually is a good family person— reliable and loving.

The Negative Side of Taurus

Sometimes the Taurus man or woman is a bit too stubborn. He won't listen to other points of view if his mind is set on something. To others, this can be quite annoying. Taurus also does not like to be told what to do. He becomes rather angry if others think him not too bright. He does not like to be told he is wrong, even when he is. He dislikes being contradicted.

Some people who are born under this sign are very suspicious of others—even of those persons close to them. They find it difficult to trust people fully. They are often afraid of being deceived or taken advantage of. The Bull often finds it difficult to forget or forgive. His love of material things sometimes makes him rather avaricious and petty.

Gemini: May 21–June 20

The Positive Side of Gemini

The person born under this sign of the Heavenly Twins is usually quite bright and quick-witted. Some of them are capable of doing many different things. The Gemini person very often has many different interests. He keeps an open mind and is always anxious to learn new things.

Gemini is often an analytical person. He is a person who enjoys making use of his intellect. He is governed more by his mind than by his emotions. He is a person who is not confined to one view; he can often understand both sides to a problem or question. He knows how to reason, how to make rapid decisions if need be.

He is an adaptable person and can make himself at home almost anywhere. There are all kinds of situations he can adapt to. He is a person who seldom doubts himself; he is sure of his talents and his ability to think and reason. Gemini is generally most satisfied

when he is in a situation where he can make use of his intellect. Never short of imagination, he often has strong talents for invention. He is rather a modern person when it comes to life; Gemini almost always moves along with the times—perhaps that is why he remains so youthful throughout most of his life.

Literature and art appeal to the person born under this sign. Creativity in almost any form will interest and intrigue the Gemini man or woman.

The Gemini is often quite charming. A good talker, he often is the center of attraction at any gathering. People find it easy to like a person born under this sign because he can appear easygoing and usually has a good sense of humor.

The Negative Side of Gemini

Sometimes the Gemini person tries to do too many things at one time—and as a result, winds up finishing nothing. Some Twins are easily distracted and find it rather difficult to concentrate on one thing for too long a time. Sometimes they give in to trifling fancies and find it rather boring to become too serious about any one thing. Some of them are never dependable, no matter what they promise.

Although the Gemini man or woman often appears to be well-versed on many subjects, this is sometimes just a veneer. His knowledge may be only superficial, but because he speaks so well he gives people the impression of erudition. Some Geminis are sharp-tongued and inconsiderate; they think only of themselves and their own pleasure.

Cancer: June 21–July 20

The Positive Side of Cancer

The Moon Child's most positive point is his understanding nature. On the whole, he is a loving and sympathetic person. He would never go out of his way to hurt anyone. The Cancer man or woman is often very kind and tender; they give what they can to others. They hate to see others suffering and will do what they can to help someone in less fortunate circumstances than themselves. They are often very concerned about the world. Their interest in people generally goes beyond that of just their own families and close friends; they have a deep sense of community and respect humanitarian values. The Moon Child means what he says, as a rule; he is honest about his feelings.

The Cancer man or woman is a person who knows the art of patience. When something seems difficult, he is willing to wait until the situation becomes manageable again. He is a person who knows how to bide his time. Cancer knows how to concentrate on one thing at a time. When he has made his mind up he generally sticks with what he does, seeing it through to the end.

Cancer is a person who loves his home. He enjoys being surrounded by familiar things and the people he loves. Of all the signs, Cancer is the most maternal. Even the men born under this sign often have a motherly or protective quality about them. They like to take care of people in their family—to see that they are well loved and well provided for. They are usually loyal and faithful. Family ties mean a lot to the Cancer man or woman. Parents and in-laws are respected and loved. Young Cancer responds very well to adults who show faith in him. The Moon Child has a strong sense of tradition. He is very sensitive to the moods of others.

The Negative Side of Cancer

Sometimes Cancer finds it rather hard to face life. It becomes too much for him. He can be a little timid and retiring, when things don't go too well. When unfortunate things happen, he is apt to just shrug and say, "Whatever will be will be." He can be fatalistic to a fault. The uncultivated Cancer is a bit lazy. He doesn't have very much ambition. Anything that seems a bit difficult he'll gladly leave to others. He may be lacking in initiative. Too sensitive, when he feels he's been injured, he'll crawl back into his shell and nurse his imaginary wounds. The immature Moon Child often is given to crying when the smallest thing goes wrong.

Some Cancers find it difficult to enjoy themselves in environments outside their homes. They make heavy demands on others, and need to be constantly reassured that they are loved. Lacking such reassurance, they may resort to sulking in silence.

Leo: July 21–August 21

The Positive Side of Leo

Often Leos make good leaders. They seem to be good organizers and administrators. Usually they are quite popular with others. Whatever group it is that they belong to, the Leo man or woman is almost sure to be or become the leader. Loyalty, one of the Lion's noblest traits, enables him or her to maintain this leadership position.

Leo is generous most of the time. It is his best characteristic. He or she likes to give gifts and presents. In making others happy, the Leo person becomes happy himself. He likes to splurge when spending money on others. In some instances it may seem that the Lion's generosity knows no boundaries. A hospitable person, the Leo man or woman is very fond of welcoming people to his house and entertaining them. He is never short of company.

Leo has plenty of energy and drive. He enjoys working toward some specific goal. When he applies himself correctly, he gets what he wants most often. The Leo person is almost never unsure of himself. He has plenty of confidence and aplomb. He is a person who is direct in almost everything he does. He has a quick mind and can make a decision in a very short time.

He usually sets a good example for others because of his ambitious manner and positive ways. He knows how to stick to something once he's started. Although Leo may be good at making a joke, he is not superficial or glib. He is a loving person, kind and thoughtful.

There is generally nothing small or petty about the Leo man or woman. He does what he can for those who are deserving. He is a person others can rely upon at all times. He means what he says. An honest person, generally speaking, he is a friend who is valued and sought out.

The Negative Side of Leo

Leo, however, does have his faults. At times, he can be just a bit too arrogant. He thinks that no one deserves a leadership position except him. Only he is capable of doing things well. His opinion of himself is often much too high. Because of his conceit, he is

sometimes rather unpopular with a good many people. Some Leos are too materialistic; they can only think in terms of money and profit.

Some Leos enjoy lording it over others—at home or at their place of business. What is more, they feel they have the right to. Egocentric to an impossible degree, this sort of Leo cares little about how others think or feel. He can be rude and cutting.

Virgo: August 22–September 22

The Positive Side of Virgo

The person born under the sign of Virgo is generally a busy person. He knows how to arrange and organize things. He is a good planner. Above all, he is practical and is not afraid of hard work.

Often called the sign of the Harvester, Virgo knows how to attain what he desires. He sticks with something until it is finished. He never shirks his duties, and can always be depended upon. The Virgo person can be thoroughly trusted at all times.

The man or woman born under this sign tries to do everything to perfection. He doesn't believe in doing anything halfway. He always aims for the top. He is the sort of a person who is always learning and constantly striving to better himself—not because he wants more money or glory, but because it gives him a feeling of accomplishment.

The Virgo man or woman is a very observant person. He is sensitive to how others feel, and can see things below the surface of a situation. He usually puts this talent to constructive use.

It is not difficult for the Virgo to be open and earnest. He believes in putting his cards on the table. He is never secretive or underhanded. He's as good as his word. The Virgo person is generally plainspoken and down to earth. He has no trouble in expressing himself.

The Virgo person likes to keep up to date on new developments in his particular field. Well-informed, generally, he sometimes has a keen interest in the arts or literature. What he knows, he knows well. His ability to use his critical faculties is well-developed and sometimes startles others because of its accuracy.

Virgos adhere to a moderate way of life; they avoid excesses. Virgo is a responsible person and enjoys being of service.

The Negative Side of Virgo

Sometimes a Virgo person is too critical. He thinks that only he can do something the way it should be done. Whatever anyone else does is inferior. He can be rather annoying in the way he quibbles over insignificant details. In telling others how things should be done, he can be rather tactless and mean.

Some Virgos seem rather emotionless and cool. They feel emotional involvement is beneath them. They are sometimes too tidy, too neat. With money they can be rather miserly. Some Virgos try to force their opinions and ideas on others.

Libra: September 23–October 22

The Positive Side of Libra

Libras love harmony. It is one of their most outstanding character traits. They are interested in achieving balance; they admire beauty and grace in things as well as in people. Generally speaking, they are kind and considerate people. Libras are usually very sympathetic. They go out of their way not to hurt another person's feelings. They are outgoing and do what they can to help those in need.

People born under the sign of Libra almost always make good friends. They are loyal and amiable. They enjoy the company of others. Many of them are rather moderate in their views; they believe in keeping an open mind, however, and weighing both sides of an issue fairly before making a decision.

Alert and intelligent, Libra, often known as the Lawgiver, is always fair-minded and tries to put himself in the position of the other person. They are against injustice; quite often they take up for the underdog. In most of their social dealings, they try to be tactful and kind. They dislike discord and bickering, and most Libras strive for peace and harmony in all their relationships.

The Libra man or woman has a keen sense of beauty. They appreciate handsome furnishings and clothes. Many of them are artistically inclined. Their taste is usually impeccable. They know how to use color. Their homes are almost always attractively arranged and inviting. They enjoy entertaining people and see to it that their guests always feel at home and welcome.

Libra gets along with almost everyone. He is well-liked and socially much in demand.

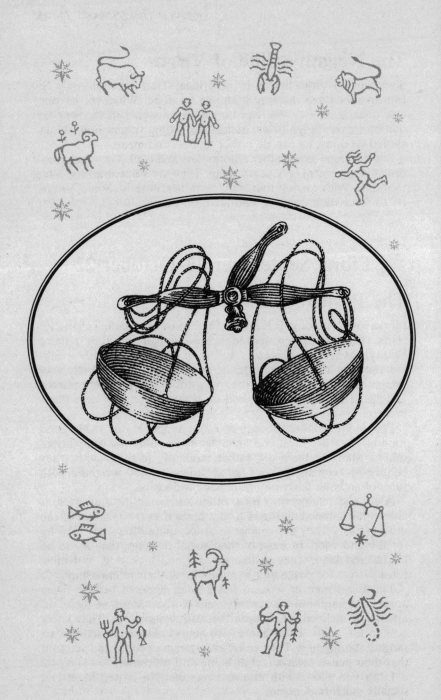

The Negative Side of Libra

Some people born under this sign tend to be rather insincere. So eager are they to achieve harmony in all relationships that they will even go so far as to lie. Many of them are escapists. They find facing the truth an ordeal and prefer living in a world of make-believe.

In a serious argument, some Libras give in rather easily even when they know they are right. Arguing, even about something they believe in, is too unsettling for some of them.

Libras sometimes care too much for material things. They enjoy possessions and luxuries. Some are vain and tend to be jealous.

Scorpio: October 23–November 22

The Positive Side of Scorpio

The Scorpio man or woman generally knows what he or she wants out of life. He is a determined person. He sees something through to the end. Scorpio is quite sincere, and seldom says anything he doesn't mean. When he sets a goal for himself he tries to go about achieving it in a very direct way.

The Scorpion is brave and courageous. They are not afraid of hard work. Obstacles do not frighten them. They forge ahead until they achieve what they set out for. The Scorpio man or woman has a strong will.

Although Scorpio may seem rather fixed and determined, inside he is often quite tender and loving. He can care very much for others. He believes in sincerity in all relationships. His feelings about someone tend to last; they are profound and not superficial.

The Scorpio person is someone who adheres to his principles no matter what happens. He will not be deterred from a path he believes to be right.

Because of his many positive strengths, the Scorpion can often achieve happiness for himself and for those that he loves.

He is a constructive person by nature. He often has a deep understanding of people and of life, in general. He is perceptive and unafraid. Obstacles often seem to spur him on. He is a positive person who enjoys winning. He has many strengths and resources; challenge of any sort often brings out the best in him.

The Negative Side of Scorpio

The Scorpio person is sometimes hypersensitive. Often he imagines injury when there is none. He feels that others do not bother to recognize him for his true worth. Sometimes he is given to excessive boasting in order to compensate for what he feels is neglect.

Scorpio can be proud, arrogant, and competitive. They can be sly when they put their minds to it and they enjoy outwitting persons or institutions noted for their cleverness.

Their tactics for getting what they want are sometimes devious and ruthless. They don't care too much about what others may think. If they feel others have done them an injustice, they will do their best to seek revenge. The Scorpion often has a sudden, violent temper; and this person's interest in sex is sometimes quite unbalanced or excessive.

Sagittarius: November 23–December 20

The Positive Side of Sagittarius

People born under this sign are honest and forthright. Their approach to life is earnest and open. Sagittarius is often quite adult in his way of seeing things. They are broad-minded and tolerant people. When dealing with others the person born under the sign of the Archer is almost always open and forthright. He doesn't believe in deceit or pretension. His standards are high. People who associate with Sagittarius generally admire and respect his tolerant viewpoint.

The Archer trusts others easily and expects them to trust him. He is never suspicious or envious and almost always thinks well of others. People always enjoy his company because he is so friendly and easygoing. The Sagittarius man or woman is often good-humored. He can always be depended upon by his friends, family, and co-workers.

The person born under this sign of the Zodiac likes a good joke every now and then. Sagittarius is eager for fun and laughs, which makes him very popular with others.

A lively person, he enjoys sports and outdoor life. The Archer is fond of animals. Intelligent and interesting, he can begin an

animated conversation with ease. He likes exchanging ideas and discussing various views.

He is not selfish or proud. If someone proposes an idea or plan that is better than his, he will immediately adopt it. Imaginative yet practical, he knows how to put ideas into practice.

The Archer enjoys sport and games, and it doesn't matter if he wins or loses. He is a forgiving person, and never sulks over something that has not worked out in his favor.

He is seldom critical, and is almost always generous.

The Negative Side of Sagittarius

Some Sagittarius are restless. They take foolish risks and seldom learn from the mistakes they make. They don't have heads for money and are often mismanaging their finances. Some of them devote much of their time to gambling.

Some are too outspoken and tactless, always putting their feet in their mouths. They hurt others carelessly by being honest at the wrong time. Sometimes they make promises which they don't keep. They don't stick close enough to their plans and go from one failure to another. They are undisciplined and waste a lot of energy.

Capricorn: December 21–January 19

The Positive Side of Capricorn

The person born under the sign of Capricorn, known variously as the Mountain Goat or Sea Goat, is usually very stable and patient. He sticks to whatever tasks he has and sees them through. He can always be relied upon and he is not averse to work.

An honest person, Capricorn is generally serious about whatever he does. He does not take his duties lightly. He is a practical person and believes in keeping his feet on the ground.

Quite often the person born under this sign is ambitious and knows how to get what he wants out of life. The Goat forges ahead and never gives up his goal. When he is determined about something, he almost always wins. He is a good worker—a hard worker. Although things may not come easy to him, he will not complain, but continue working until his chores are finished.

He is usually good at business matters and knows the value of money. He is not a spendthrift and knows how to put something away for a rainy day; he dislikes waste and unnecessary loss.

Capricorn knows how to make use of his self-control. He can apply himself to almost anything once he puts his mind to it. His ability to concentrate sometimes astounds others. He is diligent and does well when involved in detail work.

The Capricorn man or woman is charitable, generally speaking, and will do what is possible to help others less fortunate. As a friend, he is loyal and trustworthy. He never shirks his duties or responsibilities. He is self-reliant and never expects too much of the other fellow. He does what he can on his own. If someone does him a good turn, then he will do his best to return the favor.

The Negative Side of Capricorn

Like everyone, Capricorn, too, has faults. At times, the Goat can be overcritical of others. He expects others to live up to his own high standards. He thinks highly of himself and tends to look down on others.

His interest in material things may be exaggerated. The Capricorn man or woman thinks too much about getting on in the world and having something to show for it. He may even be a little greedy.

He sometimes thinks he knows what's best for everyone. He is too bossy. He is always trying to organize and correct others. He may be a little narrow in his thinking.

Aquarius: January 20–February 18

The Positive Side of Aquarius

The Aquarius man or woman is usually very honest and forthright. These are his two greatest qualities. His standards for himself are generally very high. He can always be relied upon by others. His word is his bond.

Aquarius is perhaps the most tolerant of all the Zodiac personalities. He respects other people's beliefs and feels that everyone is entitled to his own approach to life.

He would never do anything to injure another's feelings. He is never unkind or cruel. Always considerate of others, the Water

Bearer is always willing to help a person in need. He feels a very strong tie between himself and all the other members of mankind.

The person born under this sign, called the Water Bearer, is almost always an individualist. He does not believe in teaming up with the masses, but prefers going his own way. His ideas about life and mankind are often quite advanced. There is a saying to the effect that the average Aquarius is fifty years ahead of his time.

Aquarius is community-minded. The problems of the world concern him greatly. He is interested in helping others no matter what part of the globe they live in. He is truly a humanitarian sort. He likes to be of service to others.

Giving, considerate, and without prejudice, Aquarius have no trouble getting along with others.

The Negative Side of Aquarius

Aquarius may be too much of a dreamer. He makes plans but seldom carries them out. He is rather unrealistic. His imagination has a tendency to run away with him. Because many of his plans are impractical, he is always in some sort of a dither.

Others may not approve of him at all times because of his unconventional behavior. He may be a bit eccentric. Sometimes he is so busy with his own thoughts that he loses touch with the realities of existence.

Some Aquarius feel they are more clever and intelligent than others. They seldom admit to their own faults, even when they are quite apparent. Some become rather fanatic in their views. Their criticism of others is sometimes destructive and negative.

Pisces: February 19–March 20

The Positive Side of Pisces

Known as the sign of the Fishes, Pisces has a sympathetic nature. Kindly, he is often dedicated in the way he goes about helping others. The sick and the troubled often turn to him for advice and assistance. Possessing keen intuition, Pisces can easily understand people's deepest problems.

He is very broad-minded and does not criticize others for their faults. He knows how to accept people for what they are. On the whole, he is a trustworthy and earnest person. He is loyal to his friends and will do what he can to help them in time of need. Generous and good-natured, he is a lover of peace; he is often willing to help others solve their differences. People who have taken a wrong turn in life often interest him and he will do what he can to persuade them to rehabilitate themselves.

He has a strong intuitive sense and most of the time he knows how to make it work for him. Pisces is unusually perceptive and often knows what is bothering someone before that person, himself, is aware of it. The Pisces man or woman is an idealistic person, basically, and is interested in making the world a better place in which to live. Pisces believes that everyone should help each other. He is willing to do more than his share in order to achieve cooperation with others.

The person born under this sign often is talented in music or art. He is a receptive person; he is able to take the ups and downs of life with philosophic calm.

The Negative Side of Pisces

Some Pisces are often depressed; their outlook on life is rather glum. They may feel that they have been given a bad deal in life and that others are always taking unfair advantage of them. Pisces sometimes feel that the world is a cold and cruel place. The Fishes can be easily discouraged. The Pisces man or woman may even withdraw from the harshness of reality into a secret shell of his own where he dreams and idles away a good deal of his time.

Pisces can be lazy. He lets things happen without giving the least bit of resistance. He drifts along, whether on the high road or on the low. He can be lacking in willpower.

Some Pisces people seek escape through drugs or alcohol. When temptation comes along they find it hard to resist. In matters of sex, they can be rather permissive.

Sun Sign Personalities

ARIES: Hans Christian Andersen, Pearl Bailey, Marlon Brando, Wernher Von Braun, Charlie Chaplin, Joan Crawford, Da Vinci, Bette Davis, Doris Day, W. C. Fields, Alec Guinness, Adolf Hitler, William Holden, Thomas Jefferson, Nikita Khrushchev, Elton John, Arturo Toscanini, J. P. Morgan, Paul Robeson, Gloria Steinem, Sarah Vaughn, Vincent van Gogh, Tennessee Williams

TAURUS: Fred Astaire, Charlotte Brontë, Carol Burnett, Irving Berlin, Bing Crosby, Salvador Dali, Tchaikovsky, Queen Elizabeth II, Duke Ellington, Ella Fitzgerald, Henry Fonda, Sigmund Freud, Orson Welles, Joe Louis, Lenin, Karl Marx, Golda Meir, Eva Peron, Bertrand Russell, Shakespeare, Kate Smith, Benjamin Spock, Barbra Streisand, Shirley Temple, Harry Truman

GEMINI: Ruth Benedict, Josephine Baker, Rachel Carson, Carlos Chavez, Walt Whitman, Bob Dylan, Ralph Waldo Emerson, Judy Garland, Paul Gauguin, Allen Ginsberg, Benny Goodman, Bob Hope, Burl Ives, John F. Kennedy, Peggy Lee, Marilyn Monroe, Joe Namath, Cole Porter, Laurence Olivier, Harriet Beecher Stowe, Queen Victoria, John Wayne, Frank Lloyd Wright

CANCER: "Dear Abby," Lizzie Borden, David Brinkley, Yul Brynner, Pearl Buck, Marc Chagall, Princess Diana, Babe Didrikson, Mary Baker Eddy, Henry VIII, John Glenn, Ernest Hemingway, Lena Horne, Oscar Hammerstein, Helen Keller, Ann Landers, George Orwell, Nancy Reagan, Rembrandt, Richard Rodgers, Ginger Rogers, Rubens, Jean-Paul Sartre, O. J. Simpson

LEO: Neil Armstrong, James Baldwin, Lucille Ball, Emily Brontë, Wilt Chamberlain, Julia Child, William J. Clinton, Cecil B. De Mille, Ogden Nash, Amelia Earhart, Edna Ferber, Arthur Goldberg, Alfred Hitchcock, Mick Jagger, George Meany, Annie Oakley, George Bernard Shaw, Napoleon, Jacqueline Onassis, Henry Ford, Francis Scott Key, Andy Warhol, Mae West, Orville Wright

VIRGO: Ingrid Bergman, Warren Burger, Maurice Chevalier, Agatha Christie, Sean Connery, Lafayette, Peter Falk, Greta Garbo, Althea Gibson, Arthur Godfrey, Goethe, Buddy Hackett, Michael Jackson, Lyndon Johnson, D. H. Lawrence, Sophia Loren, Grandma Moses, Arnold Palmer, Queen Elizabeth I, Walter Reuther, Peter Sellers, Lily Tomlin, George Wallace

LIBRA: Brigitte Bardot, Art Buchwald, Truman Capote, Dwight D. Eisenhower, William Faulkner, F. Scott Fitzgerald, Gandhi, George Gershwin, Micky Mantle, Helen Hayes, Vladimir Horowitz, Doris Lessing, Martina Navratalova, Eugene O'Neill, Luciano Pavarotti, Emily Post, Eleanor Roosevelt, Bruce Springsteen, Margaret Thatcher, Gore Vidal, Barbara Walters, Oscar Wilde

SCORPIO: Vivien Leigh, Richard Burton, Art Carney, Johnny Carson, Billy Graham, Grace Kelly, Walter Cronkite, Marie Curie, Charles de Gaulle, Linda Evans, Indira Gandhi, Theodore Roosevelt, Rock Hudson, Katherine Hepburn, Robert F. Kennedy, Billie Jean King, Martin Luther, Georgia O'Keeffe, Pablo Picasso, Jonas Salk, Alan Shepard, Robert Louis Stevenson

SAGITTARIUS: Jane Austen, Louisa May Alcott, Woody Allen, Beethoven, Willy Brandt, Mary Martin, William F. Buckley, Maria Callas, Winston Churchill, Noel Coward, Emily Dickinson, Walt Disney, Benjamin Disraeli, James Doolittle, Kirk Douglas, Chet Huntley, Jane Fonda, Chris Evert Lloyd, Margaret Mead, Charles Schulz, John Milton, Frank Sinatra, Steven Spielberg

CAPRICORN: Muhammad Ali, Isaac Asimov, Pablo Casals, Dizzy Dean, Marlene Dietrich, James Farmer, Ava Gardner, Barry Goldwater, Cary Grant, J. Edgar Hoover, Howard Hughes, Joan of Arc, Gypsy Rose Lee, Martin Luther King, Jr., Rudyard Kipling, Mao Tse-tung, Richard Nixon, Gamal Nasser, Louis Pasteur, Albert Schweitzer, Stalin, Benjamin Franklin, Elvis Presley

AQUARIUS: Marian Anderson, Susan B. Anthony, Jack Benny, John Barrymore, Mikhail Baryshnikov, Charles Darwin, Charles Dickens, Thomas Edison, Clark Gable, Jascha Heifetz, Abraham Lincoln, Yehudi Menuhin, Mozart, Jack Nicklaus, Ronald Reagan, Jackie Robinson, Norman Rockwell, Franklin D. Roosevelt, Gertrude Stein, Charles Lindbergh, Margaret Truman

PISCES: Edward Albee, Harry Belafonte, Alexander Graham Bell, Chopin, Adelle Davis, Albert Einstein, Golda Meir, Jackie Gleason, Winslow Homer, Edward M. Kennedy, Victor Hugo, Mike Mansfield, Michelangelo, Edna St. Vincent Millay, Liza Minelli, John Steinbeck, Linus Pauling, Ravel, Renoir, Diana Ross, William Shirer, Elizabeth Taylor, George Washington

The Signs and Their Key Words

		POSITIVE	NEGATIVE
ARIES	self	courage, initiative, pioneer instinct	brash rudeness, selfish impetuosity
TAURUS	money	endurance, loyalty, wealth	obstinacy, gluttony
GEMINI	mind	versatility	capriciousness, unreliability
CANCER	family	sympathy, homing instinct	clannishness, childishness
LEO	children	love, authority, integrity	egotism, force
VIRGO	work	purity, industry, analysis	faultfinding, cynicism
LIBRA	marriage	harmony, justice	vacillation, superficiality
SCORPIO	sex	survival, regeneration	vengeance, discord
SAGITTARIUS	travel	optimism, higher learning	lawlessness
CAPRICORN	career	depth	narrowness, gloom
AQUARIUS	friends	human fellowship, genius	perverse unpredictability
PISCES	confine-ment	spiritual love, universality	diffusion, escapism

The Elements and Qualities of The Signs

Every sign has both an *element* and a *quality* associated with it. The element indicates the basic makeup of the sign, and the quality describes the kind of activity associated with each.

Element	Sign	Quality	Sign
FIRE	ARIES	CARDINAL....	ARIES
	LEO		LIBRA
	SAGITTARIUS		CANCER
			CAPRICORN
EARTH....	TAURUS		
	VIRGO		
	CAPRICORN	FIXED	TAURUS
			LEO
			SCORPIO
AIR........	GEMINI		AQUARIUS
	LIBRA		
	AQUARIUS		
		MUTABLE	GEMINI
WATER....	CANCER		VIRGO
	SCORPIO		SAGITTARIUS
	PISCES		PISCES

Signs can be grouped together according to their element and quality. Signs of the same element share many basic traits in common. They tend to form stable configurations and ultimately harmonious relationships. Signs of the same quality are often less harmonious, but they share many dynamic potentials for growth as well as profound fulfillment.

Further discussion of each of these sign groupings is provided on the following pages.

The Fire Signs

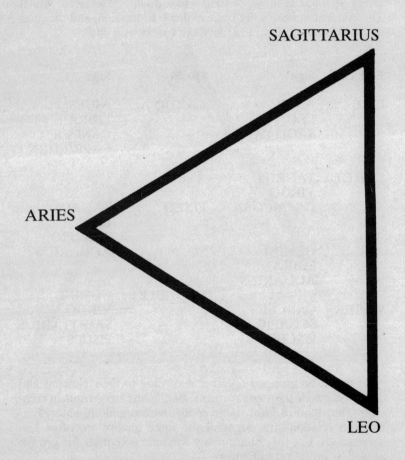

SAGITTARIUS

ARIES

LEO

This is the fire group. On the whole these are emotional, volatile types, quick to anger, quick to forgive. They are adventurous, powerful people and act as a source of inspiration for everyone. They spark into action with immediate exuberant impulses. They are intelligent, self-involved, creative, and idealistic. They all share a certain vibrancy and glow that outwardly reflects an inner flame and passion for living.

The Earth Signs

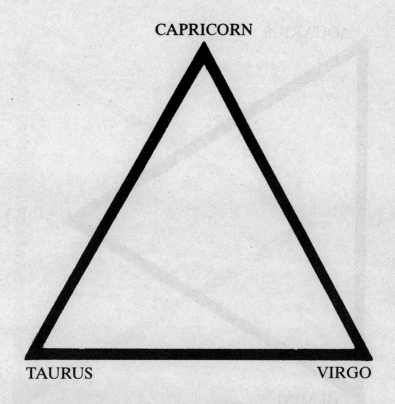

CAPRICORN

TAURUS   VIRGO

This is the earth group. They are in constant touch with the material world and tend to be conservative. Although they are all
capable of spartan self-discipline, they are earthy, sensual people
who are stimulated by the tangible, elegant, and luxurious. The
thread of their lives is always practical, but they do fantasize and
are often attracted to dark, mysterious, emotional people. They
are like great cliffs overhanging the sea, forever married to the
ocean but always resisting erosion from the dark, emotional forces
that thunder at their feet.

The Air Signs

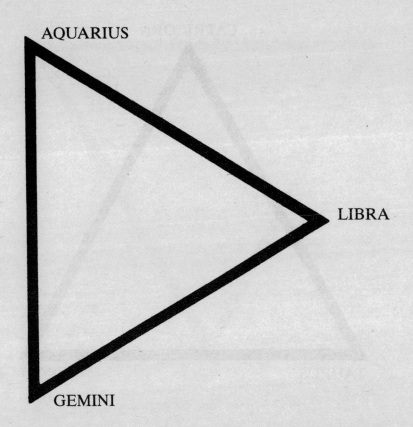

This is the air group. They are light, mental creatures desirous of contact, communication, and relationship. They are involved with people and the forming of ties on many levels. Original thinkers, they are the bearers of human news. Their language is their sense of word, color, style, and beauty. They provide an atmosphere suitable and pleasant for living. They add change and versatility to the scene, and it is through them that we can explore new territory of human intelligence and experience.

The Water Signs

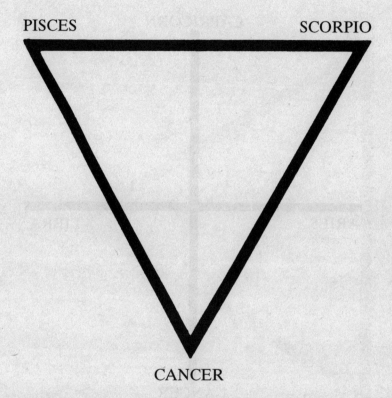

PISCES

SCORPIO

CANCER

This is the water group. Through the water people, we are all joined together on emotional, nonverbal levels. They are silent, mysterious types whose magic hypnotizes even the most determined realist. They have uncanny perceptions about people and are as rich as the oceans when it comes to feeling, emotion, or imagination. They are sensitive, mystical creatures with memories that go back beyond time. Through water, life is sustained. These people have the potential for the depths of darkness or the heights of mysticism and art.

The Cardinal Signs

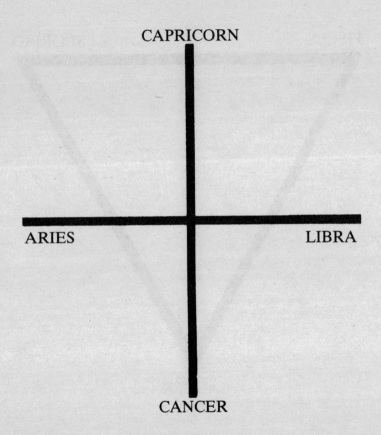

Put together, this is a clear-cut picture of dynamism, activity, tremendous stress, and remarkable achievement. These people know the meaning of great change since their lives are often characterized by significant crises and major successes. This combination is like a simultaneous storm of summer, fall, winter, and spring. The danger is chaotic diffusion of energy; the potential is irrepressible growth and victory.

The Fixed Signs

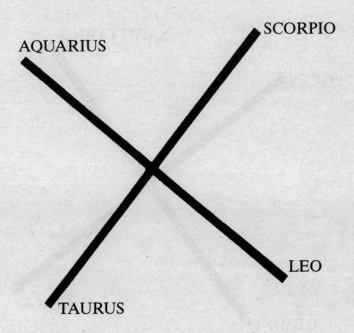

Fixed signs are always establishing themselves in a given place or area of experience. Like explorers who arrive and plant a flag, these people claim a position from which they do not enjoy being deposed. They are staunch, stalwart, upright, trusty, honorable people, although their obstinacy is well-known. Their contribution is fixity, and they are the angels who support our visible world.

The Mutable Signs

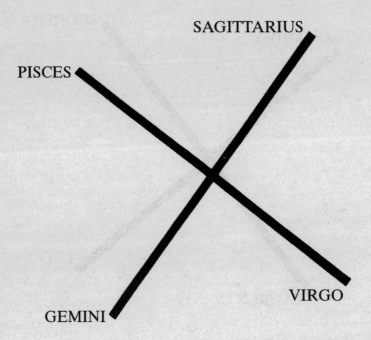

Mutable people are versatile, sensitive, intelligent, nervous, and deeply curious about life. They are the translators of all energy. They often carry out or complete tasks initiated by others. Combinations of these signs have highly developed minds; they are imaginative and jumpy and think and talk a lot. At worst their lives are a Tower of Babel. At best they are adaptable and ready creatures who can assimilate one kind of experience and enjoy it while anticipating coming changes.

THE PLANETS
OF THE SOLAR SYSTEM

This section describes the planets of the solar system. In astrology, both the Sun and the Moon are considered to be planets. Because of the Moon's influence in our day-to-day lives, the Moon is described in a separate section following this one.

The Planets and the Signs They Rule

The signs of the Zodiac are linked to the planets in the following way. Each sign is governed or ruled by one or more planets. No matter where the planets are located in the sky at any given moment, they still rule their respective signs, and when they travel through the signs they rule, they have special dignity and their effects are stronger.

Following is a list of the planets and the signs they rule. After looking at the list, read the definitions of the planets and see if you can determine how the planet ruling *your* Sun sign has affected your life.

SIGNS	RULING PLANETS
Aries	Mars, Pluto
Taurus	Venus
Gemini	Mercury
Cancer	Moon
Leo	Sun
Virgo	Mercury
Libra	Venus
Scorpio	Mars, Pluto
Sagittarius	Jupiter
Capricorn	Saturn
Aquarius	Saturn, Uranus
Pisces	Jupiter, Neptune

Characteristics of the Planets

The following pages give the meaning and characteristics of the planets of the solar system. They all travel around the Sun at different speeds and different distances. Taken with the Sun, they all distribute individual intelligence and ability throughout the entire chart.

The planets modify the influence of the Sun in a chart according to their own particular natures, strengths, and positions. Their positions must be calculated for each year and day, and their function and expression in a horoscope will change as they move from one area of the Zodiac to another.

We start with a description of the sun.

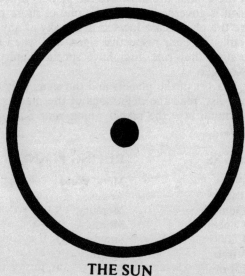

THE SUN

SUN

This is the center of existence. Around this flaming sphere all the planets revolve in endless orbits. Our star is constantly sending out its beams of light and energy without which no life on Earth would be possible. In astrology it symbolizes everything we are trying to become, the center around which all of our activity in life will always revolve. It is the symbol of our basic nature and describes the natural and constant thread that runs through everything that we do from birth to death on this planet.

To early astrologers, the Sun seemed to be another planet because it crossed the heavens every day, just like the rest of the bodies in the sky.

It is the only star near enough to be seen well—it is, in fact, a dwarf star. Approximately 860,000 miles in diameter, it is about ten times as wide as the giant planet Jupiter. The next nearest star is nearly 300,000 times as far away, and if the Sun were located as far away as most of the bright stars, it would be too faint to be seen without a telescope.

Everything in the horoscope ultimately revolves around this singular body. Although other forces may be prominent in the charts of some individuals, still the Sun is the total nucleus of being and symbolizes the complete potential of every human being alive. It is vitality and the life force. Your whole essence comes from the position of the Sun.

You are always trying to express the Sun according to its position by house and sign. Possibility for all development is found in the Sun, and it marks the fundamental character of your personal radiations all around you.

It is the symbol of strength, vigor, wisdom, dignity, ardor, and generosity, and the ability for a person to function as a mature individual. It is also a creative force in society. It is consciousness of the gift of life.

The underdeveloped solar nature is arrogant, pushy, undependable, and proud, and is constantly using force.

MERCURY

Mercury is the planet closest to the Sun. It races around our star, gathering information and translating it to the rest of the system. Mercury represents your capacity to understand the desires of your own will and to translate those desires into action.

In other words it is the planet of mind and the power of communication. Through Mercury we develop an ability to think, write, speak, and observe—to become aware of the world around us. It colors our attitudes and vision of the world, as well as our capacity to communicate our inner responses to the outside world. Some people who have serious disabilities in their power of verbal communication have often wrongly been described as people lacking intelligence.

Although this planet (and its position in the horoscope) indicates your power to communicate your thoughts and perceptions to the world, intelligence is something deeper. Intelligence is distributed throughout all the planets. It is the relationship of the planets to each other that truly describes what we call intelligence. Mercury rules speaking, language, mathematics, draft and design, students, messengers, young people, offices, teachers, and any pursuits where the mind of man has wings.

VENUS

Venus is beauty. It symbolizes the harmony and radiance of a rare and elusive quality: beauty itself. It is refinement and delicacy, softness and charm. In astrology it indicates grace, balance, and the aesthetic sense. Where Venus is we see beauty, a gentle drawing in of energy and the need for satisfaction and completion. It is a special touch that finishes off rough edges. It is sensitivity, and affection, and it is always the place for that other elusive phenomenon: love. Venus describes our sense of what is beautiful and loving. Poorly developed, it is vulgar, tasteless, and self-indulgent. But its ideal is the flame of spiritual love—Aphrodite, goddess of love, and the sweetness and power of personal beauty.

MARS

Mars is raw, crude energy. The planet next to Earth but outward from the Sun is a fiery red sphere that charges through the horoscope with force and fury. It represents the way you reach out for new adventure and new experience. It is energy and drive, initiative, courage, and daring. It is the power to start something and see it through. It can be thoughtless, cruel and wild, angry and hostile, causing cuts, burns, scalds, and wounds. It can stab its way through a chart, or it can be the symbol of healthy spirited adventure, well-channeled constructive power to begin and keep up the drive. If you have trouble starting things, if you lack the get-up-and-go to start the ball rolling, if you lack aggressiveness and self-confidence, chances are there's another planet influencing your Mars. Mars rules soldiers, butchers, surgeons, salesmen—any field that requires daring, bold skill, operational technique, or self-promotion.

JUPITER

This is the largest planet of the solar system. Scientists have recently learned that Jupiter reflects more light than it receives from the Sun. In a sense it is like a star itself. In astrology it rules good luck and good cheer, health, wealth, optimism, happiness, success, and joy. It is the symbol of opportunity and always opens the way for new possibilities in your life. It rules exuberance, enthusiasm, wisdom, knowledge, generosity, and all forms of expansion in general. It rules actors, statesmen, clerics, professional people, religion, publishing, and the distribution of many people over large areas.

Sometimes Jupiter makes you think you deserve everything, and you become sloppy, wasteful, careless and rude, prodigal and lawless, in the illusion that nothing can ever go wrong. Then there is the danger of overconfidence, exaggeration, undependability, and overindulgence.

Jupiter is the minimization of limitation and the emphasis on spirituality and potential. It is the thirst for knowledge and higher learning.

SATURN

Saturn circles our system in dark splendor with its mysterious rings, forcing us to be awakened to whatever we have neglected in the past. It will present real puzzles and problems to be solved, causing delays, obstacles, and hindrances. By doing so, Saturn stirs our own sensitivity to those areas where we are laziest.

Here we must patiently develop *method*, and only through painstaking effort can our ends be achieved. It brings order to a horoscope and imposes reason just where we are feeling least reasonable. By creating limitations and boundary, Saturn shows the consequences of being human and demands that we accept the changing cycles inevitable in human life. Saturn rules time, old age, and sobriety. It can bring depression, gloom, jealousy, and greed, or serious acceptance of responsibilities out of which success will develop. With Saturn there is nothing to do but face facts. It rules laborers, stones, granite, rocks, and crystals of all kinds.

THE OUTER PLANETS:
URANUS, NEPTUNE, PLUTO

Uranus, Neptune, Pluto are the outer planets. They liberate human beings from cultural conditioning, and in that sense are the lawbreakers. In early times it was thought that Saturn was the last planet of the system—the outer limit beyond which we could never go. The discovery of the next three planets ushered in new phases of human history, revolution, and technology.

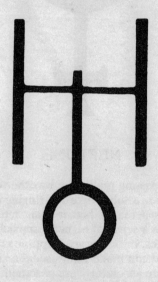

URANUS

Uranus rules unexpected change, upheaval, revolution. It is the symbol of total independence and asserts the freedom of an individual from all restriction and restraint. It is a breakthrough planet and indicates talent, originality, and genius in a horoscope. It usually causes last-minute reversals and changes of plan, unwanted separations, accidents, catastrophes, and eccentric behavior. It can add irrational rebelliousness and perverse bohemianism to a personality or a streak of unaffected brilliance in science and art. It rules technology, aviation, and all forms of electrical and electronic advancement. It governs great leaps forward and topsy-turvy situations, and *always* turns things around at the last minute. Its effects are difficult to predict, since it rules sudden last-minute decisions and events that come like lightning out of the blue.

NEPTUNE

Neptune dissolves existing reality the way the sea erodes the cliffs beside it. Its effects are subtle like the ringing of a buoy's bell in the fog. It suggests a reality higher than definition can usually describe. It awakens a sense of higher responsibility often causing guilt, worry, anxieties, or delusions. Neptune is associated with all forms of escape and can make things seem a certain way so convincingly that you are absolutely sure of something that eventually turns out to be quite different.

It is the planet of illusion and therefore governs the invisible realms that lie beyond our ordinary minds, beyond our simple factual ability to prove what is "real." Treachery, deceit, disillusionment, and disappointment are linked to Neptune. It describes a vague reality that promises eternity and the divine, yet in a manner so complex that we cannot really fathom it at all. At its worst Neptune is a cheap intoxicant; at its best it is the poetry, music, and inspiration of the higher planes of spiritual love. It has dominion over movies, photographs, and much of the arts.

PLUTO

Pluto lies at the outpost of our system and therefore rules finality in a horoscope—the final closing of chapters in your life, the passing of major milestones and points of development from which there is no return. It is a final wipeout, a closeout, an evacuation. It is a distant, subtle but powerful catalyst in all transformations that occur. It creates, destroys, then recreates. Sometimes Pluto starts its influence with a minor event or insignificant incident that might even go unnoticed. Slowly but surely, little by little, everything changes, until at last there has been a total transformation in the area of your life where Pluto has been operating. It rules mass thinking and the trends that society first rejects, then adopts, and finally outgrows.

Pluto rules the dead and the underworld—all the powerful forces of creation and destruction that go on all the time beneath, around, and above us. It can bring a lust for power with strong obsessions.

It is the planet that rules the metamorphosis of the caterpillar into a butterfly, for it symbolizes the capacity to change totally and forever a person's lifestyle, way of thought, and behavior.

THE MOON IN EACH SIGN

The Moon is the nearest planet to the Earth. It exerts more observable influence on us from day to day than any other planet. The effect is very personal, very intimate, and if we are not aware of how it works it can make us quite unstable in our ideas. And the annoying thing is that at these times we often see our own instability but can do nothing about it. A knowledge of what can be expected may help considerably. We can then be prepared to stand strong against the Moon's negative influences and use its positive ones to help us to get ahead. Who has not heard of going with the tide?

The Moon reflects, has no light of its own. It reflects the Sun— the life giver—in the form of vital movement. The Moon controls the tides, the blood rhythm, the movement of sap in trees and plants. Its nature is inconstancy and change so it signifies our moods, our superficial behavior—walking, talking, and especially thinking. Being a true reflector of other forces, the Moon is cold, watery like the surface of a still lake, brilliant and scintillating at times, but easily ruffled and disturbed by the winds of change.

The Moon takes about 27⅓ days to make a complete transit of the Zodiac. It spends just over 2¼ days in each sign. During that time it reflects the qualities, energies, and characteristics of the sign and, to a degree, the planet which rules the sign. When the Moon in its transit occupies a sign incompatible with our own birth sign, we can expect to feel a vague uneasiness, perhaps a touch of irritableness. We should not be discouraged nor let the feeling get us down, or, worse still, allow ourselves to take the discomfort out on others. Try to remember that the Moon has to change signs within 55 hours and, provided you are not physically ill, your mood will probably change with it. It is amazing how frequently depression lifts with the shift in the Moon's position. And, of course, when the Moon is transiting a sign compatible or sympathetic to yours, you will probably feel some sort of stimulation or just be plain happy to be alive.

In the horoscope, the Moon is such a powerful indicator that competent astrologers often use the sign it occupied at birth as the birth sign of the person. This is done particularly when the Sun is on the cusp, or edge, of two signs. Most experienced astrologers, however, coordinate both Sun and Moon signs by reading and confirming from one to the other and secure a far more accurate and personalized analysis.

For these reasons, the Moon tables which follow this section (see pages 86–92) are of great importance to the individual. They show the days and the exact times the Moon will enter each sign of the Zodiac for the year. Remember, you have to adjust the indicated times to local time. The corrections, already calculated for most of the main cities, are at the beginning of the tables. What follows now is a guide to the influences that will be reflected to the Earth by the Moon while it transits each of the twelve signs. The influence is at its peak about 26 hours after the Moon enters a sign. As you read the daily forecast, check the Moon sign for any given day and glance back at this guide.

MOON IN ARIES

This is a time for action, for reaching out beyond the usual self-imposed limitations and faint-hearted cautions. If you have plans in your head or on your desk, put them into practice. New ventures, applications, new jobs, new starts of any kind—all have a good chance of success. This is the period when original and dynamic impulses are being reflected onto Earth. Such energies are extremely vital and favor the pursuit of pleasure and adventure in practically every form. Sick people should feel an improvement. Those who are well will probably find themselves exuding confidence and optimism. People fond of physical exercise should find their bodies growing with tone and well-being. Boldness, strength, determination should characterize most of your activities with a readiness to face up to old challenges. Yesterday's problems may seem petty and exaggerated—so deal with them. Strike out alone. Self-reliance will attract others to you. This is a good time for making friends. Business and marriage partners are more likely to be impressed with the man and woman of action. Opposition will be overcome or thrown aside with much less effort than usual. CAUTION: Be dominant but not domineering.

MOON IN TAURUS

The spontaneous, action-packed person of yesterday gives way to the cautious, diligent, hardworking "thinker." In this period ideas will probably be concentrated on ways of improving finances. A great deal of time may be spent figuring out and going over schemes and plans. It is the right time to be careful with detail.

People will find themselves working longer than usual at their desks. Or devoting more time to serious thought about the future. A strong desire to put order into business and financial arrangements may cause extra work. Loved ones may complain of being neglected and may fail to appreciate that your efforts are for their ultimate benefit. Your desire for system may extend to criticism of arrangements in the home and lead to minor upsets. Health may be affected through overwork. Try to secure a reasonable amount of rest and relaxation, although the tendency will be to "keep going" despite good advice. Work done conscientiously in this period should result in a solid contribution to your future security. CAUTION: Try not to be as serious with people as the work you are engaged in.

MOON IN GEMINI
The humdrum of routine and too much work should suddenly end. You are likely to find yourself in an expansive, quicksilver world of change and self-expression. Urges to write, to paint, to experience the freedom of some sort of artistic outpouring, may be very strong. Take full advantage of them. You may find yourself finishing something you began and put aside long ago. Or embarking on something new which could easily be prompted by a chance meeting, a new acquaintance, or even an advertisement. There may be a yearning for a change of scenery, the feeling to visit another country (not too far away), or at least to get away for a few days. This may result in short, quick journeys. Or, if you are planning a single visit, there may be some unexpected changes or detours on the way. Familiar activities will seem to give little satisfaction unless they contain a fresh element of excitement or expectation. The inclination will be toward untried pursuits, particularly those that allow you to express your inner nature. The accent is on new faces, new places. CAUTION: Do not be too quick to commit yourself emotionally.

MOON IN CANCER
Feelings of uncertainty and vague insecurity are likely to cause problems while the Moon is in Cancer. Thoughts may turn frequently to the warmth of the home and the comfort of loved ones. Nostalgic impulses could cause you to bring out old photographs and letters and reflect on the days when your life seemed to be much more rewarding and less demanding. The love and understanding of parents and family may be important, and, if it is not forthcoming, you may have to fight against bouts of self-pity. The cordiality of friends and the thought of good times with them that are sure to be repeated will help to restore you to a happier frame

of mind. The desire to be alone may follow minor setbacks or rebuffs at this time, but solitude is unlikely to help. Better to get on the telephone or visit someone. This period often causes peculiar dreams and upsurges of imaginative thinking which can be helpful to authors of occult and mystical works. Preoccupation with the personal world of simple human needs can overshadow any material strivings. CAUTION: Do not spend too much time thinking—seek the company of loved ones or close friends.

MOON IN LEO

New horizons of exciting and rather extravagant activity open up. This is the time for exhilarating entertainment, glamorous and lavish parties, and expensive shopping sprees. Any merrymaking that relies upon your generosity as a host has every chance of being a spectacular success. You should find yourself right in the center of the fun, either as the life of the party or simply as a person whom happy people like to be with. Romance thrives in this heady atmosphere and friendships are likely to explode unexpectedly into serious attachments. Children and younger people should be attracted to you and you may find yourself organizing a picnic or a visit to a fun-fair, the movies, or the beach. The sunny company and vitality of youthful companions should help you to find some unsuspected energy. In career, you could find an opening for promotion or advancement. This should be the time to make a direct approach. The period favors those engaged in original research. CAUTION: Bask in popularity, not in flattery.

MOON IN VIRGO

Off comes the party cap and out steps the busy, practical worker. He wants to get his personal affairs straight, to rearrange them, if necessary, for more efficiency, so he will have more time for more work. He clears up his correspondence, pays outstanding bills, makes numerous phone calls. He is likely to make inquiries, or sign up for some new insurance and put money into gilt-edged investment. Thoughts probably revolve around the need for future security—to tie up loose ends and clear the decks. There may be a tendency to be "finicky," to interfere in the routine of others, particularly friends and family members. The motive may be a genuine desire to help with suggestions for updating or streamlining their affairs, but these will probably not be welcomed. Sympathy may be felt for less fortunate sections of the community and a flurry of some sort of voluntary service is likely. This may be accompanied by strong feelings of responsibility on several fronts and health may suffer from extra efforts made. CAUTION: Everyone may not want your help or advice.

MOON IN LIBRA

These are days of harmony and agreement and you should find yourself at peace with most others. Relationships tend to be smooth and sweet-flowing. Friends may become closer and bonds deepen in mutual understanding. Hopes will be shared. Progress by cooperation could be the secret of success in every sphere. In business, established partnerships may flourish and new ones get off to a good start. Acquaintances could discover similar interests that lead to congenial discussions and rewarding exchanges of some sort. Love, as a unifying force, reaches its optimum. Marriage partners should find accord. Those who wed at this time face the prospect of a happy union. Cooperation and tolerance are felt to be stronger than dissension and impatience. The argumentative are not quite so loud in their bellowings, nor as inflexible in their attitudes. In the home, there should be a greater recognition of the other point of view and a readiness to put the wishes of the group before selfish insistence. This is a favorable time to join an art group. CAUTION: Do not be too independent—let others help you if they want to.

MOON IN SCORPIO

Driving impulses to make money and to economize are likely to cause upsets all around. No area of expenditure is likely to be spared the ax, including the household budget. This is a time when the desire to cut down on extravagance can become near fanatical. Care must be exercised to try to keep the aim in reasonable perspective. Others may not feel the same urgent need to save and may retaliate. There is a danger that possessions of sentimental value will be sold to realize cash for investment. Buying and selling of stock for quick profit is also likely. The attention turns to organizing, reorganizing, tidying up at home and at work. Neglected jobs could suddenly be done with great bursts of energy. The desire for solitude may intervene. Self-searching thoughts could disturb. The sense of invisible and mysterious energies in play could cause some excitability. The reassurance of loves ones may help. CAUTION: Be kind to the people you love.

MOON IN SAGITTARIUS

These are days when you are likely to be stirred and elevated by discussions and reflections of a religious and philosophical nature. Ideas of faraway places may cause unusual response and excitement. A decision may be made to visit someone overseas, perhaps a person whose influence was important to your earlier character development. There could be a strong resolution to get away from present intellectual patterns, to learn new subjects, and to meet more interesting people. The superficial may be rejected in all its forms. An impatience with old ideas and unimaginative contacts could lead to a change of companions and interests. There may be an upsurge of religious feeling and metaphysical inquiry. Even a new insight into the significance of astrology and other occult studies is likely under the curious stimulus of the Moon in Sagittarius. Physically, you may express this need for fundamental change by spending more time outdoors: sports, gardening, long walks appeal. CAUTION: Try to channel any restlessness into worthwhile study.

MOON IN CAPRICORN

Life in these hours may seem to pivot around the importance of gaining prestige and honor in the career, as well as maintaining a spotless reputation. Ambitious urges may be excessive and could be accompanied by quite acquisitive drives for money. Effort should be directed along strictly ethical lines where there is no possibility of reproach or scandal. All endeavors are likely to be characterized by great earnestness, and an air of authority and purpose which should impress those who are looking for leadership or reliability. The desire to conform to accepted standards may extend to sharp criticism of family members. Frivolity and unconventional actions are unlikely to amuse while the Moon is in Capricorn. Moderation and seriousness are the orders of the day. Achievement and recognition in this period could come through community work or organizing for the benefit of some amateur group. CAUTION: Dignity and esteem are not always self-awarded.

MOON IN AQUARIUS

Moon in Aquarius is in the second last sign of the Zodiac where ideas can become disturbingly fine and subtle. The result is often a mental "no-man's land" where imagination cannot be trusted with the same certitude as other times. The dangers for the individual are the extremes of optimism and pessimism. Unless the imagination is held in check, situations are likely to be misread, and rosy conclusions drawn where they do not exist. Consequences for the unwary can be costly in career and business. Best to think twice and not speak or act until you think again. Pessimism can be a cruel self-inflicted penalty for delusion at this time. Between the two extremes are strange areas of self-deception which, for example, can make the selfish person think he is actually being generous. Eerie dreams which resemble the reality and even seem to continue into the waking state are also possible. CAUTION: Look for the fact and not just for the image in your mind.

MOON IN PISCES

Everything seems to come to the surface now. Memory may be crystal clear, throwing up long-forgotten information which could be valuable in the career or business. Flashes of clairvoyance and intuition are possible along with sudden realizations of one's own nature, which may be used for self-improvement. A talent, never before suspected, may be discovered. Qualities not evident before in friends and marriage partners are likely to be noticed. As this is a period in which the truth seems to emerge, the discovery of false characteristics is likely to lead to disenchantment or a shift in attachments. However, when qualities are accepted, it should lead to happiness and deeper feeling. Surprise solutions could bob up for old problems. There may be a public announcement of the solving of a crime or mystery. People with secrets may find someone has "guessed" correctly. The secrets of the soul or the inner self also tend to reveal themselves. Religious and philosophical groups may make some interesting discoveries. CAUTION: Not a time for activities that depend on secrecy.

NOTE: When you read your daily forecasts, use the Moon Sign Dates that are provided in the following section of Moon Tables. Then you may want to glance back here for the Moon's influence in a given sign.

MOON TABLES

CORRECTION FOR NEW YORK TIME, FIVE HOURS WEST OF GREENWICH

Atlanta, Boston, Detroit, Miami, Washington, Montreal,
Ottawa, Quebec, Bogota, Havana, Lima, Santiago..Same time

Chicago, New Orleans, Houston, Winnipeg, Churchill,
Mexico City... Deduct 1 hour

Albuquerque, Denver, Phoenix, El Paso, Edmonton,
Helena .... Deduct 2 hours

Los Angeles, San Francisco, Reno, Portland,
Seattle, Vancouver .... Deduct 3 hours

Honolulu, Anchorage, Fairbanks, Kodiak .... Deduct 5 hours

Nome, Samoa, Tonga, Midway.................... Deduct 6 hours

Halifax, Bermuda, San Juan, Caracas, La Paz,
Barbados..Add 1 hour

St. John's, Brasilia, Rio de Janeiro, Sao Paulo,
Buenos Aires, Montevideo..........................Add 2 hours

Azores, Cape Verde Islands...........................Add 3 hours

Canary Islands, Madeira, Reykjavik ....Add 4 hours

London, Paris, Amsterdam, Madrid, Lisbon,
Gibraltar, Belfast, Rabat ....Add 5 hours

Frankfurt, Rome, Oslo, Stockholm, Prague,
Belgrade..Add 6 hours

Bucharest, Beirut, Tel Aviv, Athens, Istanbul, Cairo,
Alexandria, Cape Town, Johannesburg ....Add 7 hours

Moscow, Leningrad, Baghdad, Dhahran,
Addis Ababa, Nairobi, Teheran, Zanzibar.........Add 8 hours

Bombay, Calcutta, Sri Lanka..................... Add 10 ½ hours

Hong Kong, Shanghai, Manila, Peking, Perth...... Add 13 hours

Tokyo, Okinawa, Darwin, Pusan.................... Add 14 hours

Sydney, Melbourne, Port Moresby, Guam.......... Add 15 hours

Auckland, Wellington, Suva, Wake................. Add 17 hours

2000 MOON SIGN DATES—
NEW YORK TIME

JANUARY Day Moon Enters		FEBRUARY Day Moon Enters		MARCH Day Moon Enters	
1. Scorp.		1. Capric.	0:11 pm	1. Capric.	
2. Sagitt.	4:33 pm	2. Capric.		2. Aquar.	8:15 am
3. Sagitt.		3. Capric.		3. Aquar.	
4. Sagitt.		4. Aquar.	0:32 am	4. Pisces	6:31 pm
5. Capric.	5:25 am	5. Aquar.		5. Pisces	
6. Capric.		6. Pisces	11:03 am	6. Pisces	
7. Aquar.	5:54 pm	7. Pisces		7. Aries	1:55 am
8. Aquar.		8. Aries	7:18 pm	8. Aries	
9. Aquar.		9. Aries		9. Taurus	7:02 am
10. Pisces	5:00 am	10. Aries		10. Taurus	
11. Pisces		11. Taurus	1:22 am	11. Gemini	10:47 am
12. Aries	1:49 pm	12. Taurus		12. Gemini	
13. Aries		13. Gemini	5:24 am	13. Cancer	1:52 pm
14. Taurus	7:39 pm	14. Gemini		14. Cancer	
15. Taurus		15. Cancer	7:46 am	15. Leo	4:44 pm
16. Gemini	10:26 pm	16. Cancer		16. Leo	
17. Gemini		17. Leo	9:12 am	17. Virgo	7:49 pm
18. Cancer	11:02 pm	18. Leo		18. Virgo	
19. Cancer		19. Virgo	10:54 am	19. Libra	11:58 pm
20. Leo	10:59 pm	20. Virgo		20. Libra	
21. Leo		21. Libra	2:22 pm	21. Libra	
22. Leo		22. Libra		22. Scorp.	6:19 am
23. Virgo	0:08 am	23. Scorp.	8:59 pm	23. Scorp.	
24. Virgo		24. Scorp.		24. Sagitt.	3:44 pm
25. Libra	4:10 am	25. Scorp.		25. Sagitt.	
26. Libra		26. Sagitt.	7:11 am	26. Sagitt.	
27. Scorp.	0:02 pm	27. Sagitt.		27. Capric.	3:52 am
28. Scorp.		28. Capric.	7:46 pm	28. Capric.	
29. Sagitt.	11:19 pm	29. Capric.		29. Aquar.	4:35 pm
30. Sagitt.				30. Aquar.	
31. Sagitt.				31. Aquar.	

Summer time to be considered where applicable.

2000 MOON SIGN DATES—
NEW YORK TIME

APRIL Day Moon Enters		MAY Day Moon Enters		JUNE Day Moon Enters	
1. Pisces	3:13 am	1. Aries		1. Gemini	11:35 am
2. Pisces		2. Taurus	11:55 pm	2. Gemini	
3. Aries	10:23 am	3. Taurus		3. Cancer	11:31 am
4. Aries		4. Taurus		4. Cancer	
5. Taurus	2:30 pm	5. Gemini	1:24 am	5. Leo	11:47 am
6. Taurus		6. Gemini		6. Leo	
7. Gemini	4:59 pm	7. Cancer	2:15 am	7. Virgo	1:58 pm
8. Gemini		8. Cancer		8. Virgo	
9. Cancer	7:17 pm	9. Leo	4:02 am	9. Libra	7:00 pm
10. Cancer		10. Leo		10. Libra	
11. Leo	10:17 pm	11. Virgo	7:42 am	11. Libra	
12. Leo		12. Virgo		12. Scorp.	0:56 am
13. Leo		13. Libra	1:28 pm	13. Scorp.	
14. Virgo	2:20 am	14. Libra		14. Sagitt.	1:19 pm
15. Virgo		15. Scorp.	9:17 pm	15. Sagitt.	
16. Libra	7:37 am	16. Scorp.		16. Sagitt.	
17. Libra		17. Scorp.		17. Capric.	1:28 am
18. Scorp.	2:36 pm	18. Sagitt.	7:10 am	18. Capric.	
19. Scorp.		19. Sagitt.		19. Aquar.	2:27 pm
20. Sagitt.	11:59 pm	20. Capric.	7:02 pm	20. Aquar.	
21. Sagitt.		21. Capric.		21. Aquar.	
22. Sagitt.		22. Capric.		22. Pisces	2:53 am
23. Capric.	11:48 am	23. Aquar.	8:01 am	23. Pisces	
24. Capric.		24. Aquar.		24. Aries	0:56 pm
25. Capric.		25. Pisces	8:08 pm	25. Aries	
26. Aquar.	0:43 am	26. Pisces		26. Taurus	7:20 pm
27. Aquar.		27. Pisces		27. Taurus	
28. Pisces	0:07 pm	28. Aries	5:09 am	28. Gemini	10:00 pm
29. Pisces		29. Aries		29. Gemini	
30. Aries	7:56 pm	30. Taurus	10:03 am	30. Cancer	10:10 pm
		31. Taurus			

Summer time to be considered where applicable.

2000 MOON SIGN DATES—
NEW YORK TIME

JULY		AUGUST		SEPTEMBER	
Day Moon Enters		**Day Moon Enters**		**Day Moon Enters**	
1. Cancer		1. Virgo	8:28 am	1. Libra	
2. Leo	9:39 pm	2. Virgo		2. Scorp.	0:56 am
3. Leo		3. Libra	10:32 am	3. Scorp.	
4. Virgo	10:20 pm	4. Libra		4. Sagitt.	9:09 am
5. Virgo		5. Scorp.	4:05 pm	5. Sagitt.	
6. Virgo		6. Scorp.		6. Capric.	8:48 pm
7. Libra	1:48 am	7. Scorp.		7. Capric.	
8. Libra		8. Sagitt.	1:31 am	8. Capric.	
9. Scorp.	8:49 am	9. Sagitt.		9. Aquar.	9:45 am
10. Scorp.		10. Capric.	1:45 pm	10. Aquar.	
11. Sagitt.	7:07 pm	11. Capric.		11. Pisces	9:35 pm
12. Sagitt.		12. Capric.		12. Pisces	
13. Sagitt.		13. Aquar.	2:44 am	13. Pisces	
14. Capric.	7:29 am	14. Aquar.		14. Aries	7:01 am
15. Capric.		15. Pisces	2:42 pm	15. Aries	
16. Aquar.	8:28 pm	16. Pisces		16. Taurus	2:06 pm
17. Aquar.		17. Pisces		17. Taurus	
18. Aquar.		18. Aries	0:45 am	18. Gemini	7:23 pm
19. Pisces	8:45 am	19. Aries		19. Gemini	
20. Pisces		20. Taurus	8:32 am	20. Cancer	11:17 pm
21. Aries	7:10 pm	21. Taurus		21. Cancer	
22. Aries		22. Gemini	1:56 pm	22. Cancer	
23. Aries		23. Gemini		23. Leo	2:01 am
24. Taurus	2:45 am	24. Cancer	5:01 pm	24. Leo	
25. Taurus		25. Cancer		25. Virgo	4:03 am
26. Gemini	7:02 am	26. Leo	6:18 pm	26. Virgo	
27. Gemini		27. Leo		27. Libra	6:23 am
28. Cancer	8:31 am	28. Virgo	6:56 pm	28. Libra	
29. Cancer		29. Virgo		29. Scorp.	10:31 am
30. Leo	8:25 am	30. Libra	8:34 pm	30. Scorp.	
31. Leo		31. Libra			

Summer time to be considered where applicable.

2000 MOON SIGN DATES— NEW YORK TIME

OCTOBER		NOVEMBER		DECEMBER	
Day Moon Enters		**Day Moon Enters**		**Day Moon Enters**	
1. Sagitt.	5:51 pm	1. Capric.		1. Aquar.	
2. Sagitt.		2. Capric.		2. Pisces	10:24 pm
3. Sagitt.		3. Aquar.	1:42 am	3. Pisces	
4. Capric.	4:43 am	4. Aquar.		4. Pisces	
5. Capric.		5. Pisces	2:14 pm	5. Aries	9:18 am
6. Aquar.	5:34 pm	6. Pisces		6. Aries	
7. Aquar.		7. Pisces		7. Taurus	4:28 pm
8. Aquar.		8. Aries	0:03 am	8. Taurus	
9. Pisces	5:37 am	9. Aries		9. Gemini	7:51 pm
10. Pisces		10. Taurus	6:13 am	10. Gemini	
11. Aries	2:52 pm	11. Taurus		11. Cancer	8:50 pm
12. Aries		12. Gemini	9:28 am	12. Cancer	
13. Taurus	9:07 pm	13. Gemini		13. Leo	9:10 pm
14. Taurus		14. Cancer	11:22 am	14. Leo	
15. Taurus		15. Cancer		15. Virgo	10:31 pm
16. Gemini	1:20 am	16. Leo	1:20 pm	16. Virgo	
17. Gemini		17. Leo		17. Virgo	
18. Cancer	4:38 am	18. Virgo	4:16 pm	18. Libra	2:02 am
19. Cancer		19. Virgo		19. Libra	
20. Leo	7:43 am	20. Libra	8:36 pm	20. Scorp.	8:13 am
21. Leo		21. Libra		21. Scorp.	
22. Virgo	10:53 am	22. Libra		22. Sagitt.	4:58 pm
23. Virgo		23. Scorp.	2:34 am	23. Sagitt.	
24. Libra	2:31 pm	24. Scorp.		24. Sagitt.	
25. Libra		25. Sagitt.	10:34 am	25. Capric.	3:55 am
26. Scorp.	7:24 pm	26. Sagitt.		26. Capric.	
27. Scorp.		27. Capric.	8:58 pm	27. Aquar.	4:26 pm
28. Scorp.		28. Capric.		28. Aquar.	
29. Sagitt.	2:41 am	29. Capric.		29. Aquar.	
30. Sagitt.		30. Aquar.	9:28 am	30. Pisces	5:28 am
31. Capric.	1:03 pm			31. Pisces	

Summer time to be considered where applicable.

2000 PHASES OF THE MOON— NEW YORK TIME

New Moon	First Quarter	Full Moon	Last Quarter
Jan. 6	Jan. 14	Jan. 20	Jan. 28
Feb. 5	Feb. 12	Feb. 19	Feb. 26
March 5	March 13	March 19	March 27
April 4	April 11	April 18	April 26
May 3	May 10	May 18	May 26
June 2	June 8	June 16	June 24
July 1	July 8	July 16	July 24
July 30	Aug. 6	Aug. 15	Aug. 22
Aug. 29	Sept. 5	Sept. 13	Sept. 20
Sept. 27	Oct. 5	Oct. 13	Oct. 20
Oct. 27	Nov. 4	Nov. 11	Nov. 18
Nov. 25	Dec. 3	Dec. 11	Dec. 17
Dec. 25	Jan. 2 ('01)	Jan. 9 ('01)	Jan. 17 ('01)

Each phase of the Moon lasts approximately seven to eight days, during which the Moon's shape gradually changes as it comes out of one phase and goes into the next.

There will be a partial solar eclipse during the New Moon phase on February 5, July 1, July 30, and December 25.

There will be a lunar eclipse during the Full Moon phase on January 20 and July 16.

2000 FISHING GUIDE

	Good	Best
January	14-18-21-22-23-24	6-19-20-28
February	5-17-18-19-20-21-27	12-16-22
March	13-17-18-19	6-20-21-22-23-28
April	4-15-16-21-26	11-17-18-19-20
May	10-18-19-20	4-15-16-17-21-26
June	2-9-14-15-16-19-25	13-17-18
July	13-14-17-18-19-31	1-8-15-16-24
August	13-14-15-18-22-29	7-12-16-17
September	5-10-11-14-15-16-27	12-13-21
October	11-12-13-16-20	5-10-14-15-27
November	4-8-9-10-12-13-14	11-18-25
December	10-11-14	4-8-9-12-13-18-25

2000 PLANTING GUIDE

	Aboveground Crops	**Root Crops**
January	7-10-11-15-16-19-20	1-25-26-27-28-29
February	7-8-11-12-16	2-3-22-23-24-25-29
March	6-10-14	1-5-20-21-22-23-27-28
April	6-10-11-17	1-2-19-20-24-25-29-30
May	4-7-8-14-15-16-17	3-21-22-26-27-31
June	4-10-11-12-13	17-18-22-23-27-28
July	2-7-8-9-10-11-15	20-21-24-25-29
August	4-5-6-7-11-12-31	16-17-21-25-26
September	1-2-3-7-8-12-28-29-30	17-18-21-22
October	1-4-5-6-10-27-28	14-15-18-19-25-26
November	1-2-6-7-28-29	11-15-21-22-23-24
December	3-4-8-9-26-31	12-13-18-19-20-21

	Pruning	**Weeds and Pests**
January	1-28-29	3-4-21-22-23-24-30-31
February	24-25	4-20-27-28
March	5-23	3-4-25-26-30-31
April	1-2-19-20-29-30	21-22-26-27
May	26-27	1-2-19-20-24-25-29
June	22-23	20-21-25-26-29-30
July	20-21-29	17-18-22-23-27
August	16-17-25-26	18-19-23-24-27-28
September	21-22	15-19-20-23-24-25-26
October	18-19	13-16-17-21-22-23
November	15-23-24	13-17-18-19-20
December	12-13-21	11-14-15-16-17-23-24

MOON'S INFLUENCE OVER PLANTS

Centuries ago it was established that seeds planted when the Moon is in signs and phases called Fruitful will produce more growth than seeds planted when the Moon is in a Barren sign.

Fruitful Signs: Taurus, Cancer, Libra, Scorpio, Capricorn, Pisces
Barren Signs: Aries, Gemini, Leo, Virgo, Sagittarius, Aquarius
Dry Signs: Aries, Gemini, Sagittarius, Aquarius

Activity	**Moon In**
Mow lawn, trim plants	**Fruitful sign:** 1st & 2nd quarter
Plant flowers	**Fruitful sign:** 2nd quarter; best in Cancer and Libra
Prune	**Fruitful sign:** 3rd & 4th quarter
Destroy pests; spray	**Barren sign:** 4th quarter
Harvest potatoes, root crops	**Dry sign:** 3rd & 4th quarter; Taurus, Leo, and Aquarius

MOON'S INFLUENCE OVER YOUR HEALTH

ARIES   Head, brain, face, upper jaw
TAURUS   Throat, neck, lower jaw
GEMINI   Hands, arms, lungs, shoulders, nervous system
CANCER   Esophagus, stomach, breasts, womb, liver
LEO   Heart, spine
VIRGO   Intestines, liver
LIBRA   Kidneys, lower back
SCORPIO   Sex and eliminative organs
SAGITTARIUS   Hips, thighs, liver
CAPRICORN   Skin, bones, teeth, knees
AQUARIUS   Circulatory system, lower legs
PISCES   Feet, tone of being

Try to avoid work being done on that part of the body when the Moon is in the sign governing that part.

MOON'S INFLUENCE OVER DAILY AFFAIRS

The Moon makes a complete transit of the Zodiac every 27 days 7 hours and 43 minutes. In making this transit the Moon forms different aspects with the planets and consequently has favorable or unfavorable bearings on affairs and events for persons according to the sign of the Zodiac under which they were born.

When the Moon is in conjunction with the Sun it is called a New Moon; when the Moon and Sun are in opposition it is called a Full Moon. From New Moon to Full Moon, first and second quarter—which takes about two weeks—the Moon is increasing or waxing. From Full Moon to New Moon, third and fourth quarter, the Moon is decreasing or waning.

Activity	Moon In
Business: buying and selling new, requiring public support	Sagittarius, Aries, Gemini, Virgo 1st and 2nd quarter
meant to be kept quiet	3rd and 4th quarter
Investigation	3rd and 4th quarter
Signing documents	1st & 2nd quarter, Cancer, Scorpio, Pisces
Advertising	2nd quarter, Sagittarius
Journeys and trips	1st & 2nd quarter, Gemini, Virgo
Renting offices, etc.	Taurus, Leo, Scorpio, Aquarius
Painting of house/apartment	3rd & 4th quarter, Taurus, Scorpio, Aquarius
Decorating	Gemini, Libra, Aquarius
Buying clothes and accessories	Taurus, Virgo
Beauty salon or barber shop visit	1st & 2nd quarter, Taurus, Leo, Libra, Scorpio, Aquarius
Weddings	1st & 2nd quarter

VIRGO

VIRGO

Character Analysis

People born under the sign of Virgo are generally practical. They believe in doing things thoroughly; there is nothing slipshod or haphazard about the way they do things. They are precise and methodical. The man or woman born under this sixth sign of the Zodiac respects common sense and tries to be rational in his or her approach to tasks or problems.

Virgo is the sign of work and service. It is the symbol of the farmer at harvest time, and so the man or woman born under this sign is sometimes called the Harvester. These people's tireless efforts to bring the fruits of the Earth to the table of humanity create great joy and beneficence. Celebration through work and harvest is the characteristic of the sign of Virgo.

Sincerity, zeal, and devotion mark the working methods of the Virgo man and woman. They have excellent critical abilities; they know how to analyze a problem and come up with a solution. Virgo is seldom fooled by superficialities, and can go straight to the heart of the matter.

Virgo knows how to break things down to the minutest detail; he or she prefers to work on things piece by piece. Inwardly, he is afraid of being overwhelmed by things that seem larger than life. For this reason, one often finds the Virgo occupied with details. His powers of concentration are greatest when he can concentrate on small, manageable things.

The Virgo person believes in doing things correctly; he's thorough and precise. He's seldom carried away by fantasy; he believes in keeping his feet firmly on the ground. People who seem a bit flighty or impractical sometimes irritate him.

Virgo knows how to criticize other people. It is very easy for him to point out another's weaknesses or faults; he is seldom wrong. However, Virgo is sometimes a bit sharp in making criticisms and often offends a good friend or acquaintance. The cultivated Virgo, however, knows how to apply criticism tactfully. He or she is considerate of another's feelings.

The Virgo person believes in applying himself in a positive manner to whatever task is set before him. He is a person full of purpose and goodwill. He is diligent and methodical. He is seldom given to impulse, but works along steadily and constructively.

Anything that is scientific, technological, and practical arouses Virgo's interest. The technical and craft aspects of the arts impress these people, and many Virgos become expert designers, graphic artists, and handicrafters. The precision so important to these disciplines is a quality Virgo possesses in abundance. Combined with imagination and flair, the attention to detail often makes Virgos first-rate artists.

Whether or not individual Virgos are talented in artistic areas, most of these people are usually very interested in anything of an artistic nature. Virgos also are great readers. They have a deep appreciation for the way the intricacies of life weave together, then unravel, and finally are rewoven into a new fabric or design.

Virgos also possess an innate verbal ability that is especially suited to the study of a language, whether the language is a machine language such as in computers or a tongue spoken by other people. Virgo has no trouble applying his or her native intelligence and skill either in a learning or teaching capacity. Virgos enjoy school. They often study a wide range of subjects, but not in great depth, in order to have a well-rounded education. Virgos like friends and colleagues to be as well-informed as they are if not more so. Virgo has a deep respect for culture, education, and intellect.

Usually, Virgo takes in stride whatever comes into his or her life. Basically, he is an uncomplicated person, who views things clearly and sharply. He has a way of getting right down to the meat of the matter. Generally a serious-minded person, he believes in being reliable. He is not one who will take great risks in life as he has no interest in playing the hero or the idealist. Virgo believes in doing what he can, but without flourishes.

Quite often he is a quiet, modest person. He believes that appearance is important and thus does his best to look well-groomed. He feels that being neat is important and dislikes untidiness in anything.

The Virgo man or woman likes to deal with life on a practical level and they usually look for the uncomplicated answer or solution to any problem or dilemma. Even if Virgos are urged to look into the mystical side of existence, they may dismiss it as being either unfounded or irrelevant.

On the whole, the Virgo person is even-tempered. He or she does not allow himself to become angry easily. He knows how to take the bitter with the sweet. But if someone does him a wrong turn, he is not likely to forget it. His good nature is not to be abused.

Health

Many persons born under this sign are amazingly healthy. They frequently live to see a ripe old age. This longevity is generally due to the fact that people born under this sign take all things in moderation. Virgo is not the type of person who burns the candle at both ends. They acknowledge their limits and avoid excess.

Frequently Virgos are small and neat-featured. Virgo women are sometimes quite attractive in a sort of dry way. Both men and women of this sign have a youthful appearance throughout life. When young, Virgos are generally very active. However, as they reach middle age and beyond they have a tendency to put on a bit of weight.

The Virgo person usually enjoys good health, although some have a tendency to be overly concerned about it. They imagine ailments they do not really have. Still, they do manage to stay fit. Other Virgos see themselves as being rather strong and resourceful, even when they are ill. For that reason they seldom feel moved to feel sorry for another ailing Virgo. Actually, serious illnesses frighten Virgos. They will do all they can to remain in good health.

The medicine cabinet of someone born under this sign is often filled with all sorts of pills, tablets, and ointments. Most of them will never be used.

As a rule, Virgo watches his diet. He stays away from foods that won't agree with him. He keeps a balanced diet and is moderate in his drinking habits. Virgos need plenty of exercise to keep the body fit. Most Virgos do not have a particular liking for strenuous sport. But the wise Virgo always will get some kind of energetic exercise, preferably a brisk and long walk, or a daily workout. Another thing that Virgos need is rest. They should get at least eight hours sleep per day.

On the whole, Virgo is a sensitive person. His nerves may be easily affected if he finds himself in a disagreeable situation. The stomach is another area of concern. When a Virgo becomes sick, this area is usually affected. Digestion complaints are not rare among persons born under this sign. Regular meals are important for the Virgo. Quick snacks and fast food may play havoc with his digestive system. In spite of this particular weakness, Virgos manage to lead normal, healthy lives. They should try to avoid becoming too concerned with ups and downs. Many of their illnesses may turn out to be imaginary.

Occupation

Virgos delight in keeping busy. They are not afraid of hard work. By nature, they are ambitious people and are happiest when they are putting their talents and abilities to good use. They can best be described as goal-directed; they never lose sight of their objective once committed. They are very thorough in whatever they undertake. Even routine work is something that they can do without finding fault. In fact, work that is scheduled—or that follows a definite pattern—is well suited to their steady natures. Virgos will put aside other things, if necessary, in order to attain a goal. They prefer to work under peaceful conditions, and will seldom do anything to irritate their superiors.

They learn well and are not afraid to undertake any kind of work—even the most menial—if it is necessary. Sometimes, however, they neglect their own conditions because they are so involved in their work. For this reason, Virgos occasionally fall ill or become a bit nervous. Any kind of work that allows them to make use of their talent for criticism will please them.

Virgo men and women usually shine as bookkeepers, accountants, teachers, and pharmacists. The cultivated Virgo person often turns to the world of science where they are likely to do well. Some great writers and poets have been born under this sixth sign of the Zodiac.

It is very important that Virgo has the kind of work that is suited to his personality. It may take a while before he actually finds his niche in life, and he may have to struggle at times in order to make ends meet. But because he is not afraid of work, he manages to come out on top.

Virgo is a perfectionist. He or she is always looking for ways to improve the work scheme or technique. He is never satisfied until things are working smoothly. He will even do more than his share in order to secure regularity and precision in a job he is doing. It is not unusual for the average Virgo to have various ideas about how to better the job they are doing, how to streamline things. They are extremely resourceful people as far as energy is concerned. In most cases, they can work longer than others, without letting it show. Because Virgo is so concerned with detail, they may seem obsessive or compulsive to co-workers.

The enterprising Virgo can go far in business if a partner is somewhat adventurous and enthusiastic, qualities which tend to balance those of the Virgo person. At times, Virgo can be quite a worrier. Battling problems large and small may prevent him from making the headway he feels is necessary in his work. A partner who knows how to cut the work and worries in half by taking advantage of shortcuts is someone the average Virgo businessperson could learn to value. People enjoying working with Virgo men and women, because they are so reliable and honest. They usually set a good example for others on the job.

If not careful, the ambitious Virgo can become the type of person who thinks about nothing else but the job. They are not afraid of taking on more than the average worker. But they can make the mistake of expecting the same of others. This attitude can lead to conflict and unpleasantness. Generally, Virgo does achieve what he sets out for, because he knows how to apply himself. He is seldom the envy of others because he is not the type of person who is easily noticed or recognized.

Virgo is a quiet person. He or she enjoys working in peaceful and harmonious surroundings. Conflict at work is bound to upset him and affect his nerves. He works well under people. He is not against taking orders from those who prove themselves his superiors. On the whole, the man or woman born under this sign does not like to be delegated with the full responsibility of a task or project. He or she would rather have a supporting or a subordinate role.

Virgo men and women frequently excel in a trade. They often make good metalsmiths and carpenters, jewelers and wood carvers. They can work in miniature, creating a variety of pleasing items.

The Virgo person is one who is very concerned about security. Now and again he may have cause to worry about his financial position. On the whole, he is conscious of the value of money. He or she is a person who will never risk security by going out on a limb. He knows how to put money away for a rainy day. Many times he will scout about for new ways of increasing his savings. Bettering his financial situation is something that constantly concerns him. When he does invest, it usually turns out to his advantage. He generally makes sure that the investment he makes is a sure thing. He does not believe in gambling or taking big risks.

Sometimes the Virgo, because of his keen interest in money and profit, is the victim of a fraud. Dishonest people may try to take advantage of his interest in monetary gain. The well-off Virgo is extremely generous and enjoys looking after the needs of others. He sees to it that those he cares for live in comfort.

Not all Virgos are fortunate enough to become extremely wealthy, but all of them work hard for what they achieve.

Home and Family

People born under this sign are generally homebodies. They like to spend as much time as possible surrounded by the things and the people they enjoy. They make excellent hosts and enjoy entertaining guests and visitors. It is important to Virgos that the people around them be happy and content. Virgo is most at ease when companions behave correctly, that is, if they are respectful of individuals' needs and property. Virgos do not like people to take advantage of their hospitality or to abuse what they consider a privilege. But on the whole Virgos are easygoing. The demands they may make of guests and family are reasonable.

A harmonious atmosphere at home is important to the person

born under this sign. As long as this can be guaranteed, Virgo remains in good humor. They are likely to have a number of insurance policies on the home, family, and possessions. They believe that you can never be safe enough.

In spite of their love of home, Virgo is likely to have an avid interest in travel. If they cannot make many changes in their environment, they are bound to make them in their home. The Virgo homemaker never tires of rearranging things. Generally, Virgos have a good sense of beauty and harmony. They know how to make a room inviting and comfortable. Change is always of interest to the person born under this sign. They like to read of faraway places, even if they never get a chance to visit them. A new job or a new home address from time to time can brighten Virgo's spirits immeasurably.

The Virgo woman is as neat as a pin. Usually she is an excellent cook, and takes care that her kitchen never gets out of order or becomes untidy even while she is working in it. She believes that everything has its proper place and should be kept there. Because she is so careful with her possessions, they often appear brand new.

Others may feel that the Virgo man or woman, because of his or her cool, calm ways, is not especially cut out to be a good parent. But the opposite is true. Virgo people know how to bring up their youngsters correctly. They generally pass on their positive qualities to their children without any trouble. They teach them that honesty and diligence are important. They instill them with an appreciation for common sense in all matters.

Although the Virgo father or mother may deeply love their children, they have a tendency to be rather strict. They are always concerned that their children turn out well. Sometimes they expect too much of them. Some of them can be old-fashioned and believe that a child belongs in a child's place. They expect this not only of their own youngsters but also of other people's children.

Social Relationships

The Virgo man or woman is particular about the friends he makes. He is fond of people who have a particular direction in life. He is inclined to avoid drifters or irresolute people. Those who have made their mark win his admiration. Virgo likes intelligent people, those who are somewhat cultured in their interests.

As a good friend, Virgo is invaluable; there is nothing he or she would not do to help someone in need. Virgo stands by friends even in their most difficult moments. The only demand he makes is that his interest in another's affairs be valued. He does not like to feel that his help is not appreciated. It is important that Virgo be thanked for even the slightest favor.

Quite often people born under this sign are rather timid or at least retiring; they have to be drawn out by others. After Virgos get to know someone well, however, they bloom. In spite of their initial shyness, they do not enjoy being alone. They like company; they like to be reassured by people. They prefer intelligent, informed people as companions. Virgo can overlook negative qualities in someone if they feel that person is basically sincere toward others. The Virgo person needs friends. In solitude, the average Virgo is apt to feel stranded or deserted. They enjoy having someone around who will make a fuss over them, no matter how small.

Virgo is a perfectionist. Sometimes they criticize others too strongly for their faults, and as a result, they may not have as many friends as they would like.

Virgo can be cliquey, enjoying a fairly closed circle of friends and acquaintances. Gossip and intrigue might be a mainstay of such a clique. The smaller the circle, the more comfortable Virgo will feel and the more chances there will be for Virgo to orchestrate the social and recreational activities. In an intimate group setting Virgo's shyness disappears, giving way to the delicious wit and clever turn of phrase basic to this verbal, mental sign.

Gala parties with lots of hangers-on and freeloaders are not Virgo's style. A typical noisy blast can be a turn-off to one who is finicky and fastidious. The mere sight of overindulgence and overfamiliarity can make Virgo long for the glamour of posh surroundings accompanied only by a lover or close friend.

Frequent home entertaining also can be a problem. The fussy Virgo will fret about all the details that must be arranged to host a successful social. Then the neat, tidy Virgo will worry about the mess created in the house after a perfect get-together. On the whole, Virgo men and women prefer socializing in a few select places known for gracious service and fine food.

Of all the signs in the Zodiac, Virgo is most drawn to human welfare issues, a fact that leads these men and women into groups whose goal is to improve people's lot in life. The Virgo dedication to a cause is remarkable. Their example is an inspiration for everyone to follow. Doing someone a good turn comes naturally to Virgo. Their qualities of service and kindness are genuine, as friends who admire and respect them will testify.

Love and Marriage

In love and romance, the person born under the sign of Virgo is not inclined to be overly romantic. To a partner, they may seem reserved and inhibited. Their practical nature prevails even in affairs of the heart. They are least likely to be swept off their feet when in love. Chances are they may flirt a bit in the beginning of a relationship, but soon thereafter they settle down to the serious side of love. Virgo standards are very high, and it may be some time before they find someone who can measure up to them. As a consequence, Virgo frequently marries rather late in life.

It is important for the Virgo man or woman to find the right person because they are easily influenced by someone they love. On the other hand, Virgo has a protective side to their nature. When in love they will try to shield the object of their affection from the unpleasant things in life.

The person born under the sign of Virgo may be disappointed in love more than once. People whom they set great store in may prove to be unsuitable. Sometimes it is Virgo's own fault. They may be too critical of small weaknesses that a partner or lover has.

Some Virgos seem prim and proper when it comes to romance. They would prefer to think that it is not absolutely necessary and that intellect is everything. It may take some doing to get such a Virgo to change this attitude. At any rate, they are not fond of being demonstrative as far as affection goes. They do not like to make a show of love in front of others.

If their lover is too demanding or forceful in the relationship, they may feel inclined to break off the affair. Virgo appreciates gentleness and consideration in love life. On the whole, they are not easy to approach. The person who finds him or her interesting will have to be very tactful and patient when trying to convince Virgo of their love.

In married life, Virgo is apt to be very practical. They are interested in preserving the happiness they have found and will do everything in their power to keep the relationship alive. It is quite important that the Virgo man or woman marry someone with a similar outlook. Someone quite opposite may misinterpret Virgo's calm and cool manner as being unfeeling. Virgo makes a faithful mate. He or she can always be depended upon. They know how to keep things in the home running smoothly. They will do what they can to preserve harmony because they dislike discord and unpleasantness. A cooperative person, Virgo is willing to make concessions if they seem necessary. In short, the Virgo man or woman can make a success of marriage if they have had the good fortune to choose the right person.

Romance and the Virgo Woman

The Virgo woman is often a serious person. She knows what she wants out of life and what to expect from people. She is discriminating in her choice of men. It may take considerable time before she will admit to herself that she is in love. She is not afraid to wait in matters of romance; it is important to her that she select the right person. She may be more easily attracted to an intelligent man than to a handsome one. She values intellect more than physical attributes.

It is important for the Virgo woman to trust someone before she falls in love with him. She will allow a relationship to develop into a love affair only after she has gotten to know the man well on strictly a companionship basis at first.

The Virgo woman is reputed to be prim and proper about sex. But this description does not tell the whole story, or even the right story. In fact, Virgo can exhibit extremes in sexual attitudes and behavior. It is an age-old dilemma, contrast, contradiction—call it what you will—between the madonna and the hooker. There is Virgo the Virgin, whose purity is renowned and whose frigidity is assumed. Then there is Virgo the Harvester, whose promiscuity is whispered and whose fruitfulness is celebrated.

Indeed, the difference between an old-fashioned Virgo and a liberated Virgo are remarkable but very hard to discern in the beginning of an affair. One thing is sure, though. Cheat on your Virgo woman, and you can kiss the relationship good-bye. That is, unless you have discussed the possibility of having an open relationship—on both sides and managed in good taste. Remember, no matter what her sexual proclivities are, the Virgo woman cannot stand vulgarity in any form.

The Virgo woman generally makes a good wife. She knows how to keep the household shipshape. She likes looking after people she loves. She is efficient and industrious. There is almost nothing she will not do for the man she loves. She is capable of deep affection and love, but must be allowed to express herself in her own way.

As a mother, she is ideal. She teaches all her youngsters to be polite and well-mannered, and constantly worries about their health and welfare. Fearing all manner of mishaps, injuries, illnesses, and minor ailments, the Virgo mother may tend to restrict the kids' freedom at play and in school. However, she always has the children's best interests at heart.

Romance and the Virgo Man

The Virgo man, practical and analytical as he is in most matters, is rather cautious when it comes to love and romance. He is not what one would call romantic. He may be shy and hesitant. It may be up to the female to begin the relationship. He may prefer not to start an affair until he has dated for a while.

Virgo is particular. If his love partner makes one false move, he is likely to dissolve the relationship. An understanding and patient woman can help him to be a little more realistic and open in his approach to love. But first she must know what kind of man she is dealing with.

The witty, talkative Virgo man enjoys flirting. But he will never press his luck nor take advantage of a compromising situation. He won't accuse you of stringing him along. It may seem as if he is waiting for you to make the next move. And you probably have to be the aggressor if the dating relationship is to get beyond the holding-hands stage and into serious lovemaking. Make sure, though, you don't go overboard with physical demonstrations of affection—especially in public places. Virgo is easily embarrassed by touching and kissing in front of other people. Any degree of sexual intimacy is strictly reserved for the bedroom.

The strong, silent Virgo type usually appeals to women who like the challenge of overcoming his apparent resistance to her feminine charms. Little does she know that he might be scared silly of making a fool of himself or of being criticized. Virgo projects his own personality traits onto people who get close to him. So he naturally believes that a woman who approaches is just as critical and faultfinding as he is. Fortunately, though, he doesn't project the egotism and chauvinism that could turn many a woman off. So if you want to play the seduction game, you will thrill to the ultimate conquest of winning this hard-to-get, nearly perfect guy.

The Virgo man enjoys family life and does everything he can to keep his wife and children happy and secure. He may want to have a hand in running the household because he feels he is more efficient than his mate. He is a calm, steady, and faithful person.

As a father he could be a bit of a fussbudget. He may not know how to communicate with his children effectively in some matters. However, he is loving and responsible. He does what he can to see that they have a proper upbringing.

Woman—Man

VIRGO WOMAN
ARIES MAN

Although it's possible that you could find happiness with a man born under the sign of the Ram, it's uncertain as to how long that happiness would last.

An Aries who has made his mark in the world and is somewhat steadfast in his outlooks and attitudes could be quite a catch for you. On the other hand, men under this sign are often swift-footed and quick-minded. Their industrious mannerisms may fail to impress you, especially if you feel that much of their get-up-and-go often leads nowhere.

When it comes to a fine romance, you want someone with a nice, broad shoulder to lean on. You are likely to find a relationship with someone who doesn't stay put for too long somewhat upsetting.

Aries may have a little trouble in understanding you, too, at least in the beginning of the relationship. He may find you a bit too shy and moody. An Aries tends to speak his mind; he's likely to criticize you at the drop of a hat.

You may find a man born under this sign too demanding. He may give you the impression that he expects you to be at his constant beck and call. You have a lot of patience at your disposal, and he may try every last bit of it. He may not be as thorough as you in everything he does. In order to achieve success or a goal quickly, he may overlook small but important details, then regret the oversight when it is far too late.

Being married to an Aries does not mean that you'll have a secure and safe life as far as finances are concerned. Not all Aries are rash with cash, but they lack the sound head you perhaps have for putting away something for that inevitable rainy day. He'll do his best, however, to see that you're adequately provided for, even though his efforts may leave something to be desired as far as you're concerned.

With an Aries man for a mate, you'll find yourself constantly among people. An Aries generally has many friends—and you may not heartily approve of them all. People born under the sign of the Ram are often more interested in interesting people than they are in influential ones. Although there may be a family squabble from time to time, you are stable enough to take it in your stride.

Aries men love children. They make wonderful fathers. Kids take to them like ducks to water. The Ram's quick mind and behavior appeal to the young. Aries ability to jump from one activity to another will suit and delight a child's attention span.

VIRGO WOMAN
TAURUS MAN

Some Taurus men are strong and silent. They do all they can to protect and provide for the women they love. In general, the Taurus man will never let you down. He's steady, sturdy, and reliable. He's pretty honest and practical, too. He says what he means and means what he says. He never indulges in deceit and will always put his cards on the table.

The Taurus man is very affectionate. Being loved, appreciated, and understood is very important for his well-being. Like you, he is also looking for peace and security in his life. If you both work toward these goals together, you'll find that they are easily attained.

If you should marry a Taurus man, you can be sure that the wolf will never darken your door. He is a notoriously good provider and will do everything he can to make his family comfortable and happy.

He'll appreciate the way you have of making a home warm and inviting. A comfortable couch and the evening papers are essential ingredients in making your Taurus husband happy at the end of the workday. Although he may be a big lug of a guy, you'll find that he's fond of gentleness and soft things. If you puff up his pillow and tuck him in at night, he won't complain.

You probably will like his friends. Taurus tends to seek out individuals who are successful or prominent. You also admire people who work hard and achieve their goals.

The Taurus man doesn't care too much for change. He's a stay-at-home of the first order. Chances are that the house you move into after you're married will be the house you'll live in for the rest of your life.

You'll find that the man born under the sign of the Bull is easy to get along with. It's unlikely that you'll have many quarrels or arguments.

Although he'll be gentle and tender with you, your Taurus man is far from being a sensitive type. He's a man's man. More than likely, he loves such sports as fishing and football. He can be earthy as well as down to earth.

The Taurus father loves the children, but he will do everything he can not to spoil them. He believes that children should stay in their place and, in adult company, should be seen but not heard. The Taurus father is an excellent disciplinarian. Your youngsters will be polite and respectful.

VIRGO WOMAN
GEMINI MAN

The Gemini man is a good catch. Many a woman has set her cap for him and failed to bag him. Generally, Gemini men are intelligent, witty, and outgoing. Many of them tend to be versatile.

On the other hand, some of them seem to lack that sort of common sense that you set so much store in. Their tendency to start a half-dozen projects, then toss them up in the air out of boredom may do nothing more than exasperate you.

One thing that causes a Twin's mind and affection to wander is a bore. But it is unlikely that an active woman like you would ever allow herself to be accused of being one. The Gemini man who has caught your heart will admire you for your ideas and intellect, perhaps even more than for your homemaking talents and good looks.

A strong-willed woman could easily fill the role of rudder for her Gemini's ship-without-a-sail. The intelligent Gemini is often aware of his shortcomings and doesn't mind if someone with better bearings gives him a shove in the right direction—when it's needed. The average Gemini doesn't have serious ego hang-ups and will even gracefully accept a well-deserved chewing out from his mate or lover or girl friend.

A successful and serious-minded Gemini could make you a very happy woman, perhaps, if you gave him half a chance. Although he may create the impression that he has a hole in his head, the Gemini man generally has a good head on his shoulders. Some Geminis, who have learned the art of being steadfast, have risen to great heights in their professions.

Once you convince yourself that not all people born under the sign of the Twins are witless grasshoppers, you won't mind dating a few to test your newborn conviction. If you do wind up walking down the aisle with one, accept the fact that married life with him will mean your taking the bitter with the sweet.

Life with a Gemini man can be more fun than a barrel of clowns. You'll never be allowed to experience a dull moment. Don't leave money matters to him, or you'll both wind up behind the eight ball.

Gemini men are always attractive to the opposite sex. You'll perhaps have to allow him a chance to flirt harmlessly. The occasion will seldom amount to more than that if you're his ideal mate.

The Gemini father is a pushover for children. See that you keep the young ones in line, otherwise they'll be running the house. He loves them so much, he generally lets them do what they want. Gemini's sense of humor is infectious, so the children will naturally come to see the fun and funny sides of life.

VIRGO WOMAN
CANCER MAN

The man born under the sign of Cancer may very well be the man after your own heart. Generally, Cancers are steady people. They are interested in security and practicality. Despite their seemingly grouchy exterior at times, men born under the sign of the Crab are sensitive and kind individuals.

Cancers are almost always hard workers and are very interested in making successes of themselves economically as well as socially. You'll find that their conservative outlook on many things often agrees with yours. They will be men on whom you can depend come rain or come shine. They will never shirk their responsibilities as providers. They will always see that their family never wants.

Your patience will come in handy if you decide it's a Cancer you want for a mate. He isn't the type that rushes headlong into romance. He wants to be sure about love as you do. If, after the first couple of months of dating, he suggests that you take a walk with him down lovers' lane, don't jump to the conclusion that he's about to make his great play. Chances are he'll only hold your hand and seriously observe the stars.

Don't let his coolness fool you, though. Beneath his starched reserve lies a very warm heart. He's just not interested in showing off as far as affection is concerned. Don't think his interest is wandering if he doesn't kiss you goodnight at the front door; that just isn't his style. For him, affection should only be displayed for two sets of eyes—yours and his. He's passionate only in private, which is something Virgo can understand and appreciate.

He will never step out of line. He's too much of a gentleman for that. When you're alone with him and there's no chance of being disturbed or spied upon, he'll pull out an engagement ring (the one that belonged to his grandmother) and slip it on your trembling finger.

Speaking of relatives, you'll have to get used to the fact that Cancer is overly fond of his mother. When he says his mother's the most wonderful woman in the world, you'd better agree with him, that is, if you want to become his wife.

He'll always be a faithful husband. A Cancer never pussyfoots around after he has taken that marriage vow. He doesn't take marriage responsibilities lightly. He'll see that everything in the house runs smoothly and that bills are paid promptly. He'll take out all kinds of insurance policies on his family and property. He'll arrange it so that when retirement time rolls around, you'll both be very well off.

Cancers make proud, patient, and protective fathers. But they can be a little too protective. Their sheltering instincts can interfere with a youngster's natural inclination toward independence. Still, the Cancer father doesn't want to see his kids learning about life the hard way from the streets.

VIRGO WOMAN
LEO MAN

To know a man born under the sign of the Lion is not necessarily to love him, even though the temptation may be great. When he fixes most girls with his leonine double-whammy, it causes their hearts to pitter-patter and their minds to cloud over.

You are a little too sensible to allow yourself to be bowled over by a regal strut and a roar. Still, there's no denying that Leo has a way with women, even sensible women like yourself. Once he's swept a girl off her feet, it may be hard for her to scramble upright again. Still, you are no pushover for romantic charm, especially if you feel it's all show.

He'll wine you and dine you in the fanciest places. He'll croon to you under the moon and shower you with diamonds if he can get ahold of them. Still, it would be wise to find out just how long that shower is going to last before consenting to be his wife.

Lions in love are hard to ignore, let alone brush off. Your resistance will have a way of nudging him on until he feels he has you completely under his spell. Once mesmerized by this romantic powerhouse, you will probably find yourself doing things of which you never dreamed. Leos can be vain pussycats when involved romantically. They like to be babied and pampered. This may not be your cup of tea exactly. Still when you're romantically dealing with a man born under the sign of Leo, you'll think up ways to make him purr.

Although he may be magnificent and magnanimous while trying to win you, he'll yowl or mew if he thinks he's not quite getting the tender love and care he feels is his due. If you keep him well supplied with affection, you can be sure his eyes will never gaze on someone else and his heart will never wander.

A Leo man often tends to be authoritarian. He can be depended upon to lord it over others in one way or another. If he is the top honcho at his firm, he'll most likely do everything he can to stay on top. If he's not number one, he's probably working on it and will be sitting on the throne before long.

You'll have more security than you can use if he is in a position to support you in the manner to which he feels you should be accustomed. He is inclined to be too lavish, though, at least by your standards.

You'll always have plenty of friends when you have a Leo for a mate. He's a natural-born wheeler-dealer and entertainer. He loves to let his hair down at parties.

As fathers, Leos tend to spoil their children. But they can also be strict when they think that the rules of the royal kingdom are being broken. You'll have to do your best to smooth over the children's roughed-up feelings.

VIRGO WOMAN
VIRGO MAN

The Virgo man is all business or so he may seem to you. He is usually very cool, calm, and collected. He's perhaps too much of a fussbudget to arouse deep romantic interests in a woman like

you. Torrid romancing to him is just so much sentimental mush.
He can do without it and can make that quite evident in short
order. He's keen on chastity and, if necessary, he can lead a sed-
entary, sexless life without caring very much about the fun others
think he's missing. In short, you may find him a first-class dud.

The Virgo man doesn't have much of an imagination; flights of
fancy don't interest him. He is always correct and likes to be handled properly. Almost everything about him is orderly. There's a
place for everything and everything in its place is an adage he'll
fall upon quite regularly.

He does have an honest-to-goodness heart, believe it or not.
The woman who finds herself strangely attracted to his cool, feet-
flat-on-the-ground ways will discover that his is a constant heart,
not one that goes in for flings or sordid affairs. A practical man,
even in matters of the heart, he wants to know just what kind of
person you are before he takes a chance on you.

The impulsive woman had better not make the mistake of kissing her Virgo friend on the street, even if it's only a peck on the
cheek. He's not at all demonstrative and hates public displays of
affection. Love, according to him, should be kept within the con-
fines of one's home with the curtains drawn. Once he believes that
you are on the level with him as far as your love is concerned,
you'll see how fast he can lose his cool. Virgos are considerate,
gentle lovers. He'll spend a long time, though, getting to know
you. He'll like you before he loves you.

A romance with a Virgo man can be a sometime or, rather, a
one-time thing. If the bottom ever falls out, don't bother reaching
for the adhesive tape. Nine times out of ten he won't care about
patching up. He's a once-burnt-twice-shy guy. When he crosses
your telephone number out of his address book, he's crossing you
out of his life for good.

Neat as a pin, he's thumbs-down on what he considers sloppy
housekeeping. An ashtray with just one stubbed out cigarette in
it can annoy him even if it's only two seconds old. Glassware
should always sparkle and shine if you want to keep him happy.
If you marry him, keep your sunny side up.

If you marry a Virgo man, instill a sense of order in the kids, or at
least have them behaving by the time he gets home. The Virgo father wants his children to be kind and courteous and always helpful
to the neighbors. The children should be kept as spotless as your
house. Kids with dirty faces and hands displease him.

VIRGO WOMAN
LIBRA MAN

Men born under the sign of Libra are frequently too wrapped up
in their own private dreams to be really interesting as far as love

and romance are concerned. Many times, the Libra man is a difficult person to bring back down to earth. It is hard for him to face reality. Although he may be very cautious about weighing both sides of an argument, he may never really come to a reasonable decision about anything. Decision making is something that often makes the Libra man uncomfortable. He'd rather leave that job to someone else. Don't ask him why, he probably doesn't know himself.

Qualities such as permanence and constancy are important to you in a love relationship. The Libra man may be an enigma to you. One moment he comes on hard and strong with declarations of his love; the next moment you find he's left you like yesterday's mashed potatoes. It does no good to wonder what went wrong. Chances are it was nothing on which you can put your finger. It's just one of Libra's strange ways.

He is not exactly what you would term an ambitious person. You are perhaps looking for a mate or friend with more drive and fidelity. You are the type of person who is interested in making some headway in the areas that interest you. Libra is often content just to drift along. He does have drive, however, but it's not the long-range kind.

It's not that Libra is shiftless or lazy. He's interested in material things and he appreciates luxuries, but he may not be willing to work hard enough to obtain them. Beauty and harmony interest him. He'll dedicate a lot of time to arranging things so that they are aesthetically pleasing. It would be difficult to call the Libra man practical; nine times out of ten, he isn't.

If you do begin a relationship with a man born under this sign, you will have to coax him now and again to face various situations in a realistic manner. You'll have your hands full, that's for sure. But if you love him, you'll undoubtedly do your best to understand him, no matter how difficult this may be.

If you become involved with a Libra man, either temporarily or permanently, you'd better take over the task of managing his money. Often he has little understanding of financial matters. He tends to spend without thinking, following his whims.

The Libra father is gentle and patient. He can be firm without exercising undue strictness or discipline. Although he can be a harsh judge at times, with the kids he will radiate sweetness and light in the hope that will grow up imitating his gracious manner.

VIRGO WOMAN
SCORPIO MAN
Some people have a hard time understanding the man born under the sign of Scorpio. Few, however, are able to resist his fiery

charm. When angered, he can act like the scorpion he is, ready to strike out and defend himself. His sting can leave an almost permanent mark. If you find yourself interested in the Scorpio man, you'd better learn how to keep on his good side.

The Scorpio man can be rather blunt when he chooses. At times, he may seem hard-hearted. He can be touchy every now and then, and this sensitiveness may get on your nerves after a while. When you feel as though you can't take it anymore, you'd better tiptoe away from the scene rather than chance an explosive confrontation. He's capable of giving you a sounding-out that will make you pack your bags and go back to Mother—for good.

If he finds fault with you, he'll let you know. He might misinterpret your patience and think it a sign of indifference. But you are the type of woman who can adapt to almost any sort of relationship or circumstance if you put your heart and mind to it.

Scorpio men are very perceptive and intelligent. In some respects, they know how to use their brains more effectively than most. They believe in winning, in whatever they do. Second place holds no interest for them. In business, they usually achieve the position they want through a combination of drive and intellect.

Your interest in home life probably won't be shared by him. No matter how comfortable you've managed to make the house, it will have very little influence on him with regard to making him aware of his family responsibilities. He does not like to be tied down, generally, and would rather be out on the battlefield of life, belting away at what he feels to be a just and worthy cause. Don't try to keep the home fires burning too brightly while you wait for him to come home from work; you might run out of firewood.

The Scorpio man is passionate in all things, including love. Most women are easily attracted to him and you are perhaps no exception. Those who allow themselves to be swept off their feet by a Scorpio man soon find that they're dealing with a carton of romantic fireworks. The Scorpio man is passionate with a capital P, make no mistake about that.

Scorpio men are straight to the point. They can be as sharp as a razor blade and just as cutting to anyone who crosses them.

Scorpio fathers like large families, generally. In spite of the extremes in his personality, the Scorpio man is able to transform conflicting characteristics when he becomes a father. He is adept with difficult youngsters because he knows how to tap the best in a child. He believes in preparing his children for the hard knocks life sometimes delivers.

VIRGO WOMAN
SAGITTARIUS MAN

The woman who has set her cap for a man born under the sign of Sagittarius may have to use a great deal of strategy before she can get him to drop down on bended knee. Although some Sagittarius may be marriage-shy, they're not ones to skitter away from romance. A high-spirited woman may find a relationship with a Sagittarius, whether a fling or the real thing, a very enjoyable experience.

As a rule, Sagittarius people are bright, happy, and healthy people. They have a strong sense of fair play. Often they're a source of inspiration to others. They're full of ideas and drive.

You'll be taken by the Archer's infectious grin and his light-hearted friendly nature. If you do wind up being the woman in his life, you'll find that he will treat you more like a buddy than the love of his life. It's his way.

You'll admire his broad-mindedness in most matters, including that of the heart. If, while dating you, he claims that he still wants to play the field, he'll expect you to enjoy the same liberty. Once he's promised to love, honor, and obey, however, he does just that.

A woman who has a keen imagination and a great love of freedom will not be disappointed if she does marry an Archer. The Sagittarius man likes to share his many interests, and he has a genuine belief in equality.

If he does insist on a night out with the boys once a week, he won't scowl if you decide to let him shift for himself in the kitchen while you pursue some of your own interests. He believes in fairness, and he is no male chauvinist.

The Sagittarius is not much of a homebody. Many times he's occupied with faraway places either in his dreams or in reality. He enjoys—just as you do—being on the go. A humdrum existence, especially at home, bores him. At the drop of a hat, he may ask you to take off with him into the wild blue yonder—his idea of a break from routine.

Sagittarius likes surprising people. He'll take great pride in showing you off to his friends. He'll always be a considerate mate; he will never embarrass or disappoint you intentionally. He's very tolerant when it comes to friends; you'll probably spend a lot of time entertaining people.

The Sagittarius father will dote on any son or daughter, but he may be bewildered by the newborn. The Archer usually becomes comfortable with youngsters once they have passed through the baby stage. As soon as the children are old enough to walk and talk, the Sagittarius dad encourages each and every visible sign of talent and skill.

VIRGO WOMAN
CAPRICORN MAN

The Capricorn man is frequently not the romantic lover that attracts most women. Still, with his reserve and calm, he is capable of giving his heart completely once he has found the right woman. The Capricorn man is thorough and deliberate in all that he does. His slow, steady approach is sure to win the one he loves.

He doesn't believe in flirting and would never lead a heart on a merry chase just for the game of it. If you win his trust, he'll give you his heart on a platter. Many times, it is the woman who has to take the lead when romance is in the air. As long as he knows you're making the advances in earnest, he won't mind—in fact, he'll probably be grateful.

But don't start thinking he's a cold fish; he isn't. Although some Capricorns are indeed very capable of expressing passion, others often have difficulty in trying to display affection. He should have no trouble in this area, however, once he has found a patient and understanding lover.

The Capricorn man is very interested in getting ahead. He's quite ambitious and usually knows how to apply himself well to whatever task he undertakes. He certainly isn't a spendthrift. Like you, he knows how to handle money with extreme care. You, with your knack for putting away pennies for that rainy day, should have no difficulty understanding his way with money.

The Capricorn man thinks in terms of future security. He wants to make sure that he and his wife have something to fall back on when they reach retirement age. There's nothing wrong with that; in fact, it's a plus quality.

The Capricorn man will want you to handle household matters efficiently. The fastidious Virgo woman will have no trouble doing so. If he should check up on you from time to time, don't let it irritate you. Once you assure him that you can handle everything to his liking, he'll leave you alone.

Although he's a hard man to catch when it comes to marriage, once he's made that serious step, he's inclined to become possessive. The Capricorn man needs to know that he has the support of his wife in whatever he does, every step of the way.

The Capricorn man wants to be liked. He may seem dull to some, but underneath his reserve there is sometimes an adventurous streak that has never had a chance to express itself. He may be a real daredevil in his heart of hearts. The right woman, the affectionate, adoring woman can bring out that hidden zest in his nature.

Capricorn makes a loving, dutiful father, even though he may not understand his children completely. The Goat believes that there are goals to be achieved, and that there is the right way to achieve them. The Capricorn father can be quite a scold when it comes to disciplining the youngsters. You'll have to step in and bend the rules sometimes.

VIRGO WOMAN
AQUARIUS MAN

You might find the Aquarius man the most broad-minded man you have ever met. On the other hand, you might find him the most impractical. Many times, he's more of a dreamer than a doer. If you don't mind putting up with a man whose heart and mind are as wide as the sky and whose head is almost always in the clouds, then start dating that Aquarius who has somehow captured your fancy. Maybe you, with your good sense, can bring him back down to earth when he gets too starry-eyed.

He's no dumbbell, make no mistake about that. He can be busy making some very complicated and idealistic plans when he's got that out-to-lunch look in his eyes. But more than likely, he'll never execute them. After he's shared one or two of his progressive ideas with you, you may think he's a nut. But don't go jumping to conclusions. There's a saying that Aquarius is a half-century ahead of everybody else in the thinking department.

If you decide to marry him, you'll find out how right his zany whims are on or about your 50th anniversary. Maybe the waiting will be worth it. Could be that you have an Einstein on your hands and heart.

Life with an Aquarius won't be one of total despair if you can learn to temper his airiness with your down-to-earth Virgo practicality. He won't gripe if you do. Aquarius always maintains an open mind. He'll entertain the ideas and opinions of everybody. But he may not agree with all of them.

Don't go tearing your hair out when you find that it's almost impossible to hold a normal conversation with your Aquarius friend at times. Usually chasing the big idea, he can overlook the vital details. Always try to keep in mind that he means well.

His broad-mindedness doesn't stop when it comes to you and your personal freedom. You won't have to give up any of your hobbies or projects after you're married. He will encourage you to continue them and to be as independent as he is.

He'll be a kind and generous husband. He'll never quibble over petty things. Keep track of the money you both spend. He can't. Money burns a hole in his pocket.

At times, you may feel like calling it quits. Chances are, though, that you'll always give him another chance.

The Aquarius is a good family man. He can be a shining example for the children because he sees them as individuals in their own right, not as extensions of himself. Kids love him and vice versa. He'll be tolerant with them as he is with adults.

VIRGO WOMAN
PISCES MAN

The man born under Pisces is quite a dreamer. Sometimes he's so wrapped up in his dreams that he's difficult to reach. To the average, active woman, he may seem a little passive.

He's easygoing most of the time. He seems to take things in his stride. He'll entertain all kinds of views and opinions from just about everyone, nodding or smiling vaguely, giving the impression that he's with them one hundred percent while that may not be the case at all. His attitude may be why bother when he's confronted with someone who is wrong but thinks he's right. The Pisces man will seldom speak his mind if he thinks he'll be rigidly opposed.

The Pisces man is oversensitive at times. He's afraid of getting his feelings hurt. He'll sometimes imagine a personal affront when none's been made. More than likely, you'll find this complex of his maddening. At times you may feel like giving him a swift kick where it hurts the most. It won't do any good, though.

One thing you'll admire about this man is his concern for people who are sickly or troubled. He'll make his shoulder available to anyone in the mood for a good cry. He can listen to one hard-luck story after another without seeming to tire. When his advice is asked, he can be depended upon to offer some wise counsel. He often knows what is upsetting someone before that person is aware of it himself.

Still, at the end of the day, the Pisces man will want some peace and quiet. If you've got a problem when he comes home, don't unload it in his lap. If you do, you might find him short-tempered. He's a good listener, but he can only take so much turmoil.

Pisces are not aimless although they may seem so at times. The positive sort of Pisces man is often successful in his profession and is likely to become rich and influential. Material gain, however, is never a direct goal for a man born under the sign of the Fishes.

The weaker Pisces is usually content to stay on the level where he finds himself.

Because of their seemingly laissez-faire manner, people under the sign of Pisces are immensely popular with children. For tots, the Pisces father plays the double role of confidant and playmate. It will never enter his mind to discipline a child, no matter how spoiled or incorrigible that child becomes.

Man—Woman

VIRGO MAN
ARIES WOMAN

The Aries woman may be a little too bossy and busy for you. Generally, Aries is an ambitious creature. She can become a little impatient with a Virgo who by nature is more thorough and deliberate than she is, especially if she feels you're taking too much time.

The Aries woman is a fast worker. Sometimes she's so fast she forgets to look where she's going. When she stumbles or falls, it would be nice if you were there to catch her. But Aries is a proud woman. She doesn't like to be criticized when she errs. The Virgo tongue lashings can turn her into a block of ice.

Don't begin to think that the Aries woman frequently gets tripped up in her plans. Many times she is capable of taking aim and hitting the bull's-eye. You'll be flabbergasted by her accuracy as well as by her ambition. On the other hand, you're apt to spot a flaw in her plans before she does.

You are perhaps somewhat slower than Aries in attaining your goals. Still, you are not inclined to make mistakes along the way. You're almost always well prepared.

The Aries woman can be sensitive at times. She likes to be handled with gentleness and respect. Let her know that you love her for her brains as well as for her good looks. Never give her cause to become jealous. When your Aries date sees green, you'd better forget about sharing a rosy future together. Handle her with tender love and care and she's yours.

The Aries woman can be giving if she feels her partner is deserving. She is no iceberg; she responds to the proper masculine flame. She needs a man she can admire and of whom she can feel proud. She can cause you plenty of heartache if you've made up your mind about her but she hasn't made up hers about you. The Aries woman is very demanding at times. Some tend to be highstrung. They can be difficult if they feel their independence is being hampered.

The cultivated Aries woman makes a wonderful homemaker and hostess. You'll find she's very clever in decorating and using color. Your house will be tastefully furnished; she'll make sure that it radiates harmony. The Aries wife knows how to make guests feel at home.

Although the Aries woman may not be keen on burdensome responsibilities, she is fond of children and the joy they bring. She is skilled at juggling both career and motherhood, so her kids will never feel that she is an absentee parent. In fact, as the youngsters grow older, they might want a little more of the liberation that is so important to her.

VIRGO MAN
TAURUS WOMAN

A Taurus woman could perhaps understand you better than most women. She is very considerate and loving. She is thorough and methodical in whatever she does. She is anxious to avoid mistakes.

Home is very important to the Taurus woman. She is an excellent homemaker. Although your home may not be a palace, it will become, under her care, a comfortable and happy abode. She'll love it when friends drop by for the evening. She is a good cook and enjoys feeding people well.

The Taurus woman is serious about love and affection. When she has taken a tumble for someone, she'll stay by him forever, if possible. She will try to be practical in romance, to some extent. When she decides she wants a certain man, she keeps after him until he's won her. Generally, the Taurus woman is a passionate lover, even though she may appear staid at first glance. She is on the lookout for someone who can return her affection fully. Taurus women are sometimes given to fits of jealousy and possessiveness. They expect fair play in the area of marriage. When it doesn't come about, they can be bitingly sarcastic and mean.

The Taurus woman is usually an easygoing person intent on keeping the peace. She won't argue unless she must. She'll do her best to keep your love relationship on an even keel.

Marriage is generally a one-time thing for Taurus. Once they've taken the serious step, they seldom try to back out of it. Taurus women need love and warmth. With the right man, they become ideal wives.

The Taurus woman will respect you for your steady ways. She'll have confidence in your common sense. She'll share with you all the joys and burdens of parenthood.

Taurus women seldom put up with nonsense from their children. It is not that they are strict, but rather that they are concerned. They like their children to be well behaved and dutiful. Nothing pleases a Taurus mother more than a compliment from a neighbor or teacher about her child's behavior.

Although some children may inwardly resent the iron hand of a Taurus mother, in later life they are often thankful that they were brought up in such an orderly and conscientious way.

VIRGO MAN
GEMINI WOMAN

You may find a romance with a woman born under the sign of the Twins a many-splendored thing. She will provide the intellectual companionship you often look for in a friend or mate. A Gemini partner can appreciate your aims and desires because she travels pretty much the same road as you do intellectually, that is, at least part of the way. She may share your interests but she will lack your tenacity.

She suffers from itchy feet. She can be here, there, all over the place. Her eagerness to be on the move may make you dizzy. Still, you'll enjoy and appreciate her liveliness and mental agility.

The Gemini woman often has a sparkling personality. You'll be attracted to her warmth and grace. While she's on your arm you'll probably notice that many male eyes are drawn to her. She may even return a gaze or two, but don't let that worry you. All women born under this sign have nothing against a harmless flirtation once in a while. But if she feels she is already spoken for, she will never let it get out of hand.

Although she may not be as handy as you'd like in the kitchen, you'll never go without a tasty meal. The Gemini woman is always in a rush. She won't feel she's cheating by breaking out the instant mashed potatoes or the frozen peas. She may not be a good cook but she is clever. With a dash of this and a suggestion of that, she can make an uninteresting TV dinner taste like a gourmet meal. Then, again, maybe you've struck it rich and have a Gemini lover who finds complicated recipes a challenge to her intellect. If so, you'll find every meal a tantalizing and mouth-watering surprise.

When you're beating your brains out over the Sunday crossword puzzle and find yourself stuck, just ask your Gemini woman. She'll give you all the right answers without batting an eyelash.

Just like you, she loves all kinds of people. You may even find that you're a bit more discriminating than she. Often all that a Gemini requires is that her friends be interesting and stay interesting. But one thing she's not able to abide is a dullard.

Leave the party organizing to your Gemini sweetheart or mate, and you'll never have a chance to know what a dull moment is. She'll bring out the swinger in you if you give her half the chance.

A Gemini mother enjoys her children, which can be the truest form of love. Like them, she's often restless, adventurous, and easily bored. She will never complain about their fleeting interests because she understands the changes they will go through as they mature.

VIRGO MAN
CANCER WOMAN

The Cancer woman needs to be protected from the cold, cruel world. She'll love you for your masculine yet gentle manner; you make her feel safe and secure. You don't have to pull any he-man or heroic stunts to win her heart; that's not what interests her.

She's more likely to be impressed by your sure, steady ways—

that way you have of putting your arm around her and making her feel she's the only girl in the world. When she's feeling glum and tears begin to well up in her eyes, you have that knack of saying just the right thing. You know how to calm her fears, no matter how silly some of them may seem.

The woman born under the sign ruled by the Moon is inclined to have her ups and downs. You have that talent for smoothing out the ruffles in her sea of life. She'll probably worship the ground you walk on or put you on a very high pedestal. Don't disappoint her if you can help it. She'll never disappoint you.

The Cancer woman will take great pleasure in devoting the rest of her natural life to you. She'll darn your socks, mend your overalls, scrub floors, wash windows, shop, cook, and do just about anything in order to please you and let you know that she loves you. Sounds like that legendary good old-fashioned girl, doesn't it? Contrary to popular belief, there are still some around, and many of them are Cancers.

Of all the signs of the Zodiac, the Cancer-born are the most maternal. In caring for and bringing up children, Cancer women know just how to combine the right amount of tenderness with the proper dash of discipline. A child couldn't ask for a better mother. Cancer women are sympathetic, affectionate, and patient with their children.

While we're on the subject of motherhood, there's one thing you should be warned about: never be unkind to your mother-in-law. It will be the only golden rule your Cancer wife will probably expect you to follow. No mother-in-law jokes in the presence of your mate, please. They'll go over like a lead balloon. Mother is something pretty special for her. She may be the crankiest, nosiest old bat. But she's your wife's mother. You'd better treat her like she's one of the landed gentry. Sometimes this may be difficult to swallow. But if you want to keep your home together and your wife happy, learn to grin and bear it.

Treat your Cancer wife like a queen, and she'll treat you royally.

VIRGO MAN
LEO WOMAN

The Leo woman can make most men roar like lions. If any woman in the Zodiac has that indefinable something that can make men lose their heads and find their hearts, it's the Leo woman.

She's got more than a fair share of charm and glamour. She knows how to make the most of her assets, especially when she's in the company of the opposite sex. Jealous men are apt to lose their cool or their sanity when trying to woo a woman born under the sign of the Lion. The Lioness likes to kick up her heels quite often and doesn't care who knows it. She frequently makes heads turn and tongues wag. You don't necessarily have to believe any of what you hear—it's probably jealous gossip or wishful thinking. Still, other women in her vicinity turn green with envy and will try anything to put her out of the running.

Although this vamp makes the blood rush to your head and makes you momentarily forget all the things you thought were important and necessary in your life, you may feel differently when you come back down to earth and the stars are out of your eyes. You may feel that she isn't the type of girl you planned to bring home to Mother. Not that your mother might disapprove of your choice, but you might after the shoes and rice are a thing of the past. Although the Leo woman may do her best to be a good wife for you, chances are she'll fall short of your idea of what a good wife should be like.

If you're planning on not going as far as the altar with the Leo woman, you'd better be financially equipped for some very expensive dating. Be prepared to shower her with expensive gifts and to take her dining and dancing to the smartest spots in town. Promise her the moon if you're in a position to go that far. Luxury and glamour are two things that are bound to lower a Leo's resistance. She's got expensive tastes, and you'll have to cater to them if you expect to get to first base with her.

If you've got an important business deal to clinch and you have doubts as to whether you can swing it or not, bring your Leo woman along to the business luncheon. More than likely, with her on your arm, you'll be able to win any business battle with both hands tied. She won't have to say or do anything, just be there at your side. The grouchiest oil magnate can be transformed into a gushing, obedient schoolboy if there's a charming Leo woman in the room.

Leo mothers are sometimes blind to the faults of their children. On the other hand, the Leo mother can be strict when she wants them to learn something. She expects her youngsters to follow the rules, and she is a patient teacher. Being easygoing and friendly, she loves to pal around with the kids while proudly showing them off on every occasion.

VIRGO MAN
VIRGO WOMAN

The Virgo woman may be even too difficult for the Virgo man to understand at first. Her waters run deep. Even when you think you know her, don't take any bets on it. She's capable of keeping things hidden in the deep recesses of her womanly soul—things she'll only release when she's sure that you're the man she wants. But it may take her some time to come around to this decision. Virgos are finicky about almost everything. Many of them have the idea that the only people who can do things correctly are Virgos.

Nothing offends a Virgo woman more than slovenly dress, sloppy character, or a careless display of affection. Make sure your tie is not crooked and your shoes sport a bright shine before you go calling on this lady. Keep your off-color jokes for the locker room; she'll have none of that.

Take her arm when crossing the street, but don't rush the romance. Trying to corner her in the back of a cab may be one way of striking out. Never criticize the way she looks. In fact, the best policy is to agree with her as much as possible.

Still, there's just so much a man can take. All those dos and don'ts you have to observe if you want to get to first base with a Virgo may be just a little too much to ask of you. After a few dates, you may decide that she just isn't worth all that trouble. However, the Virgo woman is usually mysterious enough to keep her men running back for more. Chances are you'll be intrigued by her airs and graces.

If lovemaking means a great deal to you, you'll be disappointed at first in the cool ways of your Virgo woman. However, under her glacial facade there lies a hot cauldron of seething excitement. If you're patient and artful in your romantic approach, you'll find that all the caution was well worth the trouble. When Virgos love, it's all or nothing as far as they're concerned.

One thing a Virgo woman can't stand in love is hypocrisy. She doesn't care what the neighbors say. If her heart tells her to go ahead, she does. She is very concerned with human truths. If her heart stumbles upon another fancy, she will be true to that new heartthrob and leave you standing in the rain.

She's honest to her heart and will be as true to you as you are with her. Do her wrong once, however, and it's farewell.

The Virgo mother has high expectations for her children, and she will strive to bring out the very best in them. She is more tender than strict, though, and will nag rather than discipline. But youngsters sense her unconditional love for them, and usually turn out just as she hoped they would.

VIRGO MAN
LIBRA WOMAN

Libra invented the notion that it's a woman's prerogative to change her mind. Her changeability, in spite of its undeniable charm, could actually drive even a man of your patience up the wall. She's capable of smothering you with love and kisses one day, and on the next avoid you like the plague.

If you think you're a man of steel nerves then perhaps you can tolerate these sudden changes without suffering too much. However, if you admit that you're only a mere mortal who can take so much, then you'd better fasten your attention on a partner who's somewhat more constant.

But don't get the wrong idea. A love affair with a Libra can have a lot of pluses to it. The Libra woman is soft, very feminine, and warm. She doesn't have to vamp all over the place in order to gain a man's attention. Her delicate presence is enough to warm the cockles of any man's heart. One smile, and you're a piece of putty in the palm of her hand.

She can be fluffy and affectionate, which you will like. On the other hand, her indecision about which dress to wear, what to cook for dinner, or whether to redecorate could make you tear your hair out. What will perhaps be more exasperating is her flat denial of the accusation that she cannot make even the simplest decision. The trouble is that she wants to be fair or just in all matters. She'll spend hours weighing pros and cons. Don't make her rush into a decision; that will only irritate her.

The Libra woman likes to be surrounded by beautiful things. Money is no object when beauty is concerned. There will always be plenty of flowers in the house. She'll know how to arrange them tastefully, too. Women under this sign are fond of beautiful clothes and furnishings. They will run up bills without batting an eyelash, if given the chance.

Once she's involved with you, the Libra woman will do everything in her power to make you happy. She'll wait on you hand and foot when you're sick and bring you breakfast in bed Sundays. She'll be very thoughtful and devoted. If anyone dares suggest you're not the grandest man in the world, your Libra wife will give that person a good sounding-out.

The Libra mother works wonders with children. Gentle persuasion and affection are all she uses in bringing them up. It works. She is sensitive and sensible, with an intuitive understanding of what a child needs. Her youngsters will never lack for anything that could make their lives easier and richer. Still, you will always come before the children.

VIRGO MAN
SCORPIO WOMAN
When the Scorpio woman chooses to be sweet, she's apt to give the impression that butter wouldn't melt in her mouth but, of course, it would. When her temper flies, so will everything else that isn't bolted down. She can be as hot as a tamale or as cool as a cucumber when she wants. Whatever mood she's in, you can

be sure it's for real. She doesn't believe in poses or hypocrisy.

The Scorpio woman is often seductive and sultry. Her femme fatale charm can pierce through the hardest of hearts. The Scorpio woman can be a whirlwind of passion. But life with her will not be all smiles and smooth sailing. If you think you can handle a woman who is quick to retaliate and hold a grudge, then try your luck. Your stable and steady nature will probably have a calming effect on her. You're the kind of man she can trust and rely on. But never cross her, even on the smallest thing, or she'll make you pay for it.

Generally, the Scorpio woman will keep family battles within the walls of your home. When company visits, she can be depended upon to give the impression that married life with you is one big joyride. It's just her way of expressing her loyalty to you, at least in front of others. The Scorpio woman will certainly see that others have a high opinion of you both. She'll support you in whatever it is you want to do.

Although she's an individualist, after she has married, she'll put her own interests aside for those of the man she loves. With a woman like this behind you, you can't help but go far. She'll never try to take over your role as boss of the family and she'll give you all the support you need in order to fulfill that role. She won't complain if the going gets rough, for she is a courageous woman. She's as anxious as you to find that place in the sun for you both. She is as determined a person as you are.

Although the Scorpio mother loves her children, she will not put them on a pedestal. She is devoted to developing her youngsters' talents. The Scorpio mother is protective yet encouraging. The opposites within her nature mirror the contradictions within life itself. Under her skillful guidance, the children will learn how to cope with extremes and will grow up to become well-rounded individuals. She will teach her young ones to be courageous and steadfast.

VIRGO MAN
SAGITTARIUS WOMAN

You'll most likely never meet a more good-natured woman than the one under the sign of Sagittarius. Generally, she is full of bounce and good cheer. Her sunny disposition seems almost permanent and can be relied upon even on the rainiest of days.

The woman born under the sign of the Archer is rarely malicious. But she is often a little short on tact and says literally anything that comes into her head, regardless of the occasion. Sometimes the words that tumble out of her mouth are downright cutting and cruel. But no matter what she says, she means well.

Unfortunately, the Sagittarius woman is capable of losing some of her friends—and perhaps even some of yours—through such carelessness.

On the other hand, you will appreciate her honesty and good intentions. To you, these qualities play an important part in life. With a little patience and practice, you can probably help cure your Sagittarius of her loose tongue. In most cases, she'll give in to your better judgment and try to follow your advice.

Chances are, she'll be the outdoors type and sportswoman. Long hikes, fishing trips, and white-water canoeing will probably appeal to her. She's a busy person, one who sets great store in mobility. She won't sit still for one minute if it's not necessary.

She is very friendly and likes lots of company. When your buddies drop by for poker and beer, she won't have any trouble fitting in.

On the whole, she is a very kind and sympathetic woman. If she feels she's made a mistake, she'll be the first to call your attention to it. She's not afraid to own up to her own faults and shortcomings.

You might lose your patience with her once or twice. After she's seen how upset her shortsightedness and careless comments have made you, she'll do her best to please you.

The Sagittarius woman is not the kind who will pry into your business affairs. But she'll always be there, ready to offer advice if you need it.

The Sagittarius woman is seldom suspicious. Your word will almost always be good enough for her.

The Sagittarius mother is a wonderful and loving friend to her children. She is not afraid if a youngster learns some street smarts along the way. To bolster such knowledge, or to counteract it, she may preach a bit too much for the kids. Then you can switch the focus to the practical. But you will appreciate how she encourages the children to study in order for them to get a well-rounded and broad education.

VIRGO MAN
CAPRICORN WOMAN
The Capricorn may not be the most romantic woman of the Zodiac, but she's certainly not frigid when she meets the right man. She believes in true love. She doesn't appreciate flings. To her, they're just a waste of time. She's looking for a man who means business—in life as well as in love. Although she can be very affectionate with her lover or mate, she tends to let her head govern her heart. That is not to say she is a cool, calculating cucumber. On the contrary, she just feels she can be more honest about love if she consults her brains first.

The Capricorn woman is faithful, dependable, and systematic in just about everything she undertakes. She is very concerned with security and makes sure that every penny she spends is spent wisely. She is very economical about using her time, too. She does not believe in whittling away her energy on a scheme that is bound not to pay off.

Ambitious herself, she is often attracted to the ambitious man— one who is interested in getting somewhere in life. If a man with this temperament wins her heart, she'll stick by him and do all she can to help him get to the top.

The Capricorn woman is almost always diplomatic. She makes an excellent hostess. She can be very influential when your business acquaintances come to dinner.

The Capricorn woman is likely to be very concerned, if not extremely proud, of her family tree. Relatives are very important to her, particularly if they're socially prominent. Never say a cross word about her family members. She is likely to punish you by not talking to you for days.

As a rule, she's thorough in whatever she does. The Capricorn woman is well-mannered, well-groomed, and gracious, no matter what her background.

If you should marry a woman born under this sign, you need never worry about her going on a wild shopping spree. She understands the value of money better than most women. If you turn over your paycheck to her at the end of the week, you can be sure that a good hunk of it will wind up in the bank.

The Capricorn mother is very ambitious for her children. She wants them to have every advantage and to benefit from things she perhaps lacked as a child. She will train the youngsters to be polite and kind, and to honor traditional codes of conduct. She can be correct to a fault. But the meticulous Virgo mate will not find fault with the Capricorn mother's careful ways.

VIRGO MAN
AQUARIUS WOMAN

If you find that you've fallen head over heels for a woman born under the sign of the Water Bearer, you'd better fasten your safety belt. It may take you quite a while to actually discover what she is like. Even then, you may have nothing to go on but a series of vague hunches. The Aquarius woman is like a rainbow, full of bright and shining hues. She's like no one you've ever known. There is something elusive about her.

The Aquarius woman can be pretty odd and eccentric at times. Some say this is the source of her mysterious charm. You might think she's just a screwball, and you may be 50 percent right. The

Aquarius woman often has her head full of dreams. By nature, she is often unconventional; she has her own thoughts about how the world should be run. Sometimes her ideas may seem weird, but chances are they're just a little too progressive. Keep in mind the saying: The way the Aquarius thinks, so will the world in 50 years.

She'll probably be the most tolerant and open-minded woman you've ever encountered.

If you find that she's too much mystery and charm for you to handle, tell her so and say that you think it would be best to call it quits. She'll probably agree without making a scene yet still want to remain friends. The Aquarius woman is like that. Perhaps you'll both find it easier to get along in a friendship than in a romance.

The Aquarius woman is not a jealous person and, while you're romancing her, she won't expect you to be, either. You'll find her a free spirit most of the time. Just when you think you know her inside out, you'll discover that you don't really know her at all.

She's a very sympathetic and warm person. She is always helpful to those in need of assistance and advice.

She'll seldom be suspicious even when she has every right to be. If the man she loves makes a little slip, she's inclined to forgive and forget it.

The Aquarius mother is bighearted and seldom refuses her children anything. Her open-minded attitude is easily transmitted to her youngsters. They have every change of growing up as respectful and tolerant individuals who feel at ease anywhere.

VIRGO MAN
PISCES WOMAN

Many a man dreams of an alluring Pisces woman. You're perhaps no exception. She's soft and cuddly and very domestic. She'll let you be the brains of the family; she's contented to play a behind-the-scenes role in order to help you achieve your goals. The illusion that you are the master of the household is the kind of magic that the Pisces woman is adept at creating.

She can be very ladylike and proper. Your business associates and friends will be dazzled by her warmth and femininity. Although she's a charmer, there is a lot more to her than just a pretty exterior. There is a brain ticking away behind that soft, womanly facade. You may never become aware of it—that is, until you're married to her. It's no cause for alarm, however; she'll most likely never use it against you, only to help you and possibly set you on a more successful path.

If she feels you're botching up your married life through careless behavior or if she feels you could be earning more money than you do, she'll tell you about it. But any wife would, really.

She will never try to usurp your position as head and breadwinner of the family.

No one had better dare say one uncomplimentary word about you in her presence. It's likely to cause her to break into tears. Pisces women are usually very sensitive beings. Their reaction to adversity, frustration, or anger is just a plain, good, old-fashioned cry. They can weep buckets when inclined.

She can do wonders with a house. She is very fond of dramatic and beautiful things. There will always be plenty of fresh-cut flowers around the house. She will choose charming artwork and antiques, if they are affordable. She'll see to it that the house is decorated in a dazzling yet welcoming style.

She'll have an extra special dinner prepared for you when you come home from an important business meeting. Don't dwell on the boring details of the meeting, though. But if you need that grand vision, the big idea, to seal a contract or make a conquest, your Pisces woman is sure to confide a secret that will guarantee your success. She is canny and shrewd with money, and once you are on her wavelength you can manage the intricacies on your own.

Treat her with tenderness and generosity and your relationship will be an enjoyable one. She's most likely fond of chocolates. A bunch of beautiful flowers will never fail to make her eyes light up. See to it that you never forget her birthday or your anniversary. These things are very important to her. If you let them slip your mind, you'll send her into a crying fit that could last a considerable length of time.

If you are patient and kind, you can keep a Pisces woman happy for a lifetime. She, however, is not without her faults. Her sensitivity may get on your nerves after a while. You may find her lacking in practicality and good old-fashioned stoicism. You may even feel that she uses her tears as a method of getting her own way.

The Pisces mother totally believes in her children, and that faith never wavers. Her unconditional love for them makes her a strong, self-sacrificing mother. That means she can deny herself in order to fulfill their needs. She will teach her youngsters the value of service to the community while not letting them lose their individuality.

VIRGO
LUCKY NUMBERS 2000

Lucky numbers and astrology can be linked through the movements of the Moon. Each phase of the thirteen Moon cycles vibrates with a sequence of numbers for your Sign of the Zodiac over the course of the year. Using your lucky numbers is a fun system that connects you with tradition.

New Moon	First Quarter	Full Moon	Last Quarter
Jan. 6	Jan. 14	Jan. 20	Jan. 28
2 5 3 8	2 6 1 0	7 3 1 4	2 5 9 8
Feb. 5	Feb. 12	Feb. 19	Feb. 26
4 4 7 2	2 6 8 3	1 4 7 5	8 3 2 7
March 5	March 13	March 19	March 27
0 1 5 9	0 2 6 4	7 9 7 0	5 4 9 3
April 4	April 11	April 18	April 26
3 7 2 4	8 6 9 7	4 7 2 1	1 6 9 4
May 3	May 10	May 18	May 26
7 8 1 5	3 6 4 4	7 2 1 9	5 8 3 7
June 2	June 8	June 16	June 24
2 9 4 2	2 5 3 6	1 9 6 0	5 9 4 6
July 1	July 8	July 16	July 24
4 1 0 8	2 9 3 7	7 6 2 4	4 8 3 5
July 30	August 6	August 15	August 22
8 7 1 8	8 2 6 5	1 4 8 3	7 9 4 6
August 29	Sept. 5	Sept. 13	Sept. 20
6 5 3 6	6 1 9 0	5 8 3 7	9 4 5 3
Sept. 27	Oct. 5	Oct. 13	Oct. 20
9 4 7 2	2 1 6 9	9 4 8 0	5 3 6 9
Oct. 27	Nov. 4	Nov. 11	Nov. 18
7 1 5 4	4 9 3 7	7 2 4 8	6 9 3 1
Nov. 25	Dec. 3	Dec. 11	Dec. 17
1 8 7 3	3 6 1 5	5 7 2 9	3 1 6 9
Dec. 25	Jan. 2 ('01)	Jan. 9 ('01)	Jan. 17 ('01)
7 5 8 9	6 2 5 3	8 2 6 1	0 3 7 8

VIRGO
YEARLY FORECAST 2000

Forecast for 2000 Concerning Business
and Financial Affairs, Job Prospects,
Travel, Health, Romance and Marriage
for Those Born with the Sun
in the Zodiacal Sign of Virgo.
August 22–September 22

For those born under the influence of the Sun in the zodiacal sign of Virgo, ruled by Mercury, the planet of wit and intelligence, 2000 promises to be an expansive and challenging year. The main emphasis is on cutting out the deadwood in your life so that you are free to move on to better things. You may be inspired to spend some time abroad so that you can learn about a different way of life. There is room to expand your efforts in your professional life, so that you can work on building an ever better reputation for yourself. There are apt to be some very fortunate breaks this year. Although you may have to work hard to prove yourself, the rewards should make it well worthwhile, especially in the long term. Where business and professional matters are concerned, your key to success lies in being quick to grasp opportunities and openings as soon as they come your way, then slow down to work to the best of your abilities. The year is likely to begin on a positive note for your financial affairs. A windfall may come your way, but do not necessarily take this as a sign of things to come. If you want ongoing prosperity, you will probably have to personally earn it in one way or another. More money should be freed up when you are finally able to clear a debt once and for all. Expect a high degree of fluctuation in routine occupational affairs this year. You may be shifted from one area of work to another within a short space of time. This should give you the opportunity to try out new working methods and techniques, as well as adding new skills to your resume. Opportunities for long-distance travel are likely to increase this year over last. It is wise to book more than one vacation this year so that you have a real chance to relax and wind down. Having more resources at your disposal may give you the chance to make a trip which you previously wanted to make but simply could not afford or did not have sufficient time to undertake. It is vital this year to guard your health, particularly by taking more care of your nervous system. As a Virgo you tend to live on your nerves. Too much effort and upheaval, with insufficient rest, can take a heavy toll on you. The romance in your life is likely to flourish in distant locales. Single Virgo men and women could feel tempted to embark on a holiday romance, which may turn out to be a longer term involvement than you expect. An engagement or marriage is starred from October 13 to late November.

For professional Virgo people, the doors of opportunity may take time to open. When they do, however, it could seem as though the world is at your feet. Try to be patient and wait for the best options to come along. Otherwise you risk staying in a rut and accepting options which do not really stretch you to your fullest. Once a lucky break comes and a new door is opened for you, there will be plenty of time to work out your strategies. This is a year for reaping the rewards of past efforts, but also for planting the seeds of a more prosperous future. If you want a new project to bear fruit, you must be prepared to work at it slowly but surely. Beware of making too many impulsive decisions, especially during the first half of the year. That time should be best spent reviewing what you have achieved so far and reassessing your priorities for the future. Judge your responsibilities in terms of the long-term development of your business interests. You cannot afford to allow plans to simply ride along at their own pace during the next twelve months. Your most important ventures need careful planning and constant follow-up. If you are looking for new products to manufacture or market, focus along the lines of technological style and innovation. You stand to make greater gains if you look ahead of the times. There may be opportunity to expand into unusual areas this year, particularly within the health and nutrition fields. With business investments, aim to keep a balance by plowing some of your money back into current operations and putting a certain percentage into prospecting. If there does not seem to be enough money to fulfill both options, you may be able to raise venture capital for a new project if your ideas and plans are sufficiently sound. The period between May 4 and June 16 is favored for taking brave new steps along a route that is a challenge for you.

Where finances are concerned, your luck is peaking at the beginning of the year. An unexpected windfall could come your way in January or early February. Whether this is from a gamble or a legacy, it could be quite a substantial sum. This money could free up resources to expand an area of interest which will be valuable for your future career prospects. As a Virgo you tend to be eternal students at heart. If you have cherished for some time the idea of training in a new area of work, you may at last have your chance. Think ahead to the future, however. The bonus at the start of the year may only be sufficient to cover certain expenses; you still have to find a way of creating additional income in order to make your plans viable. If you have debts to pay off, use any windfall to get them out of the way. You may be able to borrow the money you need for a specific project at a lower rate of interest compared with what you paid on a previous loan. There is also a chance that you will be able to borrow money from a parent or someone else close to you, which may not have to be repaid in any great hurry. Your mate or partner's good fortune this year may free up funds for special items which you both have wanted to purchase. If you decide to hold on to your cash this year, you may be able to take advantage of new investments which offer excellent long-term returns. The one area of life which can absorb more money than you expect is travel. If you have to travel extensively to fulfill work or personal responsibilities, you may have to foot the whole bill yourself. Allow a little leeway in your budget for the unexpected. With that in place, any sudden expenditure should be easier to deal with. The period between January 1 and February 14 can be a markedly prosperous beginning to the year, with new opportunities just waiting for you to focus on them.

Be prepared for a year of some upheaval in your routine occupational affairs. The chances are that you will be required to diversify and cover much more ground than before. Fortunately you have an aptitude for versatility, which should stand you in good stead for the likely changes. Exciting career opportunities may emerge through newly gained skills and contacts which come as a result of this upheaval. If you are looking to impress your boss or other authority figures, start thinking about innovative methods and procedures which could save time and effort. Your insights may be more significantly rewarded than you expect. There is a strong link this year between routine efforts and essential career ambitions. This should give you more chance to spend time doing what really interests you from a vocational point of view. Be sure to keep up with the latest technology and take advantage of it.

Even though time may be at a premium, there are likely to be more opportunities to travel overseas and to other parts of the country. If you are only able to take your vacation in the busy tourist season, it may not matter because you should have more cash at your disposal to make it affordable. This year you are apt to travel farther than you have ever done, especially during the first six months of the year. A new job or work role could mean you will be traveling further on a day-to-day basis to reach your destination. Commuting by public transportation may not be an unpleasant inconvenience since you can use the time to catch up on work-related reading. If you have to travel by car, however, bear in mind that it could be quite tiring. You may need to adjust your usual personal schedule in order to adapt to the stress of the road. The period between March 24 and May 3 is ideal for an unplanned trip, especially with a loved one.

It can be helpful this year to try to improve your overall health with alternative treatments for a condition which troubles you from time to time. Some of the more traditional remedies may not be suitable because the problem is so intermittent; natural cures, which work quickly, could be ideal. Be sure to get plenty of rest this year. Your nervous system may become worn down through late nights and worrying. The more sleep you can get, the better. This will help focus your mind and give your body a chance to recuperate each night. Digestive upsets can also be a source of constant trouble for Virgo people. You may discover that a particular kind of food does not agree with you. During the coming months it would be wise to avoid this food altogether in all of its forms.

Romance and marriage should be full of pleasant surprises this year. An extended trip could be like a second honeymoon for you and your marriage partner, especially if you have not had a chance to get away together in a long time. For single Virgo men and women, travel could yield romantic possibilities. You may assume that a holiday romance will only be temporary, but if you meet someone who is as fond of you as you are of them, it could be the start of a long-term relationship. It could be hard work juggling romance and career priorities. However, an understanding partner will support your ambitions. Meeting all of the exciting challenges coming your way in the year ahead will be easier with a loved one at your side.

VIRGO
DAILY FORECAST

January–December 2000

JANUARY

1. SATURDAY. Uplifting. This is an ideal day for looking ahead and planning how you can better develop your creative powers this year. There is always something new to learn, and your inquiring Virgo mind will benefit from grappling with an intriguing new subject. The accent today is on pleasure after a period of hard work; you and your loved one deserve a holiday. This is a good time to start organizing your finances so that you can afford a special treat. Youngsters will enjoy activities that demand a bit of thought; give them puzzles and games that have an element of challenge. Stay close to home later this evening; road conditions are likely to be problematic.

2. SUNDAY. Happy. Virgos who have been looking for romance may have been searching too far afield. There may well be someone close to your usual base of operations who has been expressing interest in you for some time. Look around your home to see what changes can be made to brighten it up. Your good eye for detail can pick out possibilities for appealing decorative schemes, and you should be able to create the effect you want without too much expense or upheaval. A lost items of value is unlikely to be far away. In fact, it may turn up when you do some really thorough cleaning. Think before you speak; you are apt to regret sharp words as soon as you voice them.

3. MONDAY. Volatile. Promote a spirit of harmony right from the time you get up this morning. Otherwise, family members and colleagues are apt to pull against each other, making cooperation more difficult than it need be. Romance is a tinderbox, with the slightest problem likely to spark a firestorm. If you can weather the upset, the exposure of emotions that have been kept hidden till now could make your relationship all the stronger in the future. Virgo homebuyers may be facing financial difficulties due to expenses not taken into account. However, with careful budgeting the necessary funds can be accumulated before the payment has to be made.

4. TUESDAY. Stimulating. A dynamic new business associate could breathe new life into your work routine. Although their ideas may seem a little aggressive at first, there are tips you can pick up from them for your own use. A long-term partnership is entering a phase when you alone can do a lot of valuable work improving your togetherness. It is all too easy to take one another for granted after a while. Make sure you do not fall into this trap, or life can become boring. Virgos who work from home may find this a good time to get ordinary tasks such as paperwork out of the way. Stock up on basic supplies so that your time is free for creative work.

5. WEDNESDAY. Manageable. All financial matters concerning your family are highlighted. Do not delay sorting out details of matters such as insurance; swift action is apt to benefit you in the long run. Your competitive Virgo instinct is sharp, enabling you to see ways to get ahead of the pack. A subtle approach is more likely to win the approval of superiors as well as colleagues at work. In romantic affairs, you cannot afford to be too laid-back. Unless you take the initiative, a promising relationship may slip out of your grasp. Parents may be willing and able to help if you need a lump sum for a special purchase, but do not merely drop hints; come right out and ask them.

6. THURSDAY. Beneficial. It is time for some concentrated thought about your own self-development. You may benefit by taking an evening class, or even a correspondence course. Learning to speak a new language could broaden your opportunities. There is more creative satisfaction to be obtained from your career than you might think, but you need to have confidence that you can get to the top. Find out about training in new skills that may open doors for you. The start of a new relationship is likely to put an extra spring in your step. The level of mental rapport can make all the difference. This mutual understanding should provide a strong foundation on which to build a lasting involvement.

7. FRIDAY. Tricky. Money matters could cause you some concern. As a Virgo you normally know where every penny has gone, but now your accounts may be somewhat jumbled. It is time to be extra careful with your savings and investments. Loved ones may not be carrying out promises that filled you with high hopes. In fact, they might have forgotten altogether. It is important not to swallow your disappointment; come right out and tell them you feel let down. Although you may want to begin the weekend early, be sure to finish up all urgent work before going off to enjoy yourself. Sloppily done tasks will inevitably be rejected and need to be done again.

8. SATURDAY. Slow. If you find it more difficult than usual to concentrate on household chores, it is probably because you are craving a more glamorous occupation. Unfortunately, you have to be contented with your dreams for now. It is unwise to plan a busy day because there are likely to be many interruptions, making it hard to finish whatever you start. Do not be tempted to bite off more than you can chew. Your health would benefit from a more disciplined approach to exercise. Good intentions are not enough; you need to actually go out and give your muscles a workout. Keep home entertaining simple or you will not be able to relax along with your guests.

9. SUNDAY. Unsettling. Lovers' tiffs are often little more than excuses to make up again, but something more serious could be brewing right now. If you have a real grievance, get right to the root of the matter. Otherwise your relationship could well come to a regrettable end. A family gathering may arouse old resentments and rivalries. If you step into the role of peacemaker, you run the risk of alienating both parties unless you use all your powers of diplomacy. There is the chance of a fresh start in a long-term relationship providing you both agree to allow each other some extra space. A willingness to trust is an essential ingredient of any successful partnership.

10. MONDAY. Successful. The workweek gets off to an optimistic start. If you use a little extra flattery, you can probably get colleagues to cooperate willingly with you on work that needs urgent attention. Take this opportunity to put into place details of a plan you have been considering for some time. It is never too soon to start planning for the future. A loved one may appear to be provoking you almost deliberately. If you react with anger, a full-scale argument could erupt over quite an insignificant matter. As the day goes on, it is important not to push yourself too hard. Just proceed at your own pace so that you do not get all stressed out and upset.

11. TUESDAY. Inspiring. A new mood of openness between you and a loved one should make it possible to establish more comfortable boundaries in your relationship. A shared sense of responsibility may even inspire you with romantic fervor. Certainly it will put your partnership on a sounder footing. Virgos who are living in rented property may have some difficulty concerning matters of maintenance. It might be wise to get legal advice so that you are absolutely clear about your rights; then you will be in a stronger position to get things done. News from a friend living at a distance might fill you with a desire to visit. This could be an ideal getaway for you and your mate or partner in the near future.

12. WEDNESDAY. Excellent. If you have been struggling with studies that seem a bit beyond your capabilities, take heart. This is a turning point; from now on you should be able to forge ahead with confidence. A long-delayed trip is at last in the cards. Even if you now have lost some of your enthusiasm while waiting to see if it will come off, rouse yourself to take advantage of this great opportunity. A new colleague may seem to be attracted to you, which is bound to be flattering. However, you might be happiest to keep this at the level of light flirtation rather than getting into a more involved affair which could get complicated.

13. THURSDAY. Spirited. It is full steam ahead today; you should be firing on all cylinders. Routine work could take on more interest as information comes to light that gives you an idea for improving your work prospects. Colleagues may offer financial advice that seems a little unusual, but do not be too quick to dismiss it. They may well have the knowledge necessary to know a good opportunity when it comes up. A recent event that has brought you closer to family members is giving you the chance to heal an old wound. Do not be afraid to open your heart; after all, blood is thicker than water. Profits from a recent deal should come through without delay.

14. FRIDAY. Mixed. Wheeling and dealing is not really the Virgo style. You are right to treat people who behave in this way with suspicion. Trust your own judgment if you receive a tempting financial offer; your sense of caution should guide you well. If you feel strongly about someone, there is little point pretending indifference. They are bound to become aware of your interest sooner or later, so just come out and say so without delay. A legacy from a distant relative could bring you an unexpected windfall. However, unless you are careful it may be a case of easy come, easy go. Advice from a friend may cast new light on a problem and enable you to solve it quite effortlessly.

15. SATURDAY. Solid. Taking stock of your abilities in a realistic fashion will be to your benefit. An accurate assessment of your talents will help you work out just what you can hope to achieve from your chosen career. Do not let dreams of romance lure you away from the real world. It is important to do the best with what you have got; longing for perfection is not going to get you anywhere. A long trip with a friend or loved one should blow away cobwebs and give you the chance to have some special fun together. In fact, it is preferable to get some enjoyment from the day rather than let routine chores take up most of your precious weekend leisure time.

16. SUNDAY. Cautious. Keep an eye on youngsters. Their mischievous mood could get them into trouble. Unless you are very careful, they are apt to be up to no good behind your back. Talking goes a long way toward solving problems with loved ones. However, unless you are prepared to follow up with action, words mean very little in the long run. New standards of behavior seem to be called for unless you are ready to face further difficulties. Hobbies and leisure pursuits can be more enjoyable if you find out as much as you can about the subject. Consult friends who have more experience than you, and benefit from their experience. Get to bed early tonight.

17. MONDAY. Diverse. Fresh business initiatives are likely to be well received by your associates. However, you will probably have to sell your ideas hard to make the impact you want. Virgos working in education as teachers or students can get the most out of classes by promoting a cooperative atmosphere. Once this is established, there is the chance of getting some very solid work done. Long-term objectives may have to take a backseat to daily demands on your time and energy. Naturally you are eager to realize your dreams, but even the most mundane tasks are steps on the way toward achieving your goals. Try to avoid crossing swords with your boss or other superiors.

18. TUESDAY. Changeable. A creative approach to routine work may win you the favor of those in authority. Apply your common sense and adaptability and see what you come up with. There is apt to be some tension between you and a loved one over the amount of time you spend at home. Balancing work and home life is never easy, but now it is vital to sort out your priorities. If a well-kept secret comes to your attention, the question is whether you can stay silent about it. A breach of confidence will only work against you in the end, no matter how tempting it may seem to put the information to immediate use. A friend in need is hoping for your help and support.

19. WEDNESDAY. Fair. It may be difficult to get through the day without serious disagreements with loved ones. However, do your best to keep calm and to keep the peace. Arguments that flare up now are likely to have long-term repercussions. Make time to see friends; some stimulating social contact with them will do you a world of good. Conversation should flow easily. You might even pick up some tips for developing your current leisure interests. A dearly held wish can come a little closer to fulfillment as long as you are prepared to listen to advice offered by older people. Those who love you best know you best, so listen to what they have to say.

20. THURSDAY. Problematic. As a Virgo you are usually happiest organizing daily affairs down to the last detail. However, sometimes routine chores get the best of you. This is one of those periods when you are likely to feel the need to break out. A friendship you have relied on for a long time could be causing you some concern. As hidden depths are revealed in your friend, you may start to wonder if you have ever really known them. It is wise to avoid borrowing money right now. Although you might be confident of being able to pay it back promptly, circumstances could make this problematic. An evening out is apt to become more expensive than you had planned.

21. FRIDAY. Demanding. Colleagues probably do not mean to mislead you deliberately, but a badly phrased memo may give you the wrong impression. Be sure to check the facts before taking any rash action. Youngsters' demands are apt to make inroads on your time to the extent that it may be simpler to abandon routine altogether. This is not going to hurt you for a day. As a work project reaches a crisis point, the challenge is to let go of old conceptions and reach out for new ideas. Getting some time to yourself gives you the chance to let creative thoughts come to the surface. A quiet night at home will help you wind down so that you can get a good night's rest.

22. SATURDAY. Buoyant. This is an excellent time to host a party for friends and colleagues who have invited you to their home. Pull out all the stops and give your guests something special; it should be an event to remember. Purchases made for the home are likely to be rather costly. However, it is worthwhile to spend a little extra and get good quality items. A touch of luxury is sure to cheer you up. The demands of your family are unlikely to give you much freedom, so it is probably best not to start any job that needs time and close concentration to finish. A generous donation to a charity may do more good than you might think possible, so give what you can afford.

23. SUNDAY. Smooth. Try to keep your day free of obligations so that you can relax and enjoy some peace and quiet. Looking over old photo albums and school yearbooks is bound to create pleasant feelings of nostalgia. Mulling over your family history can bring home to you just how much you value your loved ones; let them know your feelings. Serious attempts to develop your creative talents are apt to pay off. The satisfaction you get from finding out that you can achieve more than you expect will give you some much-needed self-confidence. Do not lose touch with relatives who live at a distance. Make time to sit down and write them a letter that is full of local news and gossip.

24. MONDAY. Variable. A work project in which you have invested a lot of time could be on the point of dissolution. It is probably not within your power to save it, but take comfort from the fact that you have gained lots of experience which can later be put to good use in a different setting. The opportunities for advancement held out by a superior may not seem to be coming to pass. You may have to jog their memory, or perhaps cut your losses and learn to rely on your own efforts rather than on the promises made by others. A sudden crisis in the family requires all your powers of organization and cool-headed ability. You are probably the only person who sees that things are not actually as bad as they seem.

25. TUESDAY. Good. Long-distance travel may be complicated by officials who cannot and will not bend any rules. As a Virgo you normally have the patience to deal with this kind of thing, but this time you have to grit your teeth in order to cope with the inevitable delays. An injustice at work is likely to upset you, although you probably feel it is not your place to complain. However, your conscience may hardly let you rest until you take appropriate action. For once you can afford to be a little more relaxed when it comes to money matters. Allowing yourself a few modest luxuries will hardly break the bank. A new romance may not yet give you the security you want.

26. WEDNESDAY. Favorable. Find time to go through drawers you have been meaning to empty for ages. You will probably find a lot of worthless stuff that has accumulated; be ruthless and make yourself some useful space. Home redecoration will be all the more successful if you pay careful attention to detail. It is the small touches that turn a home into a truly individual place. Talk over your financial plans with your mate or partner; they may even refine your ideas so that they will cost less than your estimate. Shopping for essentials may turn up some surprising bargains; make sure you have plenty of room to store bulk purchases of nonperishable items.

27. THURSDAY. Misleading. It is important to plan for future security, but beware of insurance plans or other schemes that appear to offer the earth. They are unlikely to fulfill their promise, and you could end up paying out a substantial sum of money for a meager return. There is apt to be an undiscussed problem undermining a close relationship. Even though it may be painful to bring it out into the open, it is essential for you to do so. The results of some research into your family history may hold a few surprises. Some of your ancestors are probably more colorful than folk tend to be in this day and age. This is something for you to be proud of and to use as an incentive in your own life.

28. FRIDAY. Sensitive. A thoughtless word of criticism from you could hurt more than you realize. Keep in mind that not everyone maintains your own high standards; sometimes it is necessary to be tolerant of the failings of other people. News of drastic changes to come at work may be something of a bombshell. However, the report could be exaggerated, and there is certainly nothing to be gained by panicking. Youngsters will benefit from some fresh air; even if it is cold, dress them up warmly so that they can get outside for a while. A surprise proposition might not be all that it seems. Before you get too excited, ask friends for their opinion of the person or company concerned.

29. SATURDAY. Eventful. Unless your car has been serviced recently and is in excellent condition, leave it at home if at all possible and use public transportation. Electrical faults could develop at an inconvenient point, leaving you in trouble. Listen carefully to loved ones; there is a chance of a misunderstanding arising from a misheard word. Because youngsters are apt to be more restless than usual and easily bored, it might take a leap of imagination on your part to keep them amused. Revive the romance in a long-term partnership by revisiting a favorite restaurant and treating yourselves to a special night out on the town.

30. SUNDAY. Starred. Your dreams are likely to stay with you when you wake up. Even the most ordinary symbolism holds some personal meaning. It would be a good idea to write down as much as you can remember. The atmosphere within the family is likely to be more harmonious than usual. Make the most of this by getting together with a few close relatives for an informal meal so that you can catch up on each other's news. A relationship which began in quite a matter-of-fact way could be turning into a real romance. The longer you know each other, the more remarkable you may find your affair. Happily, you each seem to feel the same way. This is a starred time for an engagement.

31. MONDAY. Burdensome. A sense of responsibility may be weighing heavily on you. Certainly you should take your obligations seriously, but try to delegate a little so that the burden is shared. Virgo home owners may want to check drains; inclement weather could result in a blockage which might prove problematic unless dealt with promptly. Losing your temper with a loved one will not solve anything. No matter how profound your disagreement, you both have the right to your own opinion; compromise is not beyond your reach. Patience is needed in dealing with a legal case, which is likely to drag on for some time.

FEBRUARY

1. TUESDAY. Successful. You should be right on form, eager and willing to tackle any and every task. Your Virgo talent for organization is sure to be appreciated more than usual by friends and colleagues. A small service to a family member may not seem like much to you but will be greatly appreciated and remembered for a long time. Take advantage of a good chance to complete the final details of a work project, leaving yourself free for new initiatives. Be sure you are thorough, however; work left undone now could spoil an otherwise faultless achievement. An emotional upset at home can be sorted out if you have the courage to face up to your own responsibility for it.

2. WEDNESDAY. Profitable. A creative venture has the potential for valuable development. Fortunately there is help available from a real expert; make the most of what they have to offer. Romance looks very promising. You and that special person should be finding that you have more in common than you initially thought, giving you a deeper and more satisfying understanding of each other. Right now you can afford to commit time and funds to a project that will help you climb a rung or two up the ladder of success. A wholehearted approach to self-help is bound to pay off. If you are waiting for exam results, you have little to fear so do your best not to worry needlessly.

3. THURSDAY. Buoyant. An extra spring in your step and a sparkle in your eye gives others confidence that you can achieve great things. This is a starred day to get the ball rolling, although most of your energy might need to be spent on negotiations at first. Beware of a tendency to steamroller your mate or partner into doing what you want. At the moment you can probably persuade them into just about anything, but if they agree against their will your forcefulness will eventually backfire. Youngsters have to learn the value of taking other people's feelings into account. This lesson does not usually come easily, and it is not too soon to begin teaching it to them by example.

4. FRIDAY. Bumpy. A rare mood of dissatisfaction threatens to spoil your enjoyment of the day's routine tasks. Consider how you can inject a bit more glamour into your life without losing sight of reality. Your health needs careful attention because you are more likely than usual to pick up a virus. Make sure you are eating well, and take vitamin supplements if you feel you need them. The workweek is unlikely to wind down to a quiet conclusion; new ideas for increasing cooperation among colleagues are apt to get you quite excited. However, it would be wise to work out plans fully before talking about them. Do not overindulge in food or drink if socializing tonight.

5. SATURDAY. Productive. Because youngsters take center stage today, even if you have things that need to be discussed between you and your mate or partner they may have to wait. Try to schedule a quiet time tonight to yourselves. This is an excellent time to begin a new exercise program or to join a health club. You probably need nothing extreme. A gentle exercise that tones the body such as swimming would be ideal. Sometimes it may seem that you spend too much of your free time helping others. However, this sense of consideration and thoughtfulness is in fact one of your major strengths, and you will find that friends and relatives are glad to return favors if you only ask for what you want or need.

6. SUNDAY. Variable. The day is not likely to go as planned, especially if you are hoping to get some practical work done. The gremlins seem determined to hide tools, break equipment, and cause interruptions, so you might as well just give up for now and take a break. It is usually the small details of domestic life that cause the most constant problems. Make a resolution not to get upset when family members do not do things your way; allow them their individuality. Social events are sure to be enjoyable. Although you may find yourself roped into helping behind the scenes, this will give you glimpses into your host's life you would not otherwise ever see.

7. MONDAY. Inspiring. At last your plans to develop a new job skill or to apply for a new position can be consolidated. All you needed was support from the right person, and that is now forthcoming. Legal matters may have more far-reaching consequences than you expected. In the long run, this could actually turn out in your favor, although you should anticipate the usual delays before you hear good news. For Virgos buying property, it is important to keep in mind that nothing is secure until the final papers are signed and sealed. Keep your fingers crossed, but do not bank on a sure conclusion. Try not to argue with your parents, in-laws or other older family members over trivial matters.

8. TUESDAY. Tense. Sudden and unwarranted criticism by a work associate is apt to leave you unsure of where you stand. One thing is for sure: you need to sort this out face-to-face rather than meekly accept their attack. Arrangements for a family get-together may not be going that smoothly at the moment. It is difficult, if not impossible, to please everyone, but at least you can assure them you are doing your very best. Virgos hoping to find a romantic partner should socialize as much as possible. You are bound to meet some newcomers. Sooner or later, just the right person will step into your life and may change it forever.

9. WEDNESDAY. Favorable. You can benefit from a healthier diet. Eating simple, nutritious foods does not have to be boring. Get yourself a good cookbook and experiment a little. An almost psychic intuition may lead you to find an object lost by a friend. However, it may not be so easy to locate things for yourself, so do not be tempted to become careless. The recent problem encountered by a close relative is sure to stir your sympathy. Act on your feelings and offer them whatever support you can; they are bound to be more than grateful. A romantic affair may be rousing deep emotions, giving you renewed confidence in the future.

10. THURSDAY. Uncertain. As a Virgo you are better than most at exerting the power of mind over matter because you tend to be in close touch with your body's requirements. As the need arises you can call on reserves of nervous energy in order to deal with urgent matters, but keep in mind that you need time to recuperate afterward. A romantic affair may fall prey to suspicion and doubt. Trust is essential if you are going to enjoy a close relationship. Unless you can root out these fears, the outlook for your relationship is not too bright. Because money matters may not be going your way, it would be very unwise to take unnecessary risks right now with your savings.

11. FRIDAY. Mixed. It is necessary to adopt a philosophical attitude toward your future security since there seems to be little you can do to improve it at the moment. There is no reason not to make big plans, but accept that these will take quite a long time to work out. Lack of consideration for others is not normally a Virgo fault, but you might be feeling like looking out only for number one. That is fair enough providing you do not forget that loved ones are an important part of your life. Their happiness must not be put at risk. As the day goes on, there could be a temptation to let work responsibilities slip. Relax, but do not treat your assignments with indifference or expect anyone to offer a helping hand.

12. SATURDAY. Fruitful. A shopping trip with your mate or partner is likely to be successful. You should be able to pick up items that will give you pleasure for years to come, as well as some necessities of life. Youngsters are apt to be more willing than usual to respond to firm but loving discipline. Make the most of this by giving them small tasks to do; they will enjoy the sense of adult responsibility. Older relatives with whom you have lost contact might get in touch, spurring you to resolve to be more supportive in the future. There is much that the older generation can teach to anyone who is willing to listen. A romantic affair will go better after taking a trip together.

13. SUNDAY. Stressful. Unspoken thoughts are apt to be simmering away under the surface, making the atmosphere rather tense between you and your loved ones. The sooner you get them out in the open, the better. Otherwise it will become more and more difficult to face the problem. Youngsters are likely to be particularly trying. Sooner or later they feel the need to test their will against yours, and this is one of those times. Great patience and forbearance is called for to keep them in line. Surprise the family with a mystery trip; keep the destination secret and see if anyone can guess it before you arrive. Forget household chores; you deserve to rest and relax.

14. MONDAY. Tricky. The clash of interests between work and home often flares up at this time of the week. However, at the moment there may not be a clear solution. The best you can do is aim to get out of the house this morning without having tempers flare. Virgos hoping to change jobs should attempt to get someone with influence interested in helping. Usually it is who you know rather than what you know that opens doors, so give it a try. Public speaking is never something Virgos truly enjoy; even speaking up in a meeting can make you nervous. However, as long as you know what you want to say, you should be able to make a good impression.

15. TUESDAY. Exciting. The possibility of achieving an ambition is drawing closer as you lay the groundwork for future attainments. There is no need to feel you are alone; friends and family members who can pull a few strings will be glad to help. You are apt to be put in a position of greater responsibility, perhaps as a temporary measure. However, this gives you a wonderful opportunity to show superiors just what you are capable of achieving. A sociable mood makes an evening at home a dull prospect; call a few friends to go out with you and paint the town red for once. Rumors and gossip should not be accepted as gospel truth; the motive is probably malicious on the part of one person in particular.

16. WEDNESDAY. Harmonious. This is an excellent day for meetings. Agreement can be reached more easily than usual, and some real advances made with plans that are important to you. Just make sure you get your points across clearly. A long-term relationship should benefit from a change of scene or routine. Plan a special outing for your mate or partner, or even a weekend away. The usual distractions of social life may not be satisfying to you at the moment; deeper contact is probably what you need. Investigate the numerous groups focusing on philosophy and meditation that could help point you in the right direction.

17. THURSDAY. Fair. There may be some misunderstanding between you and a friend who has been playing a larger role in your life recently. While you are happy to let the friendship develop in its own way, the other person may seem intent on a full-blown romance. If that does not interest you, it is up to you to set the matter straight. Sometimes it is wisest not to confide your dearest hopes to others. They may not appreciate how important these are, and their criticism or even lack of enthusiasm can be very upsetting. Work that has been outstanding for some time can be finished off before the weekend if you get some time to yourself and really buckle down to it. Plan on eating out tonight.

18. FRIDAY. Demanding. Your suspicions that a romantic partner is not being totally honest with you may be well founded. However, they care about you enough to reveal their feelings eventually, at which point you will have to decide what to do about the relationship. You should feel a lot healthier if you can give up a bad habit. Effort made now will pay off, so there is no excuse not to give it a try. Be careful with money, especially if you are handling a sum on behalf of other people. Make sure you get and keep records of all transactions to avoid disputes later. A good turn done for a friend or acquaintance from the kindness of your heart can cement your relationship.

19. SATURDAY. Changeable. Comments by a friend on your romantic life may seem out of order, but in fact their observations probably highlight aspects you cannot see yourself. It would be a good idea to take their words to heart and think about how you can improve your relationship. As a Virgo you usually put loved ones first without even thinking about it, but from time to time you have to assert your own needs. Doing so is entirely natural, but just guard against going over the top. Compromise is the answer so that everyone is happy. Plans for personal development have reached a turning point. It is up to you to decide if you have had enough or prefer to go on.

20. SUNDAY. Cautious. If you are planning to do practical work on your home, make sure you do not overdo it. It is all too easy to let one job develop into another, until you are at the point where you realize expert help is needed. Talking over your future plans with your mate or partner should be extremely beneficial. However, be prepared for them to put up some stiff opposition until they fully appreciate what you wish to achieve. Try to get away from home for a good part of the day; a change of surroundings will blow away the cobwebs and fill you with new ideas. You also need some mental stimulation to get out of a problem-solving bind.

21. MONDAY. Quiet. The workweek is likely to get off to a slow start. Mail may be delayed, and the phone will probably be quieter than usual. Make the most of this to catch up with unfinished tasks; conditions will doubtless heat up further into the week. Keep your calendar and address book close at hand; there is a strong possibility of appointments being changed at the last minute, forcing you to do a bit of juggling. This is not the best time to put a special personal project into operation. Action taken now is likely to be premature. Instead, do some more research and make absolutely sure you have all the information and supplies you need. A relaxing evening at home can restore your vitality.

22. TUESDAY. Stimulating. A new colleague is apt to attract you. Their air of mystery is probably quite magnetic, but you would be wise to get to know them a little better. Money matters are likely to cause a few problems because it is more difficult than usual to hold onto what you make. It would be best to have as little to do as possible with finance. However, if this cannot be avoided, get someone to check your facts and figures. Virgo singles who are looking for romance stand a good chance of attracting positive attention by playing hard to get. An air of cool detachment can sometimes be very effective, but do not appear totally indifferent.

23. WEDNESDAY. Beneficial. It is time to sit down and sort out the details of your personal finances. Do not be tempted to put off this task; it will be immensely helpful to know exactly where you stand. The possibility of being given more responsibility at work is not as exciting as promotion, but there are new skills to be learned and perhaps the potential to boost your income. You should be in fairly good physical condition if you have been sticking to an exercise program; keep up the good work. Comments from friends or colleagues on your trim appearance should certainly be encouraging. Security in a relationship depends on allowing your mate or partner some freedom even if you do not desire the same.

24. THURSDAY. Challenging. Do not expect travel to be trouble-free; there are almost bound to be hitches. If you are going a long distance, allow plenty of time. Virgos who are studying must not get overconfident. If you do, your work may become careless. Stay alert and vow to stretch yourself to the limit of your abilities. A legal matter requires some attention; papers should be signed without further delay if you want a reasonably swift result. This is one of those days when you might forget your head if it were not firmly attached, so double-check all arrangements. Any promises should be put in writing, especially if money is changing hands.

25. FRIDAY. Trying. Vacation plans are unlikely to proceed without some kind of financial problem. You could find that there are hidden costs; make sure you are absolutely clear about all the facilities. Parents or in-laws may have more to say than usual about the way you are bringing up your children. Naturally this tends to be somewhat irritating, but if you can listen to them they will probably be quite content. Virgos who are involved in selling for a living can expect a rather quiet day. Some of your usual sparkle is lacking, so it is probably best just to wind down gently toward the weekend. Take your mate or partner to a special restaurant tonight.

26. SATURDAY. Pressured. Loved ones may seem to be in a world of their own. You might find it hard even to guess what they are thinking about. If you want to get anything done, you may have to do it yourself while people around you continue their daydreaming. A family gathering should not be overplanned; once people are together, the arrangements will take second place to the joy of being in each other's company. Something nagging at your conscience is asking to be confessed and will probably not let you rest until you do so. As a Virgo you like to be thought of as perfect, but everyone makes mistakes and you are no exception, so do not be too embarrassed to ask for advice or assistance.

27. SUNDAY. Unpredictable. At last a secret admirer is ready to speak to you personally. In fact, you may have no idea that this person is interested in you, so their feelings could come as something of a surprise. For this reason you need to be very cautious about your initial reaction. Those who are closest to you know just how to upset you, and sometimes do not hesitate to make the most of this knowledge. It may be impossible to keep your temper in check, but beware of saying cruel words in the heat of the moment. Paying a little extra attention to your appearance can boost your self-confidence a great deal. If you feel good, you will look good. Get to bed earlier than usual.

28. MONDAY. Fortunate. A surge of energy and determination makes you all but unstoppable today. Put your mind to working behind the scenes so that others actually carry out the plans that you develop. Virgos who are selling a home are likely to hear of favorable developments. You can probably ask more than you actually expect to get for your property. Sometimes it helps to have challenges against which to test your wits, and this is one of those times. Now is the moment to call on all your reserves of ability in order to show other people just what you are capable of doing. If you hold back where romance is concerned, you will probably regret it as a new person comes on the scene.

29. TUESDAY. Opportune. Creative solutions to problems are near at hand providing you can think big. A recent training course has given you the necessary skills to tackle matters that you would normally refer to a superior. Romance is within your grasp; the other person is only waiting for you to make a move. If you are only interested in a lighthearted affair, think twice; whatever you initiate now is apt to last for a long time. Important negotiations that will affect your finances are unlikely to be completed without running into a few technicalities. Make sure you have the best expert assistance to keep you on the right track.

MARCH

1. WEDNESDAY. Productive. Frank discussion is the key to a successful day. Any doubts you have about current plans should be mulled over so that arrangements can be modified if necessary. If you and your mate or partner are failing to see eye-to-eye, it may help to write down just how you view the situation. Emotions tend to get in the way of clear expression when you are trying to thrash things out between you; this exercise can put problems in better perspective. For once you can take a bit of a risk with funds. As long as you are confident, there is the possibility of making a good return. All the same, however, do not commit more than you can afford to do without for a while.

2. THURSDAY. Satisfactory. There is no point making a martyr of yourself; ask for assistance with a difficult task and it will be gladly given. The results of some recent overindulgence may begin to show, as your friends and family members are probably not slow to point out. Your sense of pride is undoubtedly strong enough to enable you to start saying no when necessary. You and your mate or partner may feel inclined to talk about more serious subjects than usual. This can actually be very good, deepening your relationship as long as you remain tolerant of each other's point of view. Try to find some time to be with an older relative who would welcome a surprise visit.

3. FRIDAY. Fair. Your mate or partner may deliberately hold back some news for a reason that is not yet clear. Until this matter is brought out into the open, the atmosphere at home is likely to remain tense. Work off some of your surplus energy outdoors, if possible. Sometimes it is not appropriate to express negative emotions, but they always come out somehow; hard physical work can be a positive channel for them. It is apt to be more difficult than usual to get involved in work with any enthusiasm. If your heart simply is not in it, any important project should be postponed until you can give your best. Watch your spending or you may waste money merely to please a salesperson.

4. SATURDAY. Tense. The weekend is unlikely to begin peacefully because your nerves are on edge. Although the temptation is to snap at loved ones, do not blame them for your uncomfortable mood. Romance should be handled with kid gloves or your love life may take an unexpected turn for the worse. You cannot afford to take for granted that the other person wants the same as you do from the relationship; your expectations might be entirely different. If you are looking for a gift for a friend, be bold and go for an unusual item of jewelry or accessories. At the very least, what you buy will be a talking point. Make sure expensive purchases are adequately guaranteed, and save receipts.

5. SUNDAY. Promising. A more open attitude of mutual trust can rejuvenate a long-term relationship. There is no better time than the present to initiate this new phase. Youngsters may regard you as a playmate rather than an authority figure; relax and join in their games. A phone call from a friend could bring important news of a new development in their life. Your support will be very much appreciated, even if you only offer to listen as they talk through the problem. Close family members may be upset with you for no reason you can detect. It might be best simply to stay out of their way for a while until they regain their good humor.

6. MONDAY. Uplifting. As the workweek gets underway there is an exciting new opportunity for expanding your creative work. Just do not let self-doubt trip you up at this crucial time. Virgos who have been having difficulties in a close relationship have the chance now to make a fresh start. As long as you both agree not to let petty differences come between you, there is every possibility of making a go of it this time. A long-drawn-out legal case is finally coming to a conclusion, lifting a heavy weight from your shoulders. This could be a lesson to think twice before getting involved in a lawsuit unless it is absolutely necessary as a matter of principle.

7. TUESDAY. Exciting. An unexpected cash windfall from a relative could enable you to splurge without having to worry about the expense. Make the most of this chance to fulfill a long-held wish. A new acquaintance is likely to have a powerful physical attraction, which may be mutual. However, before you get involved be aware that if you have little else in common, the relationship will not be easy to sustain. Interesting facts related to your work may come to light during the course of routine research. This is apt to give you a whole new perspective on what you are able to contribute on a daily basis. Relax your tired nerves tonight in a soothing bath.

8. WEDNESDAY. Good. Your thoroughness and grasp of detail should serve you well when you are asked to investigate a financial matter. There should be information that you can apply to your own personal savings plan as well. The indirect approach is best in romantic matters. If you make your feelings too obvious, the other person may draw away from you. In fact, they will probably be more interested in you based on your show of strength. A cluttered desk and drawers need to be cleared out thoroughly. This is a job that Virgos are usually good at, so get to work; you never know what you could find. Keep private papers well hidden from prying eyes.

9. THURSDAY. Buoyant. Because this is a day with plenty going on, you need to keep a cool head to know where you are. It is important to prioritize so that you do not overlook essential tasks. All learning is favored. If you get the chance to enroll in a course that may be of use in your career, do not hesitate. Even a subject that seems a bit offbeat might come in handy one day. For Virgos who have been keeping quiet about an attraction to someone at work who is already involved romantically, the situation may be changing. Be alert for the possibility that this person will soon be available and probably interested in you.

10. FRIDAY. Confusing. Clear thinking may not be your strong suit today; for some reason you are not apt to be as quick and alert as usual. It is probably because you have been working too hard recently and now could really do with a good rest. Virgos who are engaged in studies might find teachers rather harsh in their judgments. You need to put in some extra effort to come up to their expectations, but the discipline will actually be good for you. Interruptions to your daily routine can be very distracting. It could help to list exactly what you have to accomplish by the end of the day so that you do not fall behind. Cheer yourself up by beginning to plan a getaway to a better climate.

11. SATURDAY. Disconcerting. Be really careful what you say and to whom. Ill-chosen words can give your listener the entirely wrong impression. People may be listening more closely than you realize, and taking your words to heart. Because youngsters are likely to be full of nervous energy, urge them to play out of doors for at least part of the day. At the same time, keep an eye on them; otherwise there is no telling what they might get up to. Romantic matters may not be going your way at the moment. There may seem to be no pleasing that special person in your life. Try to find out what is wrong by asking a mutual friend. A decision about your career direction cannot be put off much longer.

12. SUNDAY. Spirited. A yearning to get away from the dull realities of everyday life is foreseen. It would be ideal to spend the day at some romantic spot where you can enjoy the beauty and lose yourself in dreams. This is not the best time to spend at home. Differences of opinion are likely to spoil the atmosphere, whereas in another environment it may be easier to get along with each other. A pet might need more exercise than usual, and a brisk walk would not do you any harm either. It is also a good idea to involve youngsters in pet care as much as possible in order to develop their sense of responsibility. Avoid socializing this evening.

13. MONDAY. Lively. You should wake up this morning with a real feel of a fresh start and plenty of energy. Make the most of this opportunity by concentrating on important jobs; do not fritter away your valuable time on petty matters. If financial matters between you and your mate or partner need to be on a sounder footing, do not delay discussing possibilities and then taking action. Arrangements made now are likely to be clear, businesslike, and successful. During the course of the day you may find yourself at odds with a superior. The best course of action is to hold your tongue, letting your actions speak louder than words. A sociable evening should round off the day nicely.

14. TUESDAY. Profitable. This busy day is likely to keep you on your toes. Because all lines of communication are open, it may be difficult to keep track of the amount of information that is coming in. A strong sense of organization is needed to stay on top of it all. If you have been waiting for money to come through, you should be in luck. Be sure to put it safely into your bank account as soon as possible. A sense of wanting to help may lead you to get involved with a group dedicated to making the world a better place. Everyone has something to contribute, and you are no exception; it is a very good time to offer your services to a worthy cause.

15. WEDNESDAY. Rewarding. A long-term partnership often tends to become rather undemonstrative, but tender words are still capable of thrilling a loved one's heart. Virgos involved in home renovations may not be too satisfied with the progress. The level of inconvenience might seem almost intolerable to your orderly Virgo nature, but the final results will be worth all you have put up with. If you have been hesitating on the brink of making a proposal, pluck up your courage and go ahead. Your eloquence and depth of feeling are almost bound to produce just the answer you want. Jumping to conclusions before you have all the facts can be a major mistake.

16. THURSDAY. Tricky. Information passed on to you about opportunities at a distance is unlikely to be accurate. Rather than get too excited, check it for yourself. Protect your health; going to an extreme with any kind of diet or exercise regime can be as harmful as overindulgence. Try to avoid both ends of the spectrum; work on finding out what is right for you personally. Financially it is important to keep a low profile. Tempting investment ideas may be dangled in front of you, but right now you do not have funds to risk. Getting time to yourself can be difficult; be firm and tell other people they will have to wait until you have met a current deadline.

17. FRIDAY. Changeable. Although the day probably does not get off to a promising start, by evening you should be able to look back on at least one job well done. You can do your best if you work in privacy. That way a lot of loose ends can be cleared up, enabling you to make a clean start next week. Memories of a past relationship may be aroused with news of an old flame. Although this person might seem to want to reenter your life, the past is past. It is unlikely that your passions will be rekindled. Computer equipment could be troublesome, with an unexpected failure that causes you to lose valuable information. Be sure to back up all important files at regular intervals.

18. SATURDAY. Opportune. You are apt to be in high demand among friends who see you as an asset at any social event. Once you are among people you know, your shy Virgo exterior drops to reveal someone who can be the life and soul of any party. Like everyone else, sometimes you want to have your cake and eat it, too. Unfortunately life is not like that very often. Sooner or later you must make a decision so that loved ones are not hurt. If you are shopping for yourself, splurge for a change. Sometimes it does you good to buy an item you really like on the spur of the moment. Family commitments can seem restricting but nevertheless must be honored. Do not renege on a promise.

19. SUNDAY. Tranquil. A quieter mood prevails, probably making you attracted to the idea of solitude. This is a fine time to start giving your path of self-development some deeper thought. You may even want to ponder the meaning of life with the help of a religious or philosophical book. Arrange a trip for loved ones that has some educational value. Everyone in the family can benefit from learning, and there is no reason the outing cannot be enjoyable too. Older family members might have words of wisdom to share if only you give them a fair hearing. Although their experience of life may be quite different from yours, another perspective can be very valuable to you in making a major decision.

20. MONDAY. Fair. You may have gotten yourself into a bind where a close relationship is concerned. If your back is against the wall, let the other person know whether their company is more important to you than your independence. A partner may seem to be stifling your creativity. Try to talk this over rather than seething silently with resentment. It could be that the other person does not realize what they are doing. Virgos who are waiting for a lawsuit to be settled should shortly be able to heave a sigh of relief. The process is bound to be stressful, but soon you will be able to once more look ahead with confidence and enthusiasm.

21. TUESDAY. Stimulating. Investing more money in your home might stretch your resources, but in the long term it will probably pay off. Discuss with your mate or partner positive improvements you can make to your environment. Parents and other relatives can bolster your sense of self-worth by bestowing unexpected praise. Perhaps they never before really let you know how proud they are of your achievements. Improvements to your health can be consolidated by making sure you do not get into a rut with your exercise and diet routine. Boredom can cause a surprising amount of stress, while mental stimulation keeps you young. It is never too late to take up a new hobby or interest.

22. WEDNESDAY. Stressful. Money matters can all too easily come between you and a loved one. At the root of this is trust; shared funds must be handled scrupulously by both of you. There is little to be gained by losing your temper because a romance is not giving you the support you think you deserve. Possibly the other person considers that your relationship is not yet close enough for that kind of demand to be made. After all, you have friends to whom you can turn for consolation and encouragement. Youngsters are likely to be extra curious. Unless you have plenty of time and patience today for long explanations, it might be a good idea to share their care with another adult.

23. THURSDAY. Difficult. A love relationship is entering a new phase that is less easygoing than before. If one of you falls prey to jealousy and possessiveness, there is little hope of developing a healthy partnership. Such a problem needs to be nipped in the bud if it crops up. Money may vanish as soon as you receive it, but there is probably a simple explanation. If you sit down and total up your weekly expenditures, they are bound to be higher than you budgeted. Virgo drivers are not usually impatient, but today watch out and do not take any foolish risks while in heavy traffic. Think carefully before getting involved with a neighbor.

24. FRIDAY. Relaxing. A quiet hour or so alone can give you a chance to catch up on your correspondence. For once you might actually enjoy writing letters you usually regard as an obligation. Virgo singles who are looking for love might want to scan the personals column of a favorite magazine or newspaper. You have little to lose. After all, there could be just the right person out there hoping to hear from someone like you. This is a good time to finish off a report that is half-written, but do not begin anything new unless absolutely necessary. The weekend should begin peacefully. Use this quiet evening to recoup your energy and make plans.

25. SATURDAY. Happy. You and your mate or partner can bond closer if you socialize together more. Even though it is important for both of you to have separate friends and interests, sharing some activities gives you a deeper sense of togetherness. Virgos who are hoping for romance should try frequenting places such as art galleries and bookshops. It is easy to get into conversation with someone in such places, and topics of mutual interest are bound to occur. Shopping for the home should be more successful than usual. Look in out-of-the-way places such as antique and thrift shops; you could pick up some unusual items at a very reasonable price.

26. SUNDAY. Unpredictable. From time to time it seems small household items seem to have a life of their own: if they do not want to be found, there is little you can do about it. When things turn up missing, it is probably simplest just to wait for them to appear in their own good time rather than spend hours searching. A romantic affair may be developing depths of emotion that take you out of the everyday world. At first you are likely to feel slightly uneasy, but it will do you a world of good to be shaken loose from your familiar routine for a while. If doing your best for loved ones does not seem to be enough, perhaps you should not try so hard.

27. MONDAY. Exciting. Your strong urge to get ahead should make the day more active and exciting than usual. For once you are not willing to take a backseat, so get out and show exactly what you can do. If you enjoy sports, you are likely to get great satisfaction from pitting yourself against the odds. Just be careful you do not overestimate your physical powers and strain a muscle. The results of an exam or test might come as a pleasant surprise since you may not have expected to do as well as you did. Virgos are known for underestimating their talents, but this is a time to make sure you get the praise due you for your achievements.

28. TUESDAY. Challenging. The results of a moment of financial carelessness could come back to haunt you. There is nothing much to be done except take this as a lesson to be learned. Creative endeavors are highlighted. Have faith that you can achieve good results. Every time you reach what appears to be the limit of your talent, regard that as a challenge to be overcome. Later in the day a quieter, more thoughtful mood prevails, enabling you to look to the future and plan ahead rather than getting overwhelmed by daily tasks. It will help if you and your loved one put your heads together to discuss ways of improving your mutual lifestyle.

29. WEDNESDAY. Smooth. Your social life is apt to be less busy than usual, giving you a chance to catch up with private leisure interests. Youngsters may take up more of your time, although their playful mood makes them a pleasure to be with. Think about keeping a record of their activities since their childhood years go so quickly; photos and videos should not be only for special occasions. Take some time to clear up small chores that have been on your mind for some time. This is a good opportunity to get better organized and also to ensure that you have fulfilled all obligations to colleagues. Promises are all too easy to forget, especially when you are busy.

30. THURSDAY. Demanding. It might be necessary to bite your tongue when friends or associates voice views that strike at the foundations of your beliefs. Unless an argument is appropriate, it is probably wise to keep quiet until a more propitious moment for a discussion. If you feel rather lackluster, it may be that you have been neglecting your diet due to your busy schedule. It is all very well to go without a meal here and there, but once this becomes a habit your health is bound to suffer. Your own work may have to be shelved for a while so that you can help out a colleague. Just make sure that superiors know there is a good reason for the delay.

31. FRIDAY. Deceptive. Your best efforts at getting ahead may be undermined, perhaps through jealousy. It might be a good idea to set the facts before someone who can act on your behalf. Take it easy as much as possible; low physical vitality makes you more susceptible than usual to an infection. Pamper yourself a bit; you deserve it. The desire to go it alone breaks through your usual Virgo sense of service to others. Try to schedule some time this weekend for activities that are purely for your own pleasure. You probably will not be able to entertain yourself tonight, so arrange an evening out on the town with friends who know you well.

APRIL

1. SATURDAY. Uplifting. You are not likely to settle down to a lazy day. For one thing, loved ones will probably badger you to take an interest in the wide world around you. This is an excellent opportunity for expanding your mental horizons. Any leisure activity should have some serious content that gives you something to get involved with wholeheartedly. If you are playing a sport, there is every chance of scoring a success. Your concentration and muscle coordination are better than usual. If you set your heart on winning, there is a good chance of doing so. It would be preferable to spend time with your mate or partner rather than socialize with groups of friends. Enjoy a concert or a theatrical production this evening, but do not stay out too late.

2. SUNDAY. Rewarding. Practical work on your home can be tackled with confidence. All the changes you make now are likely to be lasting, but discuss them with family members before beginning anything drastic. For once it is possible to go into depth with your parents or in-laws about problems you usually find hard to discuss. They are apt to be much more understanding than you expect, so that grievances or doubts from the past can be cleared up to everyone's benefit. No matter how well youngsters are doing at school, a little extra homework help at home is sure to be useful. This is a good way for you to learn something, too. Settle down with a good book this evening rather than watching TV.

3. MONDAY. Good. Virgos setting off for work this morning may feel rather reluctant to get into the swing of things. This is the kind of day when you far prefer to deal with the more gentle aspects of your job. Negotiate rather than be forceful. There should be no need to resort to the courts to settle a dispute. As long as you can be reasonably objective, it should be possible to resolve your differences by discussing them alone or with the help of a mediator. Close relationships can enter a phase of understanding and harmony as long as you relax your demands on the other person. Stop and consider how much they mean to you, then act accordingly.

4. TUESDAY. Manageable. It is time to put joint finances on a new footing. Pooling resources cannot only be very effective but also bring you closer together. An unusual experience may give you pause as you wonder about the hidden reality behind all that is happening. Occult subjects should be approached with caution, although there is much to be discovered. If your sense of wonder is stimulated, that is a definite plus. The end of a small project may leave you eager to try your powers of investigation on a larger matter. Your Virgo patience and ability to piece bits of information together stand you in good stead in figuring out a puzzling situation.

5. WEDNESDAY. Successful. You can stand out boldly from your colleagues if you have the courage to put your original plans into action. Do not be shy about becoming a force to be reckoned with for once. A romantic prospect may appear out of the blue, with someone you never considered in that light. Although their lifestyle may seem unusual to you, there is probably much for each of you to learn. Even if you have been wary about studying new technology, sooner or later you are going to have to make some sort of effort. Look into enrolling in a training course. Once you shed your doubts and fears, a whole new world might open up for you.

6. THURSDAY. Challenging. If you come across a good opportunity for bettering yourself, grab it. However, if you hold back through lack of confidence, a valuable chance may be lost. You can make your mark if you really want to do so. For once you can afford to go out on a limb. Your Virgo intuition and hunches will almost certainly pay off. Long-distance travel for business can be extremely effective. It pays to take a long-term view and make your plans accordingly. Pull out all the stops and you should have good reason to be pleased with yourself. A sense of responsibility toward those in your care cannot be handed off to someone else, no matter how competent they seem to be.

7. FRIDAY. Changeable. It may seem as if your normal routine is threatened. Instead of allowing yourself to get upset, regard this as a challenge. Open yourself to the possibilities of improving your efficiency. Clashes with the boss, a teacher, or another superior are unlikely to be fruitful or useful in any way. Unless your criticisms have been carefully thought through and are well presented, you run the risk of being ignored at best. As the day progresses, hitches in communications can be ironed out. It should become possible to reach agreement on issues that earlier were

APRIL—VIRGO—2000 / **159**

dividing you and your colleagues. Surprise your mate or partner with a special night out on the town.

8. SATURDAY. Positive. Although not obvious, you may have an admirer who up until now has been too shy to come forward. In fact, they may need some encouragement on your part to reveal their feelings, so the next step is up to you. As you finally decide with your mate or partner on plans for your mutual future security, make sure you are both committed to the idea. There is no use one saving while the other spends, so clarify matters before going any further. Sometimes you need a break from the real world; escaping into fantasy can be healing and refreshing. A film or a concert this evening can give you a glimpse of beauty and romance in the purest sense.

9. SUNDAY. Cautious. A small health problem can be cleared up by taking extra care with your diet. As a Virgo you tend to be prone to digestive problems, so it is vital to avoid foods that upset you. An open attitude toward sharing household chores can improve home relationships immensely. As long as everyone takes part in mutual responsibilities, there is nothing to be gained from being too dictatorial. Try to get out of the house, even if only for a walk. The fresh air will do you and loved ones good, taking you out of yourselves. Guard against provoking an argument that could spoil this otherwise upbeat day and evening.

10. MONDAY. Fortunate. All meetings scheduled for today are likely to have a very positive outcome. As long as everyone can agree on general principles, there is no reason plans cannot go ahead immediately; details will be worked out along the way. Friends could introduce you to a whole new outlook on life through courses they have recently taken. While you might be a little skeptical of their enthusiasm, they probably have valuable insights to offer. A personal wish is now within your grasp as long as you have confidence that you can achieve it. This is just why you have been developing your talents; do not hold back. Socializing may make a dent in your budget but be worth it.

11. TUESDAY. Exciting. You may have fallen under the spell of an attractive colleague or neighbor, and they are probably not indifferent to you either. At the moment, pleasure can be gained by just enjoying the interplay between you; push the relationship further and reality is apt to intrude. Some extra work could make it possible to salt away more savings than usual. Do not fritter away the money; spend it on a really special purchase. Aimless socializing is unlikely to satisfy you; what you crave is good conversation and meaningful debate. Older acquaintances who have had more life experience than you have a lot to offer. Do not waste time listening to gossip or worrying about it.

12. WEDNESDAY. Disconcerting. If you have important issues to discuss with your mate or partner, try to do so in the early part of the day. Pressure and stress could wear both of you down toward the afternoon, making agreement more difficult to reach later. Colleagues cannot always be relied upon to give you a helping hand out of the goodness of their hearts. Not everyone is as obliging as you, and there are times when it may be simpler and quicker to go it alone. Memories of a past love affair may be revived when you hear an old song. Cherish these reminders of a former time but do not give your current loved one any cause to be jealous.

13. THURSDAY. Productive. Make the most of the day by getting down to tasks that have been hanging around unfinished for a while. It can be especially satisfying to get letters to friends and relatives out of the way; they will be delighted to hear from you. Put forward a plan for improved use of your own money or company funds. Your Virgo attention to detail should persuade the other people who are involved that the scheme is viable. Later in the day be prepared to encounter resistance from those who consider themselves experts. Your best course is probably to quietly go on with what you are doing since their objections might just be a lot of hot air.

14. FRIDAY. Slow. Current conditions offer an ideal chance to tidy up loose ends before the weekend. Do not spoil this opportunity by allowing other people to pressure you. There is no cause for rush, so just proceed at your own pace. Today's more introspective mood inclines you to solitude. A period of quiet reflection can give you insights into your life and relationships that will be of great value. Later in the day you may feel like coming out of your shell and taking an active part in all that is going on around you. Consider sprucing yourself up with a change of hair color or overall image. Loved ones will probably be pleased to go along with your plans this evening, so just relax and have fun together.

15. SATURDAY. Strenuous. As long as you know what you want, your efforts to get it will be rewarding. However, nothing worth having comes easily. You will probably be put through a few hoops before reaching your goal. Vacation plans may be taking up more time than you expect but it is well worthwhile sorting out all the details before you depart. Make sure you have adequate home protection and you will feel more comfortable and able to enjoy yourself. If family obligations seem to be getting the best of you, stand back and consider whether other relatives can take a turn. Do not become a doormat, allowing loved ones to take you for granted; do only your fair share.

16. SUNDAY. Challenging. Going through financial records is likely to be less relaxing than you imagine. Your Virgo sense of orderliness has not been as active as usual, so figures may not add up. If it all seems too confusing, it may be wise to drop this work for now. Youngsters may be determined to oppose you and upset your plans for the day. This is a good moment to assert your authority and let them know there are rules of behavior that must not be broken. Find time to check on home security. There are bound to be weak spots that can be strengthened quite easily, improving all the family's peace of mind. Be prepared for an important phone call to be interrupted.

17. MONDAY. Lucky. You may receive news before anyone else about developments at work. However, it is probably best to keep it to yourself until the time is right. An unusual opportunity to add to your income should not be dismissed just because it has never been tried before. This might actually give you an opportunity to add another notch to your belt. Property negotiations are likely to be profitable as long as you are able to agree on basic terms that suit you. You have to be more forceful than usual in order to get what you feel is fair. Romance can come your way if you are prepared for a relationship that involves you in powerful emotions.

18. TUESDAY. Demanding. A crisis point has been reached between you and your mate or partner over shared resources. Somehow you have to balance personal needs against the necessity of laying a sound foundation for the future. Impulse buying is not usually appealing to you, but the chance discovery of a beautiful item for your home may lead you to act out of character. This thing of beauty is sure to be a joy forever. Honesty is the best policy when dealing with your colleagues. You can persuade them to accept your view, but first make sure you are really confident about taking responsibility for the plans you are promoting. Failure can come back to haunt you.

19. WEDNESDAY. Confusing. It is very important to listen carefully or you may easily misunderstand what others are saying. If in doubt, ask them to repeat; do not be shy about it. Confirmation can save difficulties later on. Contracts and written statements need to be carefully checked. It would be very unwise to sign anything you have not read, including all of the small print. Your car is unlikely to run smoothly even over a short distance. Make sure the tires have the right pressure before you set off. A trip might turn out to be rather expensive, so bring along spare funds or a credit card with a low balance due in case of an emergency situation.

20. THURSDAY. Frustrating. On this frustrating day plans are unlikely to work out. Probably the best attitude for you to adopt is to expect the unexpected and not let it shock you. Local travel may be slowed by delays due to heavy traffic, so if you have an important appointment do not set off late. If youngsters' schooling does not seem to be going as well as would hope, you may feel that teachers are being somewhat harsh. Naturally they expect high standards, but it is up to you to boost your children's confidence when they receive criticism. Tempers may run rather high in the family. To avoid arguments at home, you need to exercise a fair measure of self-control.

21. FRIDAY. Inspiring. A more sympathetic attitude from members of the family can lead to their offer of help in sorting out your everyday problems. Family should stick together, and this is the proof. A romantic affair seems to be giving you a great deal of pleasure. At the moment you and that special person in your life are probably both seeing the world through rose-colored glasses. Make the most of this phase; it probably will not last forever. A more informed interest in the arts could enhance the quality of your life. Such sources of inspiration provide assurance that there is more to life than everyday reality. Consider taking a course in art or music appreciation.

22. SATURDAY. Satisfying. Get down to some real cleaning and clearing up at home. Enlist the help of loved ones. Thorough work done now will be immensely satisfying. Do not allow relatives to play on your sense of guilt in order to manipulate you into doing what they want. You are an individual and have the right to tell others when they are intruding in your life. Structural problems at home can be avoided by prompt action; call in expert help. Your attraction for an acquaintance may have to be kept secret for a while. At the moment this person is apt to be rather vulnerable emotionally, and it would be unfair to take advantage of this no matter how tempting it may be.

23. SUNDAY. Stimulating. A lost piece of jewelry that you long ago gave up on ever seeing again may turn up quite unexpectedly. This is a lesson to keep better track of precious pieces; it might be a good idea to consider insurance as well. Virgos who have been hoping for romance can find it by looking long and hard enough. Do not reject an offer that promises to take you out of your usual social sphere; new company could be very stimulating. This is not the sort of day when you will be happy doing housework and gardening. Plan on getting together with loved ones and friends for an unusual day somewhere that is new to you. Make sure you have a camera handy; you could take some excellent shots.

24. MONDAY. Calm. This comparatively laid-back day eases you into the working week. The accent is on mental activity. Schedule your time to make plans rather than put them into action. Long-distance travel for business purposes is likely to have a strong element of pleasure as well. You might make contacts that you wish to pursue on a social level, and it may be possible to begin building a network of distant friends. Exams and tests of your knowledge should not pose much of a problem providing you have prepared adequately. The only thing you need to watch is a tendency to write too much on some questions and then have to skimp on others.

25. TUESDAY. Tricky. No matter how persuasive the evidence, do not rush into committing funds to any project that seems even the least bit risky. You will probably feel far more comfortable doing your own research and confirming facts and figures for yourself. For once in your life the prospect of a usual vacation may seem rather tame; you are more likely to be attracted to something considerably more adventurous. Get some brochures of vacation packages that focus on sports activities; you might learn something new. A good sense of timing is necessary when you overhear comments that could be a bombshell in your daily work. Be cautious about spreading rumors.

26. WEDNESDAY. Uncertain. If a course of study is not turning out to be what you expected, you might be tempted to drop out. However, there could still be something of value to be learned. It would be a shame not to get some value for your tuition money. Expert advice cannot always be trusted. If you feel any doubt at all about the financial recommendations you are being given, get a second opinion. The results of a medical test may be rather unclear. There is probably nothing to worry about, but ask the doctor to explain the matter fully so that you completely understand. Your mind may not easily focus on what you are supposed to be doing, and small items can easily be mislaid.

27. THURSDAY. Stressful. Colleagues are apt to be more touchy than usual. Catty remarks may irritate you. Working in a bad atmosphere does no one any good. If you are at fault in any way, an apology is in order. Youngsters may try to shock you for the sake of it. The worst thing you can do is laugh at them. Instead, appreciate that they are learning to assert their individuality for the first time. You may be more prone than usual to stress. It could be helpful to learn some simple breathing exercises that can be done on the spot when necessary. A quiet evening at home will probably be much more enjoyable than going out with your friends.

28. FRIDAY. Promising. A private word with someone in the know could give you access to useful advice. There is no need to broadcast this even to friends. Just let your mate or partner know what you are planning; otherwise keep it to yourself. Merely because someone is not wearing their heart on their sleeve does not mean they are not interested. You are bound to pick up signals if they want to see more of you, so the ball is now in your court. At last it is possible to get to the bottom of a relationship problem by facing up to some hard truths. As long as you both are gentle with each other, even uncomfortable facts can be dealt with so that you can make a fresh start.

29. SATURDAY. Variable. A better atmosphere at home can be promoted by taking an interest in loved ones' activities. Even if you are not normally attracted by their leisure pursuits, it is thoughtful to take them seriously. Shopping for household goods could cause upsets, particularly over cost. Compromise may be more difficult than usual, so it might be wise to put off making important purchases until you calm down. A friend's advice given off the cuff may provide insight into a matter you are pursuing. Although there may not be much you can do about it right now, make a note to investigate further at the first opportunity you get. Be sure to check reliable sources.

30. SUNDAY. Spirited. All sporting activities should go well. Disciplined effort is the key. As long as you keep your mind on the game, you have a good chance to win. A friendship that began with a meeting of the minds may be developing into a physical attraction as well. This gives the relationship a whole new slant, so think very carefully about the implications before you continue. Try to get some quiet time to catch up on your reading. With your mind hungry for new information, it is vital to search out a sense of life's purpose that can give meaning to all of your activities. Keep home entertaining simple and you are sure to enjoy it more.

MAY

1. MONDAY. Fulfilling. The inspiration that beauty brings may fill you with a desire to buy something really special. Go ahead; there are times when everyone needs reassurance that there is more to life than everyday routine. If you are planning a longer journey than usual, consider taking a friend along for company. With a companion the time will pass quicker and the whole trip be more enjoyable. A legacy may involve more participation from you than expected. However, this is likely to bring you back into contact with distant relatives, which is no bad thing. It would be a shame to drop out of touch once again after you renew your relationship.

2. TUESDAY. Buoyant. Your nerves could receive a real tonic from an alternative form of therapy. Consult a qualified expert, and remember that as a Virgo you are usually highly receptive to any kind of physical remedy and need only low doses. Getting comfortable with a new computer program may not seem the ideal way of passing a couple of hours but actually could be very rewarding. Although you might be a little lost at first, you should be able to pick it up quickly, and then it will probably feel like a new toy. Break out of your usual routine and give yourself more time for creative work. The results could surprise you, since routine can be a straitjacket for the mind.

3. WEDNESDAY. Deceptive. Check all travel arrangements very carefully. In particular, make sure that accommodations have been properly booked. Otherwise you could waste a day or so in hassles once you get where you are going. Criticism of a plan for improving efficiency may not be wholly objective. Someone may not be playing straight; try to get a third party to intervene in order to provide a more balanced view. A superior could attempt to expand your job description but not offer any additional pay. Do not fall prey to flattery; try to maintain your independence. Revise written work; it may not be as good as it appears to you right now.

4. THURSDAY. Expansive. Now is your chance to expand your mental horizons by taking up a whole new field of study. This could change your life if your attitude is open enough, so go for it wholeheartedly. A colleague who can put in a few words on your behalf may be willing to help you get useful training. Do not hold back from asking for their assistance; there will certainly be a time in the future when you will be able to return the favor. Older relatives living at a distance could be causing some concern. This may even reach the stage where you feel obliged to visit them, but the inconvenience to you will undoubtedly be outweighed by their pleasure.

5. FRIDAY. Variable. There seems to be little chance of winding down gently toward the weekend. A sudden crisis demands immediate attention and quick action by you. If you keep your head, you can impress those in charge very favorably, so it is worth summoning all your energies. You need to act with a greater sense of responsibility than usual. Decisions made now are apt to be crucial and will have long-term effects. Carefully weigh the pros and cons. Romance is in the air, although at the moment you may not be quite sure how it is going to develop. As long as you are prepared to take the first step, all should be well.

6. SATURDAY. Tricky. If you are trying to save money, it is vital that you and your mate or partner get on the same wavelength. Otherwise it is all too likely that one of you will succumb to temptation, leading to unnecessary arguments. A new love relationship may not be giving you all that you hoped for. The other person may be rather elusive and unreliable. If you suspect they have something to hide, you are probably on the right track. Pay some attention to the physical structure of your home, which might not be as sound as it should be. Call in expert help if necessary; do not attempt complicated repairs by yourself unless you have the training and experience.

7. SUNDAY. Pleasant. This relatively quiet day gives you a much needed chance to rest and restore your energy. Make this a time of relaxation; let household chores remain undone for a while. If you are entertaining, there is no need to go to a great deal of trouble for your guests. The atmosphere should be so friendly that they will be quite content to enjoy the company and conversation, so do not plan anything formal. For Virgo singles, a romantic affair looks promising, but you could spoil things if you rush it. At the moment you should just be getting to know each other better and finding out whether your dreams and aspirations are in harmony.

8. MONDAY. Inspiring. You have the opportunity today of inspiring your colleagues, friends, or students with high ideals. Do not be afraid to rise to loftier heights of thought than usual. You should be easily able to persuade other people of the truth of what you are saying. Travel is favored. If you are setting off today on the journey, it is likely to be trouble-free. Make sure you have cash for immediate use when you arrive at your destination so that you can get a snack or a taxi without any delay. If you are in charge of youngsters, you could spend a lot of time answering their incessant questions. Be prepared to be challenged by their insights and to answer with words they can understand.

9. TUESDAY. Challenging. It is often true that you get what you need rather than what you want, although that is seldom much comfort at the time. Right now you have lessons to learn about the limits of your own talents, which are all the more valuable for being challenging. You can probably do your best work if you find a quiet place to concentrate in solitude. Backlogs can be cleared up in little time, so do not put off doing what are usually rather tedious chores; today you can rip right through them. If news of a friend who dropped out of sight some time ago wakens memories of happy times, give them a call to catch up on all the news.

10. WEDNESDAY. Stressful. At the moment it might seem that you cannot do anything right. Because superiors are unlikely to be totally satisfied with your best efforts, it can be quite a struggle for you to resist giving up. However, hang in for as long as you can. Youngsters can be very disruptive of your daily routine, not responsive to discipline that usually is effective. You may need to find another way of appealing to their reason or demanding their obedience. A thoughtless word could hurt a loved one much more than you think. Sometimes casual remarks hit a tender spot. If this is the case, a swift and sincere apology can do a lot to mend matters. Do not jump into a new relationship just because you are feeling lonely or angry.

11. THURSDAY. Sensitive. There is a strong possibility of electrical equipment causing problems. Information could be scrambled. It might be wise to rely on old-fashioned pen and paper to take important notes. Colleagues may have mistaken ideas that they are welcome to contribute to a work project you consider your own. Although it may be awkward, let them know exactly where your responsibility ends and theirs begins. Diversions and problems can hold up long-distance travel. Be prepared for lengthy delays. Make sure you take something to read if using public transportation. Do not take out your frustrations on youngsters or other people who are dependent on you, even if it is hard to be patient.

12. FRIDAY. Beneficial. Help is at hand to aid you in putting a personal plan into action. You should not have to delay matters through lack of funds; money is available if you know where to look. A friend in the know can probably pull strings on your behalf. Your physical well-being is better than usual. However, you may still be tempted to overindulge in favorite high-calorie foods, but try to resist. Dress to impress for a special evening out. This could be one of those occasions when you meet someone with whom you have instant rapport. Do not let parents or other older relatives get you down with criticisms of your earnings. You are the one who knows what is the right career path to pursue.

13. SATURDAY. Fair. Plans for going out are likely to be disrupted by the urgent need to get certain household tasks done. It would be wise not to attempt a journey too far afield. You will be happier if you stay close to home. If you can find time for a visit to a local park or garden, you should really benefit. All the family will probably enjoy being outdoors. Do not expect to be athletic; just get some gentle exercise. Obligations to others may cut into the day. Although you may feel resentful at first, the time will come when the tables are turned. Your expert knowledge could help a friend in need who is struggling to make a major decision. You can even help by just listening.

14. SUNDAY. Good. A romantic involvement should be giving you an even more secure sense of your own self-worth. When others show that they appreciate you, it is much easier to feel genuine self-confidence, so lap up any and all praise and do not be too modest. A greater feeling of security can be fostered by considering what is really valuable to you. Material goods are useful, but your loved ones undoubtedly mean much more to you. Be sure to tell them so. Some exercise in the fresh air is bound to get your blood flowing and stretch the tension out of your muscles. Entertaining at home should be a fairly low-key affair. Keep the guests to those whose company you enjoy most.

15. MONDAY. Opportune. By making a clean sweep of the daily tasks you can free yourself to face the unexpected. You are unlikely to have a spare minute to yourself, so brace for a busy day. You should be able to cope very well. A reshuffle of staff could mean that you have to take on extra responsibilities for a while. However, there is likely to be a financial gain so that it is all worthwhile. This is a good time to arrange a medical checkup primarily for the sake of getting advice rather than anything else. As a Virgo you seldom go to excess, but you are prone to stress which can be just as upsetting to your health. Work off extra energy with an evening walk or jog.

16. TUESDAY. Confusing. If others look at you somewhat blankly when you speak, it is probably because you are not expressing yourself clearly. You need to keep your mind on what you are saying, so pull yourself together and concentrate. A neighbor might ask a favor you are not too eager to grant. You may have the feeling that you are being pushed to the edge, so it would be simplest just to say no right away and mean it. Be prepared for travel difficulties in your immediate locality. Even if your car appears to be in good working order, it is likely to develop a mysterious problem that could leave you stranded. Silence is golden where your loved ones are concerned.

17. WEDNESDAY. Exciting. Virgo singles who are looking for romance should not be disappointed. Someone you have been slightly in awe of may actually see you as an equal, and a desirable one at that. Long-distance travel should be extremely enjoyable. A business trip may be financially more successful than expected. Make sure you get all due credit for your part in the proceedings. Tests of your knowledge may rouse you to heights of achievement that you have rarely managed. Now that you know just what you can do, there is no excuse to settle for anything less. Try not to overindulge in rich foods tonight or you may suffer for it when you try to sleep.

18. THURSDAY. Demanding. Restrictions on your promotion prospects might seem unbearable at the moment. However, in the long run you will probably see that a move now would not have been in your best interests. Lack of funds could be holding you back from the vacation you really want. However, there is still much that you can do on a tight budget. You might want to get together with friends and see if you can book accommodations at group rates. A romantic affair might be doing more harm than good. If the other person is constantly critical of your ideas, your self-confidence can be undermined. If you allow them to get away with it now, they may just intensify their negative comments.

19. FRIDAY. Unsettling. Disagreements over domestic matters could escalate unless you are willing to be more conciliatory. Any harsh words spoken now are going to be remembered for a long time, so try not to get carried away by the feelings of the moment. Your health can take a dramatic turn for the better if you listen to what your body is telling you. Most of the time your instincts are a sound guide to what you need, but modern living can lead to the body's wisdom being ignored. A superior might criticize a decision you had to make in a hurry. If you feel your action was correct, defend yourself; otherwise apologize and then do not look back.

20. SATURDAY. Chaotic. It could be a case of too many cooks spoiling the broth, as loved ones come up with ideas for an unusual day trip. To avoid spending all day arguing over what to do, choose one option and then put your foot down and be firm. If you are involved in a property deal you might suddenly get cold feet and want to pull out. Doing so is likely to cause a good deal of bad feeling, so wait a while before making a final decision. There is a real possibility of encountering aggressive behavior on the part of someone you thought was a friend. It is up to them to work out the problem; do not be tempted to step in and try to help if they see you as a threat.

21. SUNDAY. Quiet. Settle back for a quiet day. Let the phone ring if you do not feel like answering. Gentle work in the garden should be good exercise and also mentally relaxing. Relations within the family are less stressful than usual. In fact, you might be inspired to make your peace with a relative who has been a thorn in your side for quite a while. There should be plenty of time for a favorite leisure pursuit, the more creative the better. Try to involve youngsters if appropriate; they might learn something useful while having fun with you. Since all appears quiet on the romantic front, be careful not to rock the love boat.

22. MONDAY. Profitable. The workweek begins in quite an upbeat atmosphere. After the refreshing weekend you are bound to be full of new ideas. An opportunity to invest may seem a little out of your reach, but if you can commit a small amount of money there might be a very good return. The more creative aspects of a current project need not worry you. Colleagues and friends are ready and willing to help and are bound to be pleased that you are taking such a close interest in the work. Youngsters should not rebel against your discipline, so take this chance to instill in them some additional ideas about responsibility. It is surprising how much even young children can understand concepts that are put to them simply.

23. TUESDAY. Promising. A romantic liaison is on the horizon. This is likely to bring you a great deal of pleasure, although you might want to keep part of yourself uninvolved because the relationship may not last very long. Creative writing is favored; even if you only have a report to write, you should be able to do so in an attractive and easy-to-read style. A business lunch is likely to become more of a social occasion. However, make sure you get the subject under discussion wrapped up before turning to lighter topics. Virgos who are looking for a better job may want to ask for some assistance from former colleagues; they may know of openings that have not yet been advertised.

24. WEDNESDAY. Favorable. If you need to act quickly to beat the opposition, get a move on. Thinking on the spur of the moment should be easier than usual, and you should also be able to pull something out of a hat. Communications between superiors and colleagues are allowing all kinds of small problems to be sorted out. You may find yourself acting as spokesperson, in which case you are bound to get credit for your tactful approach. This is a good time to purchase electrical equipment for your home. Problems are unlikely; all the same, be sure to keep receipts and guarantees in a safe place. Try not to overdo physically as your reserves of energy are lower than usual.

25. THURSDAY. Difficult. Just as you think you have reached an agreement regarding routine matters, the others involved may seem to backtrack and deny everything said earlier. Naturally this is going to be rather annoying, but losing your temper will not help. Just this once you might have to admit defeat. Recent problems may have left their mark on your nervous system. Even though you are now back on course, you are not yet out of the woods and need to be gentle with yourself. Fortunately there may be news of a job opening that is just up your alley. Although this opportunity is timely, do not pin all of your hopes on it; many other people are pulling out all the stops in their efforts to get this desirable position.

26. FRIDAY. Disquieting. At the moment there may be little peace wherever you turn. Superiors are showing signs of cracking down, and loved ones may be brooding over problems of their own. Do not be taken in by the friendly appearance of a new acquaintance. Wait until you know them better before giving them your full confidence; it is all too likely that they have a hidden agenda of their own. A romantic liaison is reaching a turning point. The other person in your life may begin to demand to know your long-term intentions. You will not be able to sit on the fence forever, but the very fact that you find it difficult to make a decision should tell you something.

27. SATURDAY. Uplifting. Loved ones fully appreciate how important a personal project is to you. They are probably willing to commit time to assist you in reaching your goal, and their participation will make the final achievement all the sweeter. Older people are not usually all that willing to accept advice from their children, but now your parents may be all too happy to listen to your suggestions for improving their well-being. Your Virgo interest in health and hygiene certainly has something to teach them. Oddly enough, you may be in love without even realizing it. Your feelings for a close friend may have developed quite quietly but powerfully.

28. SUNDAY. Auspicious. This can be a truly significant day if you have the courage to search your heart and mind with complete honesty. Now is the time for you to discover a deeper sense of meaning in your life. You may have a sense that all this has been thought out before. It is certain that you will have a memorable time if you go on a short trip; you may return again in future years. Squabbles among youngsters can affect you and your mate or partner if you are not very careful. Whatever you do, avoid taking sides or a civil war could break out. Romance should be pleasant; do not spoil it by making demands you know will be refused.

29. MONDAY. Reassuring. An apology could come out of the blue for an action you dismissed from your thoughts some days or weeks ago. However, it obviously has been preying on the other person's mind, and now it would be kind of you to assure them you are ready to forgive and forget. Virgos who are hoping to improve overall prospects need to take a subtle approach. There are many small ways of making yourself indispensable, and your naturally helpful nature should enable you to do so without difficulty. Property negotiations should go ahead without a hitch. Any doubts should be stifled because it is natural to be a little nervous when big changes are afoot.

30. TUESDAY. Happy. Romance is sometimes found in the most ordinary places. A chance encounter in an elevator or a glance exchanged across a restaurant can lead to a passionate affair, but only if you are brave enough to let yourself go. Financially, things are looking up. The results of your recent efforts to save are beginning to show. This should prove to you that it is well worth your while putting away even small amounts on a regular basis. The important thing is to do so regularly. Your social life is likely to revolve around good conversation and exciting ideas. Do not hesitate to become involved in a group of like-minded people; you are bound to make new friends while having a good time.

31. WEDNESDAY. Disconcerting. You are apt to be all fingers and thumbs, which is not at all typical. If you feel rather flustered, it is probably for a romantic reason; there is nothing to be ashamed about that. A job prospect that seemed almost too good to be true is likely to turn out to be disappointing. Perhaps you should set your sights slightly lower and be more realistic about what you can do. A long journey could involve you in all kinds of complications. It would be unwise to take on commissions for other people because your hands will be full. If you decide to go out to a restaurant tonight, eat and drink in moderation.

JUNE

1. THURSDAY. Frustrating. There could be a battle of wills developing between you and your mate or partner. It would be unwise to let this get out of hand; sooner or later one of you is going to say something you are likely to regret. Virgos who work from home may find it difficult to deal with the demands of daily life as well as job responsibility. Better organization is needed so that you do not find yourself spending too much time on domestic matters. Distant business connections may not be all that reliable. It can be a challenge getting a contract fulfilled on time; you may have to issue a stern warning or two before you see action. Do not let a neighbor intimidate you.

2. FRIDAY. Stimulating. This busy day suits you perfectly as you hum with energy and are raring to go. As long as you are working along the right lines, setbacks are unlikely. It should be considerably easier than usual to persuade others to cooperate. Virgos looking for a new job can take this opportunity to renew efforts. You need something you can be enthusiastic about; it will be a waste of time pursuing an opening that does not truly excite you. Relationships with parents and other older relatives can be improved by opening your heart on a topic you do not normally discuss. You may be surprised how understanding and sympathetic they are.

3. SATURDAY. Unsettling. If you are hoping for a pleasantly romantic weekend, you are in for a shock. A loved one has been waiting for this chance to pour out hurt and resentment that have been boiling up for quite a while. You may not even be sure what exactly you did wrong. It can be more difficult than usual to reach an agreement on the subject of home redecorating. Some measure of compromise will be necessary, but the question is just how much you are prepared to back down for the sake of peace. A social event is likely to be full of thrills and chills. Arguments may erupt among other guests; do your best to stay out of the fray.

4. SUNDAY. Easygoing. This is not the kind of day you should spend alone. Fortunately the phone is bound to ring. Invite some friends to your home for a relaxed meal, but do not go overboard on the preparations. Everyone will have a far better time if you keep things casual. Plans for the future need some fine-tuning. It would also be a good idea to discuss them with loved ones, who are bound to come up with some positive ideas of their own. In fact, you can ignite new thoughts in each other. Try to include youngsters in your activities as much as possible. They can be a breath of springtime with their innocent observations and love of life.

5. MONDAY. Useful. The friendly relations you have cultivated with certain colleagues should be paying off. Now you are able to rely on their support when you propose new work projects. All forms of cooperation are favored. You can get a lot more done working as part of a team rather than independently. If you meet someone who appears suitable as a romantic partner, it would be foolish to let them get away. Business meetings are likely to be more productive than usual. Although negotiations might be complicated, the final results should be satisfactory. You can persuade someone of the value of your ideals if you really want to win a convert to your cause.

6. TUESDAY. Productive. It is not always wise to take work home, but for once this offers the best chance for putting the finishing touches to an important task. You should be able to concentrate better in solitude, so make it clear to family members that you must be left alone for a while. Entertaining at home can have rather unexpected results. It will probably become clear to you that something is going on between two of your guests; you may even end up playing Cupid. Be especially careful of your health right now. Pushing yourself too hard may only result in jangled nerves and an upset sleep pattern, so take it easy and maintain your sense of humor.

7. WEDNESDAY. Uncertain. You may have placed too much trust in a colleague who is actually less reliable than you supposed. Now you could be left to clear up their mistakes. Do not hesitate to let them know exactly how let down you feel. The results of a course of study may not produce the raise or other benefits which you hoped to achieve. You may have let your expectations get too high this time, but do not let this keep you from trying other lines of self-development. Loved ones may intrude on your leisure time with demands for assistance which strike you as unreasonable. There are limits to putting others first, so assert yourself for once.

8. THURSDAY. Challenging. A feeling of boredom indicates that there are certain areas of your life that you have outgrown. However, you may still be projecting an image which does not fit the person you have become. It is time to consider a major change. Close family members may be rather intrusive into your private life. Although they probably only mean to be helpful, if you need more privacy you will have to make that clear to them. Put the cares of the world behind you and organize a fun night out with some of your friends. Problems shrink into perspective when you are all relaxing together; this kind of effortless support is what friendship is all about.

9. FRIDAY. Changeable. Even though superiors expect a lot from you, it may soon be clear that what they are proposing is a change in your job responsibilities. Take some time to think over your feelings about this rather than reacting on the spur of the moment. There is no point bending over backward to please anyone if they are only going to take advantage of you. Show a bit more forcefulness and they are more likely to treat you with added respect. If you feel your talents are not being properly put to use in your present position, find out about courses that could lead to more suitable opportunities. Keep evening plans flexible so you can accept a last-minute invitation.

10. SATURDAY. Smooth. Shopping can be more successful than usual, especially if you take a fairly laid-back approach. Be prepared to spend some time leisurely looking; there is no telling what special items you could find at a sale. Money should not be much of a problem at the moment. You do not have to keep as tight a hand as usual on the purse strings. This more relaxed attitude is fine for a while, just as long as you do not lose control altogether. A family gathering can give a deeper sense of togetherness to the different generations. Youngsters will benefit from the company of older relatives.

11. SUNDAY. Buoyant. Social events should bring you into contact with new acquaintances. These are likely to be people whose outlook on life is different from yours. Their attitude can be quite refreshing. It is time to get out of the rut of your usual routine. Take up a new activity that will get your adrenaline going. A more challenging sport could liven up weekends immensely. There is not much point worrying about the cost of a day out with friends.

Go ahead and enjoy yourself; everyone deserves a treat from time to time. It might be harder than usual to keep your temper with youngsters, but a tolerant attitude will make this a pleasanter day for everyone.

12. MONDAY. Opportune. Buckling down to work with renewed enthusiasm should prove profitable. A new initiative offers you the chance to make some extra cash, which would certainly come in handy. If you are thinking of changing jobs you might suddenly see possibilities where you currently are. There is no need to act rashly; take your time before making a decision. Meanwhile, do your best in your current job. As the afternoon goes on you may become a little forgetful. Make a note of chores and appointments; otherwise you are likely to wake up with a jolt in the middle of the night realizing you neglected something important. Be sure to return library books or video rentals.

13. TUESDAY. Mixed. An appeal to a neighbor for assistance can lead to a new friendship. In fact, this could be the beginning of a new social circle as you are brought together by common interests and concerns. Travel conditions are good. If you do not have a means of transportation, friends seem more than willing to provide a ride. There is a distinct possibility of a rift occuring between you and a brother, sister, or other relative. Try not to listen to secondhand news; it is bound to be misleading. Arguments could blow up over nothing at all. Be prepared for interruptions in phone conversations, especially a long-distance call.

14. WEDNESDAY. Sensitive. A longed-for getaway might not live up to your expectations. What looks wonderful in a brochure may turn out to be rather dull. Perhaps next time you should save up for a really exotic break. If youngsters do not appear to be fulfilling their potential in some school subjects, it is more likely due to a clash of personality between them and a teacher than any lack of ability. You may want to discuss this with the adult involved. Virgos who travel for a living may be hoping for a raise in salary, only to be disappointed once again. It may be time to start looking for a new position or at least a job transfer.

15. THURSDAY. Tricky. There is apt to be more going on at home than meets the eye. Youngsters may be rather furtive. However, whatever they are hiding is undoubtedly more shocking to them than it will be to you. A quick look around the house is probably enough to convince you that some changes need to be made. Redecorating can give the place a whole new aura, especially if you do a really thorough job. Keeping fit can be time-consuming, but there are exercises that can be done in your spare time and in private if you wish. Achieving your ideal weight will make you feel a whole lot better about your health and appearance, especially in a bathing suit.

16. FRIDAY. Fair. Sometimes even the closest friend can get on your nerves, making it difficult for you to keep cool. However, if you keep in mind all the times you have supported each other, it should be easier to be tolerant. Tension between the claims of career and home are coming to a head. It is not possible to give both of these your full undivided loyalty, so one is going to have to receive a bit less attention. Virgos considering buying a house may find the process rather complicated, even overwhelming. It should not take long, however, to become familiar with proceedings. This is a big step toward future security and demands careful consideration and professional advice.

17. SATURDAY. Demanding. All the tact and diplomacy in the world is not enough when loved ones are really ready for a good argument. If you take a passive stance they will only become angrier. There is nothing to do but slug it out and at least clear the air. Try to spend some time putting personal plans into action. If you let the day fritter away on household chores, you will only end up feeling frustrated. Try not to let friends persuade you into activities that do not appeal. They may be convinced that you will have a good time, but you know better. There is little point putting up a false front and then berating yourself for not saying no.

18. SUNDAY. Quiet. Social events may have made quite a dent in your budget in recent weeks. Begin restricting your activities a little, even though you hate to feel you are missing out on any fun. As a friendship begun through mutual interests develops, you may begin to realize that the other person is becoming increasingly important to you. Sooner or later you will want to find out just how they feel about you. Youngsters need their imaginations stimulated; there is more to life than sitting in front of a television. It will not hurt to stretch their capabilities by spending time in the library or suggesting games that are suitable for a slightly older age group. Spend the evening at home rather than going out.

19. MONDAY. Reassuring. A gamble seems to be paying off as a new business connection comes through for you. Make sure you take credit for having the initiative to push forward into new areas. All creative work is favored. If you test yourself to the limit, you may be surprised at what can be achieved. It is crucial to have enough self-confidence to persuade others to go along with your ideas. Do not turn down an opportunity to learn a new skill. Curiosity keeps you young. You are not in a position to be complacent about your current level of practical knowledge. Relax with a few friends tonight but get to bed on time.

20. TUESDAY. Deceptive. If your mind is preoccupied with wondering where you stand in a romantic affair, it is unlikely you are going to perform efficiently on the job. Do your best to put these thoughts aside until a more appropriate time so that colleagues and the boss do not lose patience. Rumors of a workforce reduction could be flying around your place of employment. However, it would be premature to act on such dubious information, which may have no basis in truth at all. As a Virgo you tend to have a delicate digestive system; a diet of plain food is advisable. Overindulgence may not only upset but weaken you, although once in a while it might be worth the suffering.

21. WEDNESDAY. Disconcerting. It can be harder than usual to get routine tasks accomplished when other people are constantly interrupting and asking you for advice. In the end you may need to point out that they would benefit from working things out for themselves sometimes instead of running straight to you. Do not become discouraged if loved ones are somewhat critical of creative work you feel is especially good. Their opinion is not necessarily objective; you probably know in your heart what the true value is. A new acquaintance may have a powerful physical attraction. Before you get involved, however, consider what the cost might be in terms of current relationships.

22. THURSDAY. Variable. Although the day gets off to a rather frustrating start, things should look up during the morning. However, be prepared to put in some difficult work that would have to be done all over again if not up to the required standard. Spreading yourself too thin is likely to backfire. There is only so much you can expect to do before your health suffers, so do not make a martyr of yourself; doing so will not be appreciated anyway. Relations between you and your mate or partner should be smoother than usual. Concentrating on what draws you together rather than on your disagreements can be a useful exercise. Do not let the telephone interrupt your private time together.

23. FRIDAY. Changeable. Work should quiet down early for the weekend, so if you are eager to start on a new project you will just have to be patient. Check that all communications equipment is working; faults may develop without you noticing. Keep your calendar close at hand in case appointments have to be changed on short notice. Try to schedule your time to be as flexible as possible. Transportation may cause some problems. If you can avoid a journey during the course of the day, you can save yourself some hassle. Lunch with colleagues can be a pleasant way of getting to know them better; you are bound to share interests outside work.

24. SATURDAY. Spirited. As long as you are prepared to rise above the petty details of everyday routine, this can be an enjoyable day. If you let yourself get bogged down in humdrum tasks, you will just have a feeling of wasted time. Intervention in a close relationship is not always welcome, but if you see friends cutting each other down emotionally you can hardly stand back and do nothing. In fact, an objective view from someone like you might be just what they need to restore their relationship. Be prepared for shopping to take you farther afield than usual. You should be able to find some unusual stores selling goods you cannot get elsewhere.

25. SUNDAY. Lively. Although team sports are not usually your favorite pastime, today you might be quite flattered when friends ask you to join in. Even if you are only a reserve, the feeling of participation will be beneficial. Malicious gossip may be making the rounds; you are probably in a position to know just how untrue it is. It is up to you to set the record straight, even if that means an unpleasant confrontation with an acquaintance. Romance is a bit problematic at the moment. All relationships need constant work in one way or another. You cannot expect to drift along forever without making any effort to change and improve.

26. MONDAY. Chancy. Financial affairs need very careful handling. There is an appealing proposal that can really play havoc with your savings if you do not know what you are doing. Get expert advice before making any move. A friend who promised you support seems inclined to make excuses now that it is crunch time. At least now you know not to rely on them again. Others will be genuinely helpful. A little research can clear up a work problem that has stressed relationships between you and your colleagues for some time. There is no need for you to be at loggerheads, but it may suit someone else for this to happen. Stay home tonight and shut out the world.

27. TUESDAY. Cautious. Allow self-doubt to creep in and the day is likely to be far more difficult than necessary. If you have confidence in yourself, you should be able to draw on powers of inspiration that will see you through. A romantic affair threatens to founder on differences of belief. You must decide which is more important to you: your principles, or the companionship of someone who loves you. Speaking up in public may be rather stressful, but to get a point across in a meeting it will be necessary to do so. Clear diction, good eye contact, and well-chosen words will stand you in good stead. Round off the day with dinner out, and treat your mate or partner.

28. WEDNESDAY. Problematic. The best way to approach other people is in a conciliatory mode. Listen to what they have to say, and use your judgment. Setting yourself up in opposition to them will get you nowhere. Chores could keep you from more personal pursuits until there is hardly enough time left to make it worthwhile starting. It is all too easy to relegate creative self-development to second place, but in fact it should be central to your life. Give your frayed nerves a tonic with a massage or leisurely bath to smooth out the tension in your muscles. Do not be too quick to judge someone you just met; appearances can be very deceptive. Just keep an open mind.

29. THURSDAY. Promising. Although there is a danger of taking on too much, it should do you a world of good to expand your mind by delving deeper into a subject. Even philosophy can be understandable if well taught, as well as highly illuminating. The outlook is fair for travel. Do not overload yourself with luggage if you are going a long distance. It is impossible to prepare for every eventuality, so you just have to accept an element of chance. An unusual job opportunity could come your way unexpectedly. Unless it is vital that you respond immediately, it would be wise to take some time to think it over and then to discuss it with loved ones.

30. FRIDAY. Auspicious. At last it seems there is the chance of a real move forward toward a personal goal. Your hard work will be rewarded, but you probably need some expert assistance or training. More responsibility is coming your way at work, which could mean longer hours. Even if the money is good, be sure to consider the repercussions on your private life. Sometimes it is necessary to stand up and be counted, and this is one of those occasions. Fortunately you are on the right side. A courageous act can only do you credit. Do not be afraid to speak your mind to parents, in-laws, or other older relatives.

JULY

1. SATURDAY. Tense. If you are entertaining at home, be prepared for the get-together to go less than smoothly. Unless you have been very careful in picking your guests, differences of opinion could escalate and spoil the whole atmosphere. All sporting activities are favored. Remember it is the game that counts; whether or not you win should be unimportant as long as you played well. You may feel more protective than usual toward loved ones. There might even be some of your friends you would prefer to keep away from your relatives, but do not go so far as to hamper their freedom. Wind down before bedtime, or you may be awake for most of the night.

2. SUNDAY. Pleasant. At last it is possible to tell a close friend your strong attraction to them. This could be the start of a satisfying relationship, so do not be shy. Youngsters can bring a great deal of unconscious humor to the day; all you have to do is listen. Of course, it would be quite unwise to laugh at them; the jokes should be shared. Social events are likely to go well as long as guests are kept entertained. Because boredom can throw a long shadow over proceedings, there should be plenty to eat, drink, and talk about. Friends are willing to give you loving support if you have a problem; do not hesitate to tell them what is on your mind.

3. MONDAY. Fair. There are apt to be some odds and ends of tasks left over from last week that require immediate attention. At first you might feel resentful that other people have taken for granted that you will help tie up remaining loose ends, but there is satisfaction to be gained from making sure all is finally in order. Charity begins at home; do not forget that today. You can hardly refuse to come to the assistance of a family member who needs some aid, and your generosity will not be forgotten. Usually your memory is good, but everyone slips up on occasion, so do not be surprised if you do so once in a while. However, do not try to cover up a mistake or ignore an apology you should offer.

4. TUESDAY. Demanding. The reaction of your boss or other superiors to written work may be more critical than you expected.

Although this will come as a blow, if you look at your work with an impartial eye you should begin to see what they mean. Someone who has been a guru or a mentor to you for a while may now seem to have feet of clay. This does not mean that all you have learned from them is invalid, just that they are a fallible human being; you need to realize that and treat them accordingly. If you allow interruptions to get you upset, not only your work but your health can suffer. Tell colleagues they must allow you some peace and quiet.

5. WEDNESDAY. Pressured. In your heart you know that you are doing yourself no favor by challenging superiors whose position makes them all but invincible. Even if you feel you have a valid complaint, there are better ways of making them. Now more than ever it is vital to keep promises to friends, who are probably relying on you more than you think. All may not be quiet on the home front. A close family member wants to involve you in a quarrel which is really none of your business. If you succumb to pressure, it will be almost impossible not to take sides. Some time alone would be deeply refreshing this evening.

6. THURSDAY. Auspicious. A call from a friend could put you back in touch with someone you had given up as out of your life forever. This is likely to bring a whole new dimension to your life, as old memories are revived and a former relationship is renewed. It is essential to stand on a point of principle at work. Speak up now and others will respect the air of authority you radiate. If you choose to remain silent instead, you are bound to berate yourself for some time. Business meetings can become a forum for exchanging useful information about all kinds of leisure pursuits. Just like you, no one really wants to spend all of their time working; play is important for mental and physical vitality.

7. FRIDAY. Spirited. Try to keep your temper; when roused you tend to let fly with words that can be extremely wounding. Colleagues will not soon forget unjust criticism, which may be held against you for a long time. Youngsters seem full of mischief and are likely to be a real handful. If you can get a friend to help out with them, the day will be that much easier. There should be a chance for you to work on a creative self-development project. Every ounce of effort put in will eventually bear fruit, so do not hold back. An opportunity to put in some overtime could bring in useful extra cash that can be put toward an important purchase; make sure it is not frittered away.

8. SATURDAY. Lively. Give home security some extra attention. It might be a good idea to buy some new locks, especially if you live in an urban area. You can get the most out of the day by concentrating on daily chores. If these tasks are left undone, they will prey on your mind. Do the necessary shopping and what is necessary around the house before going out on the town. Social events can cost more than you bargained for. It is not always a simple matter keeping all loved ones happy. Doing so today might entail some sacrifice on your part. Time spent in the open air should be particularly enjoyable and refreshing, but guard against sunburn.

9. SUNDAY. Confusing. A romantic partner may not share your views on where the relationship is going. While this special person may want a companion for an active social life, you might prefer something more intimate. This disagreement needs to be addressed and resolved before you go any further. Do not let yourself be dragged away from an activity that you enjoy just to please friends and loved ones. Sometimes it is necessary to insist on having your own way, even though your actions may come as a shock to others. Your finances might spin out of control unless you make sure that all of your accounts are in apple-pie order and bills have been paid.

10. MONDAY. Variable. Sometimes it can be useful to write down your hopes and aims for the future. Put the paper somewhere safe, then take it out and look at it from time to time to check how far you have progressed toward your goals, or if your aims have changed. Local travel is not likely to be problem-free. There may be cuts in public services, and road repairs could cause irritating holdups. You are apt to be expressing yourself less clearly than usual. Curb a tendency to ramble on at length; your listeners will simply lose interest and stop paying attention. Go out with a group of friends to a new restaurant tonight or to a sports event. Do not overspend your budget despite temptation.

11. TUESDAY. Good. If you have been given a work assignment that seems a little too much to handle, request some assistance from colleagues. There is no point doing a bad job when a good one can be done by two people, even if asking for help does hurt your pride somewhat. It is not unusual to be attracted to those who teach you. The situation of student and teacher has a certain power, but beware of confusing this with a romantic attachment. Keeping better control over your money should give you a greater sense of security. Spendthrift friends can accuse you of being dull, but they will change their tune when you are able to afford luxuries beyond their reach.

12. WEDNESDAY. Sensitive. There are times when it is tempting to lose sight of reality in favor of chasing a dream. As a Virgo you are normally too hard-headed to do so, but now there is a real danger of squandering your energy on a wild goose chase. Extra responsibilities at work may keep you on the job for longer hours than usual, sparking off resentment if loved ones feel neglected. Just try to explain to them that there is no alternative for a while, but some little gifts to assure them of your continued affection wouldn't go amiss either. An argument among family members could cause a long-term rift unless someone acts quickly to restore the peace.

13. THURSDAY. Satisfactory. Although it may not be obvious to others, you have come a long way during the past few months. The biggest difference is in your understanding of what life is all about. This gives you an air of quiet confidence. The reappearance of a former lover might not be all that welcome in your present circumstances. They may still have the ability to stir your heart-strings; it may be a struggle to resist the seductive attraction of shared memories. Home redecoration can go ahead now that final doubts have been overcome. A more modern look will give your rooms a dynamic atmosphere that enhances all of your activities.

14. FRIDAY. Productive. Virgos who work from home may be tempted to take off early for the weekend. Although there should be nothing urgent to claim your attention, rather than relax you can use the time to clear up paperwork and sort out your finances. As the day goes on it becomes increasingly easy to think ahead. Concentrate on finding more time for creative pursuits; as a Virgo you tend to underestimate the value of your talents. Youngsters should not cause any major problems, and may even enjoy quieter pursuits such as you reading to them or going for a walk together. Take this chance to introduce them to some of your own favorite childhood activities.

15. SATURDAY. Fortunate. This is an excellent day for going through closets and drawers and throwing out items that have accumulated over the years. Although some are bound to bring back memories, you should be enjoying the present in the belief that you are now making happy memories for future times. Romance is going through a quiet phase, but there is plenty happening behind the scenes. Once the first flush is over, it is time to begin the process of consolidating a truly sound relationship. Be careful not to overstretch yourself, especially in making social engagements. You cannot be everywhere at once, even if you wish you could accept every invitation.

16. SUNDAY. Stimulating. You can get the most out of the day by making sure it does not pass without you learning something new. There are many places to visit which can give you better insight into aspects of life that interest both you and your loved ones. Try to find time to hone your skills at a favorite hobby; even if this means you have less time to dedicate to other people, it will be worth it. If you have had difficulties in your love life, you might feel as if the point of no return has been reached. The decision is yours: is the other person good enough for you or has the relationship played itself out? Youngsters are apt to be in high spirits and require extremely patient handling.

17. MONDAY. Stressful. The workweek begins with a bang, as overdue mail arrives and the phone rings with inquiries all needing urgent attention. Do not get snowed under; ask for help. Unfortunately a mistake you made during the past few weeks may now be discovered. If you had admitted the error at the time, the matter could have been ironed out fairly easily; now it will not be so simple, or straightforward. Sometimes showing sympathy for others can work against you, as less scrupulous people do not hesitate to take advantage. Try to harden your heart a little; after all, you are used to keeping a stiff upper lip, and there is no reason why others should not do so as well.

18. TUESDAY. Erratic. Your usual ability to juggle several balls in the air at once may temporarily desert you. However, panicking will only add to the chaos, so pull yourself together and tackle tasks one by one. A pet may cause a few worries by acting out of character. A visit to the vet might be in order, just to be on the safe side; odd behavior can be an early symptom of illness. If you allow yourself to get too stressed, there is a risk of having a small accident. It is all too easy to make a slip when you are in a hurry and thinking of something else. Changes in routine at work can be for the good, opening up new possibilities for creative input.

19. WEDNESDAY. Disconcerting. If you have unrealistic views about your own talents, sooner or later someone is bound to point out the truth. By all means feel confident in your abilities, but do not lay claim to a level of skill that you do not yet possess. A business prospect in which you have invested quite a lot of time may not appeal to an associate. All you can do is try to persuade them; in the end the decision must be theirs. Loved ones may have reached the limit of their tolerance when it comes to letting you rule the roost. Even though you are certain that you know best, they have a point of view that must be accommodated. Give in occasionally to prove you can do so.

20. THURSDAY. Beneficial. The best way to get decisions made is through free and frank discussion. An exchange of views gives everyone a chance to have their say; the resulting cross-fertilization of ideas is bound to be beneficial. The hopes and wishes for the future that your mate or partner cherishes should become a part of your life almost as much as theirs. If you truly care for someone, you will be as eager for their achievements to be realized as for your own. There is no point arguing about who is to blame when problems occur at home. The first priority should be to sort out the situation, not to make a loved one feel guilty. Avoid a power battle with parents or in-laws.

21. FRIDAY. Promising. Your finances should be looking up. The practice of putting away savings where you cannot get at them easily can pay off. However, restrain yourself a while longer from withdrawing money until you accumulate a really useful sum. Romance may appear just when you had begun to think you were in for a period of solitude. This is likely to be an affair that appears serene to outsiders but is actually brimming over with emotional intensity. If you mislay a sentimental item begin your search at home. It could even be that youngsters have picked it up without thinking. Your mate or partner will appreciate a romantic evening out on the town, perhaps including dancing.

22. SATURDAY. Good. Today it is more important than usual to spend some time alone. There are a lot of personal issues you need to mull over in private, and for once it will only complicate things to discuss them with your loved ones. Even though a friend may ask for your help, it could be wiser to offer emotional support rather than financial assistance. In the long run they will have to solve the problem themselves; loaning or giving money is only going to be a temporary measure at best. You will feel all the healthier if you cut down on caffeine and nicotine. Since the Virgo system tends to be rather delicate, you are more susceptible to these substances and their effects than more hardy people.

23. SUNDAY. Mixed. Get a secret off your chest. If you continue to brood over it, others are bound to guess there is something up. You may have blown the matter out of proportion; confessing is likely to have less of an impact than you expect. A friend may be taking more interest than is natural in your personal financial affairs, perhaps working up to asking you to go into partnership with them for a pet project. In that case you must use your good Virgo business judgment. Do not let nagging doubts undermine your faith that you can achieve a lifelong ambition. You have more than enough time to reach your goal, and you can then use it as a stepping-stone toward further aims in the future.

24. MONDAY. Deceptive. Keep a low profile throughout the day. There is every possibility of being made a scapegoat for recent problems at home or work. This would be grossly unfair, but unfortunately someone has to be in the firing line; this person could well be you. Although you have learned through hard experience that colleagues do not always remember their promises, once again it seems you have placed your trust in someone who is going to let you down. This time, do not let them get away with it; confront them with their failure and insist on an explanation. Caring for an elderly relative can be costly in terms of time and commitment, but the gratitude you receive will be ample payment.

25. TUESDAY. Demanding. There is nothing to be gained by getting on your high horse when a loved one refuses to take you seriously. If you are honest, you should realize that you sometimes make little jokes at their expense, so you can hardly complain when they do the same. Virgo singles who are looking for love are unlikely to have an easy time getting close to a new acquaintance. They are apt to be somewhat opinionated; unless you are prepared to compromise a great deal, you may expend a great deal of energy pulling against each other. Exam results should turn out better than expected, but this is no reason to rest on your laurels.

26. WEDNESDAY. Unpredictable. A projected trip may have to be canceled due to local transportation problems. This is bound to be frustrating, especially if you have spent a lot of time preparing. However, the work you have done will doubtless be useful in a different context at a different time. Taking a more active part in group activities can lead to pleasant new social contacts. There are bound to be some clubs meeting locally that would interest you. Virgos looking for work may be able to get some assistance from a former employer. At the very least, an appreciative reference will stand you in good stead. Be proud of a recent romantic conquest but do not brag about it.

27. THURSDAY. Sensitive. You may not yet be over a past love affair. Memories can come back to haunt you to the point of dreaming about your former lover. Be careful that you do not indulge too much in fantasies or they could become more vivid than reality. You may have trouble with routine work as nothing comes together. In the end it may be simpler to give up rather than struggle on without achieving anything positive. Make sure you lock the house securely during your absence; carelessness could cost you an unwanted visit. Consider those who are less well-off than you; not everyone has the advantages you take for granted. Do what you can to lend a hand.

28. FRIDAY. Favorable. The workweek ends on a cheerful note with the completion of an important project. If there is any cause for celebration, do not hold back. Work done on behalf of others may seem thankless at the time, but undoubtedly you will be able to call in a favor when you need one. It is unlikely you will enjoy a boisterous evening out; arrange with your loved one to see a movie or simply stay at home. As a relationship finally comes to an end, it is bound to leave you with some feelings of regret. However, it is far better to finish it now rather than let it drag on amid increasing bitterness. It will be easier for you both to pick up the pieces once you are emotionally free. Goods offered to you at a very cheap price may be too hot to touch.

29. SATURDAY. Challenging. Even if you thought a romantic affair was settling down nicely, you are in for a surprise. The other person may suddenly appear to be showing signs of restlessness. Unless you can keep their interest, there is every possibility of them finding someone else. There have been so many demands on your time and attention recently that you may have almost lost sight of your own needs. Now is the time to withdraw and recover a sense of self. You and your mate or partner might benefit from leaving youngsters with friends for a while so that you have some peace in order to discuss domestic problems and then simply to enjoy the quiet.

30. SUNDAY. Tricky. You are likely to be in demand socially. The only difficulty might be deciding which event to attend. Normally Virgos do not argue with friends, but someone's behavior may have become so outrageous that you feel there is no other reasonable course of action. You cannot afford to be associated with a person who could tarnish your good reputation. Try to recoup your energy by napping for an hour or two this afternoon. If you have not been paying proper attention to your diet recently, get back on track. Parents may lend a helping hand with a loan that you need for a necessary repair for your home or your car.

31. MONDAY. Buoyant. Travel is highlighted. A trip taken now is almost bound to bring you in touch with people who will remain friends for some time to come. Extending your hospitality to acquaintances could cement the relationship. Finally you can put the mistakes of the past behind you and strike out in a new career direction. You should be able to pinpoint where your talents lie and how you want to use them to best advantage. This would be a good time to make a firm resolution to give up a habit you know is bad for you. Tell friends and loved ones what you are going to do so that they can give you their support and help keep your willpower strong.

AUGUST

1. TUESDAY. Disconcerting. It may feel as if you are wading through mud during the early part of the day. Tasks that usually take no time at all are likely to be slow going. You need to summon up all of your reserves of patience and persistence in order to finish. Spare a thought for relatives who are living at a distance. They will appreciate a call, especially if you have been out of touch for some time. When it comes to studying for an important test or interview, you can be your own worst enemy. By now you must realize that the only surefire way of succeeding is to do your homework thoroughly. Hoping to scrape through is probably courting disaster. Avoid mixing business with pleasure in any way.

2. WEDNESDAY. Manageable. Once a long-buried family secret comes to light, a great deal of odd behavior among your relatives should suddenly make sense. It can be a relief all around to finally know the truth; now the past can truly be put behind you. If you are looking for a new home, try searching off the beaten track. There is bound to be a suitable house tucked away somewhere, just waiting to be discovered by you. An act of kindness from a close relative can help you out of a tight spot. You are not likely to forget that you owe them a favor; all the same, make sure they know how much you value their assistance. Try to keep all of your options open.

3. THURSDAY. Easygoing. This is the sort of day when work becomes plain sailing. It should be much easier than usual to get your points across, which makes other people more willing to help you. Conferring with experts can make your life immeasurably easier. Their knowledge is available to be used, so do not pretend you know it all. You can now take a real step toward achieving a personal aim. Any setbacks should be treated as challenges, since it is certain you can overcome them as long as you have a positive attitude. While your finances may be in a slightly dubious state, you should soon receive money owed to you that can be used to finance an important project.

4. FRIDAY. Excellent. The end of the workweek brings good news for all romantic Virgos. Someone with whom you have been working may disguise their admiration for you no longer. All you have to do is decide whether or not you want to get involved emotionally. Some extra work you did recently may qualify you for a bonus. This is a sure sign of appreciation for your sense of responsibility, so you are justified in feeling proud of yourself. Money spent on your home will probably turn out to be a good investment when you decide to sell. Any work that improves the value of your property is bound to enhance your future finances. Restore your energy with a peaceful evening at home.

5. SATURDAY. Opportune. Once in a while you are able to make a real deal with an impulse purchase. Electrical goods offer surprising savings. A fresh approach to health care for yourself and your family may be needed. Any habit tends to offer diminishing returns after a while, so try to alter your routines of diet and exercise. Stick to healthy principles; avoid fads. Friends can be rather challenging about your personal beliefs. Although you may not be able to persuade them to adopt your views, it can be a worthwhile exercise to have to defend yourself. A more cautious attitude toward savings should produce effective results.

6. SUNDAY. Misleading. At first it may not be clear just why a romance is not working out well. Although the other person may seem loving, they may feel a lack of mental rapport with you. A long trip may be something of a disappointment whether you travel alone or with a companion. In particular, youngsters are apt to be easily bored, so take along plenty to keep them entertained. You may also be feeling rather restless and in need of a change of image. It can do a lot for your self-confidence to indulge in some new clothes; put aside a sum of money for that purpose. Misunderstandings with loved ones are likely to occur unless you pay more attention to their tone of voice as well as their actual words.

7. MONDAY. Mixed. Although it may seem as if meetings are an uphill struggle, actually you should be able to communicate your plans very clearly. Superiors are likely to take action on your advice. A friend's youngster may make an uncannily accurate remark about what you thought of as your private life. Let this be a warning that little ears are listening when grown-ups talk and that they understand more than you might realize. Do not take a colleague's word that you can let routine tasks slip. If you fall far behind now, it will take a long time to catch up. A neighbor's help with a do-it-yourself job could be more trouble than it is worth.

8. TUESDAY. Chancy. There may be a real problem with a new deal just being negotiated. It would be extremely unwise to get involved now. Beware of others trespassing on your good nature; give someone an inch and they are apt to take a mile. It is important to keep your energy level high. If you allow your strength to be drained, there is a likelihood of picking up a virus. Long-haul travel has more than the usual quota of complications and delays. Although those in authority might be officious, no matter how irritated you become it is vital to respect the customs of the area where you are traveling. Do not give up a personal project solely because of family obligations.

9. WEDNESDAY. Challenging. Having idealistic plans is to be commended, but sometimes it is necessary to compromise for the sake of practicality. You may have to give up hope of achieving perfection, but that does not mean impressive goals are not still within your grasp. Virgos who have been working toward a better job may be placing too much faith in a colleague's promises. Consider whether they really have the clout they claim and if you would be just as well off doing a bit of self-promotion. Trying to manipulate loved ones seldom pays dividends because they are bound to sense something is up; mistrust can be the only result. Do not let parents or in-laws exert emotional blackmail.

10. THURSDAY. Tricky. Even if you hear a rumor in which you are implicated, it would be unwise to react without advance thinking. In fact, the best course might be to let the truth speak for itself. Hearing from a former acquaintance with whom you cut ties is likely to arouse your anger. They may not have got the message that you do not want them in your life, so this time spell it out clearly. Wind down a creative project so that there is space to begin something new. All that you have learned can be applied to other areas of your life and is bound to be immensely useful. Differences within the family can be cleared up if everyone has the will to give in a little.

11. FRIDAY. Rewarding. Someone at work may slip you news that can make all the difference in the way you approach a job interview. Take this information to heart; it could put you far ahead of the competition. Complaining about a superior's behavior behind their back can get you into more trouble than you suppose. If you have a genuine grievance, have the courage to discuss it face-to-face. Your nerves are more easily jangled than usual, especially by youngsters. This is a good time to learn a relaxation technique that you can practice on the spot whenever necessary. Spend the evening doing whatever you want rather than relying on friends.

12. SATURDAY. Harmonious. Shared memories of past experiences can bring family members closer together. Get out photo albums and indulge in some pleasant nostalgia. There is no telling what might be hidden in attics or obscure closets. Rummaging through them could reveal articles of value, even saleable antiques. It can be very surprising what collects in a house over the course of years. Find time for a leisure activity that allows you to forget the pressures of everyday life. It is not important to take a creative project too seriously; just give yourself a space where you can be at peace for a while. Keep romance on an even keel and do not make demands on your mate or steady date.

13. SUNDAY. Lively. You could be tempted to overdo as a burst of early morning energy makes you feel almost unstoppable. Unless you are careful, however, this feeling will evaporate with nothing major being achieved. Sporting activities should be very satisfying, even if winning is not the outcome. Just the healthy exercise can be very beneficial. There is no point upsetting others for the sake of asserting your own wishes if you are only going to end up feeling guilty about it. Keep a sense of proportion and try to arrange some sort of mutually agreeable compromise. Pets could turn up missing if you do not keep a sharp eye on them; be careful, as they may not be easily found. Get to bed earlier than usual tonight.

14. MONDAY. Demanding. You may have angered or annoyed someone without realizing it. Now they are making it very plain that there is a problem that needs to be sorted out. Romance is a thorny issue at the moment. A relationship can act as a catalyst to bring to the surface all kinds of emotions, and these need respectful handling. Inevitably you will sometimes be torn between spending on yourself and on your home. If recent redecorating made a hole in your pocket, you may have to cut back on personal items for a while. However, with a little careful planning, this phase will pass and you should soon be able to indulge yourself again.

15. TUESDAY. Disappointing. Hopes of a job promotion may seem to be fading at the moment. Take heart, however. Sooner or later just the right position will become vacant. Your health should be a priority. If you continue to carry on the way you have been doing, there will be a price to pay. You cannot expect to push yourself beyond your physical limits forever: a change of lifestyle seems necessary right now. Memories of the past could undermine your present happiness. It is easy to forget the more difficult times. Consider whether life was really better then than it is now. You might have to accept criticism from a superior if recent work was below your usual high standards.

16. WEDNESDAY. Opportune. Some slightly unorthodox methods could hasten the conclusion of a deal. Just be sure that the other party concurs fully with the arrangements. You have terrific motivation right now to sort out a long-standing family problem. Once you decide that enough is enough, everyone should be able to behave like adults. Disagreements with a business associate can escalate out of proportion unless you are both prepared to see reason. This is probably not a clear-cut case of right versus wrong, so get together and work out a remedy. Spend quality time with your mate or partner this evening; leave the television off.

17. THURSDAY. Tranquil. For Virgos who have been through emotional turmoil recently, the dust seems to be settling at last. This can take a lot longer to get over than is generally realized, but you probably already feel an inkling of the peace that will one day be yours once again. Compromise with colleagues is the name of the game. For once you just do not have the energy to get worked up over a matter of pure principle. This may bring home to you what a nuisance you have been on a previous occasion. Where romance is concerned, it would be wise to keep quiet if you want to continue on your present course. Discussion of practical matters such as joint finances can come later.

18. FRIDAY. Favorable. Some financial advice passed on in private could be useful for improving your future security. It is possible for even the small investor to make a good return on money once you know what you are doing. Virgos who are getting nervous about a job interview have no need to do so. Draw on your inner resources and have confidence in your worth. The Virgo talents of organization and efficiency can be invaluable to employers. The old adage about a healthy mind in a healthy body applies to you right now. It is vital to care for your emotional well-being as well as your physical health. Allow yourself to be drained and there could be problems requiring medical advice.

19. SATURDAY. Satisfying. The weekend begins with a sustainable surge of energy and a strong desire to fix up your home. Tackle some of the clearing and cleaning tasks that have been put off for a long time. Enlist the help of family members, too. The solution of a mystery is probably right under your nose. Look for the simplest explanation and you will be on the right track. Reviving past memories can sometimes be healing, especially if they have been deliberately buried in your subconscious. Even painful recollections lose a great deal of power simply by being looked at in the bright light of day. If you are thinking of buying or adopting a pet, consider your home's limitations of space as well as your everyday lifestyle before deciding.

20. SUNDAY. Inspiring. An old family feud at last stands a chance of being cleared up for once and for all. It is time to forgive and forget so that life can go on as before. You may find it useful to keep a container handy for your loose change. This can come in surprisingly handy when you are caught short of cash. Youngsters may seem slightly withdrawn, but they are probably only in an imaginative world of their own. Rather than risk breaking the spell, leave them to pursue their dreams; just keep an eye on them from time to time. Visit an art gallery to get your fill of beauty; the soul needs feeding as much as the body. Going with your mate or partner can bring you closer together.

21. MONDAY. Problematic. You may get the distinct feeling that someone is keeping you in the dark about developments at work. Their motive may be to get an advantage over you, so do your best to find out exactly what is going on. It can be more difficult than usual to pursue private studies. Your powers of concentration are apt to be weak. It might be a good idea to get some physical exercise before settling down to work. Travel is subject to disruptions. If you are setting off on a long-distance trip, make contingency plans in case of a delay or detour. A smile can work where a long face does not, and it will keep your opposition guessing.

22. TUESDAY. Variable. It may not be possible to persuade your boss or another superior of the value of your idea for increasing creative output. If you really believe you have hit upon something important, you may simply have to go ahead and prove it by your own independent actions. This is one of those times when youngsters are apt to question your authority at every turn. Probably nothing you say will satisfy them until their mood changes for the better. There could be delays before money you are owed reaches you. In fact, it might be smart to jog the memory of the person concerned, who may be withholding funds deliberately. Do not drive yourself too hard; relax a little during the day as well as this evening.

23. WEDNESDAY. Strenuous. Even though you are likely to be pleased to be given greater responsibility at work, your new duties may not be going over too well with your colleagues. You need to tread very carefully at first to avoid causing jealousy and resentment. Doubt that you can fulfill a personal dream is not going to give you the positive energy you need. Sometimes when you are thrown back on your own resources it may seem hard to press on, but every forward step takes you closer to your goal. Loved ones may try to make you feel guilty for not being as ambitious as some other people. However, your achievements are not solely in the conventional world of paid employment.

24. THURSDAY. Good. Try a fresh approach to health care, with more attention to the subtle signals of your body. It can be very instructive to sit quietly for a few minutes each day and tune in to how your body is reacting. There comes a point when you can no longer compromise for the sake of a quiet life. Even at the risk of being unpopular, it is vital sometimes to stand up for yourself and what you believe to be right. If others seem to be projecting a more professional image than you, it could be time to smarten yourself up a bit. First impressions can be crucial, so it is worth spending some time and money to create a positive persona.

25. FRIDAY. Enjoyable. The workweek ends on a sociable note, with numerous invitations for the weekend ahead. You should be in a more extroverted mood than usual, so it will do you good to get out and about. As a Virgo you normally are rather reticent when it comes to speaking out in a meeting, but that is not the case at the moment. In fact, you have a valuable contribution to make, so it would be a shame to keep quiet. Doing your bit to make the world a better place will also improve your own self-image. Do not buy into the idea that an individual cannot make a significant difference. Every little bit helps, and you might even inspire others to support a worthy cause that is close to your heart.

26. SATURDAY. Smooth. Relax into the weekend by forgetting the household chores. Enjoyment should be your priority; put duty on the back burner for a while. Loved ones will help you further self-development plans as long as they are included. This shared activity is bound to bring you closer together. If you are organizing a social event, make sure the guests will lack for nothing. As long as you create a warm atmosphere, the get-together should go smoothly. Your hopes for the future depend largely on your own efforts. Sometimes it is useful to sit back and mull over how much you have already achieved, and do not be overly modest in your self-assessment.

27. SUNDAY. Cautious. There is a danger of boring or even alienating loved ones if you get carried away about a favorite subject. They could accuse you of having a one-track mind, and they might be right. Ideas of what should be yours by right may not match up with reality. Consider all the elements of your life that you take for granted; then you may realize there is a great deal for which to be grateful. A persistent infection could be undermining your health. Instead of being stoical, make an appointment with your doctor and get it treated properly. Put youngsters to bed early so that you can have a peaceful night as you prepare for the workweek.

28. MONDAY. Erratic. It is always painful to find out that your trust has been misplaced. An acquaintance may have used you rather cynically to get what they want. Part of your feeling is probably hurt pride that your judgment could be so much at fault. Today's rather chaotic conditions make it hard to get organized. Your attention is apt to be pulled first in one direction and then another, so that tasks have to be left half-finished or passed on to someone else for final touches. Even though you might be reluctant to express your anger about a loved one's behavior, burying your hurt is not a good alternative. Confront the issue once your feelings have cooled down. Avoid making any threats.

29. TUESDAY. Chancy. Do not take chances with your health. Aim for moderation in all things; excess in any direction soon catches up with you. A rather shady financial proposition might seem attractive at first glance, but it would be very unwise to get involved in a scheme that could backfire badly. And even if you did gain by it, there would be little pleasure as your conscience would not let you gloat. Make a resolution to leave self-doubt behind and forge ahead with your personal development. You will not get anywhere by focusing on your faults; celebrate your talents and strengths for a change. Put your personal stamp on a group project.

30. WEDNESDAY. Useful. This is a good time to sort out financial paperwork. You may be able to find better ways to make your money work for you; the first step is to figure out exactly where you stand. Some useful shopping can be done, particularly for essentials. Stock up now and you can free some time for more interesting pursuits. Your employer may seek to keep you in your current position at work. However, if you are beginning to feel restless, it could be time to stretch your wings. Prepare a detailed plan of action before making any move. Loved ones may feel rather insecure and would welcome some extra-special attention from you this evening.

31. THURSDAY. Satisfying. A small pay raise could make it possible to at last buy a luxury item. Be firm with yourself, banking this extra money before you are tempted to spend it on everyday living. The attention of someone who is a little older than you might be flattering, but consider whether your emotional reaction goes any deeper. It would not be wise to get involved too lightly if the other person appears to be quite serious about establishing a relationship. This is an excellent time to buy a new outfit; your judgment of what suits you is accurate. Do not purchase anything too radical; a classical style will be most appropriate and the best value.

SEPTEMBER

1. FRIDAY. Exciting. An original idea for making money by using your Virgo talents could strike you out of the blue. This might really be a winner, so jot down your first thoughts and promise yourself to develop them later on. Spend some time sorting through old letters and keepsakes. Although many have sentimental value, there are periods from your past that would be best left behind with nothing that reminds you of them. Try to finish off a task that has been hanging fire; you should then feel all the more inspired to begin a new project. Savings should be earmarked for your home rather than for personal items or gifts to other people. Keep evening entertainment simple.

2. SATURDAY. Sensitive. There is apt to be a conflict between the way you want your life to develop and the direction in which circumstances are pushing you. It is no use just hoping this problem will solve itself; you have to consider how you can bring about positive changes. No relationship is without its upsets, and right now you may be getting more than your fair share. Taking a hard line and refusing to compromise is not going to help the situation. Local shopping is likely to leave you feeling dissatisfied; be sure to keep receipts in case you want to exchange purchases later on. Be careful with alcohol; your tolerance is lower than usual.

3. SUNDAY. Happy. Romance is about to enter your life from a most unexpected direction as you begin to see an acquaintance in a new light. Giving support in times of need can teach you more about each other than months of superficial socializing, providing a firm basis for long-term understanding and trust. Trips could cause a few upsets, particularly if youngsters get overly tired. It would be unwise to go too far or visit a place that may be boringly over the heads of younger family members. The ability to assert yourself might be put to the test as close relatives tell you what to think. Do not be afraid to follow your own good instincts.

4. MONDAY. Fair. A real battle of wills may be developing between you and a superior at work. Unfortunately any tendency to mutiny on your part can only do you damage; in fact, this is likely to be something of a no-win situation. Necessary renovations and repairs to your home may cost more than you expect. Tighten your belt and cut back on luxuries for a while. Neighbors can be more helpful than usual; do not hesitate to ask if you need someone to look after plants or pets while you are away. Expect delays to local journeys; heavy vehicles could hold up traffic for some time. Relax tonight with a quiet meal at home rather than going out.

5. TUESDAY. Disquieting. Look around your home with a critical eye and you may be surprised at how much needs changing. It is important to have an environment that reflects your moods and induces calm and serenity. Differences of opinion with loved ones can escalate out of control unless you are firm with yourself. Much may be said in the heat of passion that you profoundly regret, but words once spoken cannot be called back. The end of a relationship is likely to leave you feeling lonely, at least for a while. It may seem now as if you will never fall in love again, but time heals all wounds. Do not take on too much responsibility at work; no one will thank you for it.

6. WEDNESDAY. Opportune. This is a good time to consider moving. If you have needed a bigger place for some time, figure out what you can afford and start looking. Electrical gadgets can make life easier; do not struggle with manual tools in the kitchen or yard more than you need to. Virgos who work from home can spend some useful time getting odds and ends of tasks out of the way in preparation for a clear start on a new project. There is no point putting off the crucial moment when you must pluck up courage and begin. In fact, the sooner you get going the better. Few words are needed to express your true emotions. When it comes to your love life, action is bound to speak volumes.

7. THURSDAY. Exacting. Do not invest too much time and emotion in a new romantic affair in hopes that this will be the one true love of your life. Time alone will tell whether the relationship is going to last. Let it develop slowly and it stands a better chance of maturing fully. Financially you could be tempted in several directions. However, current funds are probably not sufficient to cover everything you want, even if you leave your family's needs out of the equation. Making a go of a creative venture can be a struggle at the best of times. You are bound to hit slow, unproductive periods, but hopefully these will be balanced by periods when you can make enough money to build up your bank account.

8. FRIDAY. Starred. A bit of quick thinking should enable you to stake your claim in the jobs market. Do not hesitate if you hear about a promising position; go for it without delay. An older colleague could have sound financial advice to offer. You can only benefit from their experience, and they will probably be pleased to help you. This is a starred time to give youngsters a greater sense of responsibility. They are likely to relish being treated in a more grown-up way, responding with touching seriousness. Virgos on the lookout for love should try to meet the friends of friends. You will then have some common ground right from the start. Just beware of getting too involved too soon.

9. SATURDAY. Manageable. Do not be surprised if you have trouble with a home appliance. Rather than try to fix it yourself, call in someone who knows exactly what they are doing. Where romance is concerned, you are courting heartache if you put too much trust in someone who has a negative reputation. You may think that you will be able to change them, but old habits die hard; sooner or later they are bound to let you down. Concentrate on practical chores for a satisfying sense of achievement. It will do you good to see results, even if other people are unappreciative or do not even notice. Careful handling of funds should enable you to have a really good evening out on the town, with no expense spared.

10. SUNDAY. Harmonious. A day out with your loved ones would be ideal. All the family can relax in peaceful surroundings, and a greater sense of togetherness should bind you to one another. Better organization can make this a starred day. As a Virgo you know how to please others by giving them just what they want, but do not forget to take into account your own wishes even when you are caring for others. A friend may reveal in confidence something said by a loved one that makes you feel more secure about the relationship. Someone you recently met may be too shy to reveal feelings to you just yet, but that will change with time.

A pet can give great pleasure and even a new lease on life to an elderly relative.

11. MONDAY. Erratic. Malfunctioning electrical equipment can play havoc with your daily routine. It may be impossible to access computerized records, so some business will just have to be put aside for the moment. There is no point flying off the handle just because colleagues do not work to your high standards. The best you can do is set an example, then hope they follow your lead. When you are engaged in practical tasks, try not to fall prey to impatience. In the long run you will only slow matters down, since you are bound to make mistakes or produce sloppy work that needs to be redone. A romantic involvement based on physical attraction is not likely to endure very long.

12. TUESDAY. Demanding. Just as it seems you are getting ahead in your job, a setback may occur. However, it would be more positive to regard this as an obstacle to be overcome. On no account should you give up trying to get ahead. Financial restraints could prevent you from putting a business plan into operation. There is little you can do about this right now. It would not be wise to borrow money in the hope of being able to repay it quickly. Domestic arguments about trivial matters can be surprisingly draining emotionally. Just wait until you recover your sense of perspective, then discuss the matter. You may have to admit that your usual way of doing something is not the only option.

13. WEDNESDAY. Challenging. You and your mate or partner may have reached a point where you cannot go back in the relationship, and yet you cannot see a smooth way ahead. Neither of you should act hastily. It may help to have some time apart from each other in order to get your bearings. As one door closes, another one opens; this is certainly true where matters of self-development are concerned. Even if you feel you have come to the end of one period of your life, there is no reason not to initiate a new phase right away. A legal decision is likely to be reached quite soon. While waiting for it you are bound to be somewhat tense, but it will not help to get agitated about the eventual outcome.

14. THURSDAY. Lucky. A sudden windfall can give your finances a much needed boost. You will probably get much more pleasure spending at least some of it on necessary items instead of socking it all away. A romantic affair should be much more enjoyable if you allow each other some independence. The time you spend together will be all the more pleasurable for having separate concerns. Property negotiations are likely to be put in motion quite quickly. You will have to move swiftly in order to keep up with the process and make sure you get the best deal. Work offers you some scope for putting your basic ideals into action. This cannot only do you good but may inspire other people as well.

15. FRIDAY. Promising. A legacy could bring you some family property that is poignant with memories. At first this may be painful to deal with, but in time you will appreciate having custody of items that carry traces of your own history. A business decision that has been pending for some time could suddenly appear quite simple and obvious. You have probably been working on the solution unconsciously, and now you should be able to act with confidence. Do not make a move to improve your future security without consulting your mate or partner. Even if financial matters are usually left to you, it is vital that they understand and approve in advance what you are going to do.

16. SATURDAY. Spirited. The most satisfying way to approach the day is to make it a time for freeing yourself from the past. Do not hesitate to get rid of old possessions that have been weighing you down for some time. Or you may want to plan a radical change of color scheme for your house. You need physical exercise to tone muscles and pep up your whole system. Take care, though, that you do not go overboard and strain yourself, especially if it has been some time since you were active. An old friend could contact you after a lapse of years. Together you will want to catch up with news of other acquaintances with whom you have both lost touch. As a result, there may be some surprises in store.

17. SUNDAY. Pressured. Plans for a day out may dissolve away as more pressing concerns take center stage. However, it would be a pity to deny yourself inspiration, so be sure to find some time for some pure pleasure and indulgence. It might be wise to keep youngsters away from water, or at least keep a close eye on them. This is one of those times when you can all too easily lose your sense of direction. You know in your heart that there is more to life than the daily grind, but now you have to figure out how to go about incorporating more satisfying activities into your schedule. A more assertive mood may lead to arguments with loved ones if you are not careful and considerate.

18. MONDAY. Strenuous. Sometimes you may feel as if you are beating your head against a brick wall as other people just do not seem to see the value of your input. It can be an uphill struggle to implement improvements at home or at work. Make sure your diet is balanced; any lack of essential nutrients is bound to have an effect on your stamina. It is important to build up a reserve of strength rather than scraping by on nervous energy. Your parents or other relatives may have had a deeper influence on you than you are now prepared to admit. Stop and ask yourself whether you might not be seeking their approval even when it is no longer necessary. Remember that you are a free and responsible person.

19. TUESDAY. Inspiring. You should have no shortage of ideas for money-making schemes. Some of them may be a little wild, but that is no reason for not giving them a whirl. Do not pit yourself against a colleague who has considerably more influence than you. Doing so will be wasted energy. A far better approach is to try to persuade them to your view. Virgos who are looking for a new job may find an opening that would make better use of newly acquired talents. In this situation there is no such thing as overselling yourself; just go for it. An act of self-sacrifice on your part is likely to be repaid tenfold, not now but later when you may be in need.

20. WEDNESDAY. Excellent. Fortunately it is fairly easy for you to live on your wits when necessary. Thinking on your feet can save the day when an important deal seems in danger of falling through. Once you have achieved a goal, your sense of satisfaction may not last all that long. What is needed now is a fresh mountain to conquer. You are armed with the confidence of your recent success. Learning a new computer skill could come in handy, even for use at home; youngsters might be very helpful in explaining how to proceed. If a fresh romantic prospect has entered your life you should have a renewed sense of hope and optimism. Love makes the world go around, so do not hold back through shyness.

21. THURSDAY. Mixed. The day may get off to a scratchy start. Little things are apt to upset you more than usual, as if you are looking for an excuse to lash out at other people. Where personal plans are concerned, you can no longer put off a major decision. Even if you have to make sacrifices in some other area of your life, the eventual reward will be worth it. Now is not the time to get itchy feet; an important project should be absorbing most of your energy, and it is vital to see it through to the very end. Work put in now should stand you in good stead later on; others who are involved will appreciate your efforts. Donate some time or money to a good cause.

22. FRIDAY. Disquieting. If you have been letting your financial situation slip recently, do not let this go on any longer. Review your accounts investments to see just what is needed to get back on an even keel. Friends are inclined to spread gossip that could be harmful to you and your loved ones. You may have no idea how the rumors originated, but it is essential to stop them as soon as possible. There is only so much you can do to support other people when they need your assistance. Eventually they have to start standing on their own feet. If you take on too much of their responsibility, you will not actually be helping them in the long run.

23. SATURDAY. Reassuring. Domestic concerns are apt to be at the forefront of your mind. A shopping trip can be organized with military precision, the emphasis being on essentials rather than luxury items. A solid sense of self-worth is sure to come from learning to value your achievements more highly. Loved ones should be eager to support you with their respect and love. In romance, be prepared to take the rough with the smooth. Upsets with your mate or partner can actually have a positive aspect because in that way you learn how you both cope when life is less than perfect. Take it easy later in the day to relax your tired nerves. Get to bed earlier than usual.

24. SUNDAY. Beneficial. This quiet day need not be uneventful. There is much for you to talk over with loved ones. Now would be a good moment to delve into a subject that requires some deep thought and emotional honesty. A past romantic relationship may still have a hold on your heart. Some ties are never really broken, but you nevertheless need to realize that life moves on, and so must you. If you are planning a day out, consider going farther afield than usual. You are bound to benefit from a taste of freedom, and a day out in the country could give you a whole new lease on life. Conversation with friends can be difficult because just this once you may be on totally different wavelengths.

25. MONDAY. Changeable. Because you are apt to feel a bit fragile this morning, if you can work by yourself so much the better. Take the opportunity of a fairly quiet start to the day to clear up financial paperwork; be sure bills are paid before they are due. Sometimes you have to put your trust in a person who has your security in their hands. Fortunately your Virgo instincts are usually infallible. In this case you are right to have faith in a new acquaintance. It may be frustrating not to have more freedom of choice in your work. You might have reached a stage where once you prove that you can act responsibly as a truly independent agent, new opportunities will start coming your way.

26. TUESDAY. Rewarding. A friend who is in the know can give you a helping hand with your finances. Their suggestions may be unlike anything you would have thought of for yourself, but that is no reason not to at least seriously consider their advice. Taking up a gentle form of exercise could be just what you need to tone up physically. You should be able to take pleasure in the exercise itself, rather than just doing it for the sake of keeping fit. Family obligations might stand in the way of personal fulfillment. However, honoring your promises and duties can be a good means of developing your character, so do what is expected in as generous a spirit as possible.

27. WEDNESDAY. Fair. A romantic affair may be in the doldrums as that special person in your life reads adverse criticism into everything you say. This is a problem they have to deal with, but it will help if you try to find out just why they feel so vulnerable. Short journeys are unlikely to be uninterrupted. Your car could develop a problem that puts it out of action for a short time; make sure you get expert help rather than trying to do repairs yourself. There is a fresh chance to put your future finances on a sounder footing. Pooling resources with your mate or partner increases the possibilities for profitable new investment.

28. THURSDAY. Productive. Virgo collectors could find a valuable new piece by looking in the least likely places. This is a time to think seriously about getting some additional insurance; it is easy to forget how high the cumulative worth of a collection can be. Do not begrudge putting in overtime at work; the extra money will come in handy, and your positive attitude is sure to be noted by higher-ups. Resolve to break the habit of snacking and to eat proper meals at regular intervals. It is also important to keep in mind that nourishment should have more than physical value; your mind and emotions need healthy and regular feeding as well.

29. FRIDAY. Variable. You may find yourself talking on and on. If you are telephoning, you will have only yourself to blame if the toll charges are astronomical. Virgos who work with the written word can get a lot accomplished. A light touch should make reports and letters a pleasure to read. If you are in charge of youngsters, prepare to answer a multitude of questions. There is no use saying that curiosity killed the cat when, in fact, this is how everyone learns to find their way around in the world. A recent bout of nervous exhaustion may have taken a toll on your health. You need to learn to recognize the signs that you have reached the limits of your physical and mental capabilities.

30. SATURDAY. Good. Romance is in the cards. All you have to do is declare your interest. Make a special effort to please a newcomer. Do not ask anything for yourself beyond the pleasure of their company. Shopping for gifts should be successful. Your instinct will tell you what would particularly appeal to friends and loved ones; it will be worth spending a little over your budget to get something very special. Conversations can be interrupted and never finished, leaving room for misunderstandings on both sides. It is all too easy to imagine what someone has said because that is what you wanted to hear. All promises made today should be put in writing.

OCTOBER

1. SUNDAY. Confusing. You will not be able to comprehend what is being said unless you listen closely. Today you are more inclined than usual to daydream, making concentration a real effort. Sometimes the best ideas come to you in your dreams. They might need to be interpreted, but your sleeping mind can be a source of true wisdom. Keep an eye on youngsters. They may be more elusive than usual, ducking out of sight as soon as you turn your back, so some extra vigilance is necessary. A lull between periods of work gives you the chance to catch your breath. At those times you should be able to get a better idea of what the final results will be like.

2. MONDAY. Exciting. There should be plenty going on today, including in your romantic life. If you have stirred up quite passionate feelings in someone new on the scene, you now have the choice of either fanning or quenching the flames. Do not let loved ones put a brake on your ambitions just because they have not fulfilled their own. They should be glad to see you aiming high; after all, they will be able to bask in reflected glory when you achieve your goal. A more conciliatory approach to a family problem may work in a situation where confrontation has failed. Follow the principle of live and let live and you will not go far wrong. You should be able to sleep soundly all through the night.

3. TUESDAY. Mixed. Investment in property can be a great means of securing your future. However, it is vital to use your good Virgo judgment and also seek advice from those who are familiar with the market. You need to keep a tight rein on your temper all day long as loved ones seem determined to drive you to the limits of your tolerance. An argument now could have serious consequences that you would regret too late. The discovery of old family photographs may make you feel more connected with the previous generation. Although these relatives led lives very different from your own, their basic concerns were the same. Your garden or potted plants need some extra attention as the season changes.

4. WEDNESDAY. Chancy. You may be inspired to make a real effort to get a better job. However, this might not be straightforward. You would be wise to expect to have to put in a lot of time and effort before seeing results. A reckless mood can make you feel like throwing caution to the winds where romance is concerned. A bold move might pay off, but first consider how much you could lose if it backfires. Your financial situation should be looking up, thanks to a period of hard work. It would be a good idea to look into opportunities for additional investment rather than go on a spending spree. Make time for socializing with friends or neighbors tonight.

5. THURSDAY. Smooth. Virgo writers should feel inspiration flow from the moment you wake up. Gather your energy and get to work as soon as possible; if you wait too long your enthusiasm is apt to wane. A romantic affair will go more smoothly if you are honest in talking about your hopes. Let that special person in your life know where they stand, so that they know what to expect from you. A more authoritative approach with youngsters may work better than trying to relate on their own level. Sometimes children need the comfort of being sure who is in charge and what they cannot get away with. Do not be persuaded to take up a new hobby just because a friend thinks you will enjoy it; find your own pleasures.

6. FRIDAY. Successful. Parents or other older relatives can be a great help when you need to consult someone about the practicalities of life. Even if you would not usually ask their advice, there are times when it may be invaluable. For once, you can benefit from taking a hard-line stand at work. Do not just be a cog in the machine; make your boss and co-workers sit up and take notice. A better sense of discipline will soon show results where your health is concerned. It can be easier than you think to stick to a healthy diet; resisting temptation is just a matter of practice. Your innate sense of responsibility will get you noticed if you are hoping for career advancement.

7. SATURDAY. Tranquil. The day is likely to get off to quite a slow start. It may be hard to wake up. Your dreams are apt to seem more vivid than reality and may well have a message for you; try to remember the details and to write them down before they fade. People will not be deceived by any attempt to disguise the truth. If you have something to confess, be honest about it. Shopping can fray your nerves. Youngsters will quickly get bored if you take them along; you may have to give in and go home with some items yet to buy. Later in the day a family event should improve relations between young and old. Warmer appreciation of each other could lead to more frequent contact.

8. SUNDAY. Erratic. Because loved ones may be decidedly touchy, it might be best to stay out of their way for a while. Do not make hard-and-fast plans, especially for practical work. It would be wiser to be open to whatever may turn up during the course of the day. Only tackle tasks that can be dropped at a moment's notice. A romantic affair with someone outside your usual sphere of interest can be both stimulating and unsettling. While you will learn a lot from each other, do not let them cast doubt on your own basic beliefs. Any desire to shock someone for the sake of it must be curbed; you could actually cause considerably more offense than you expect.

9. MONDAY. Uneasy. A somewhat uneasy atmosphere prevails this morning as no one seems to trust anyone else. Rumors are apt to be flying with no clear idea of who is responsible for them. If you are feeling constricted at work, there are lessons to be learned from the experience. It may be time to spread your wings and try something a little more ambitious. Relations with your mate or partner may be going through an awkward period because neither of you is really willing to sit down and discuss what is wrong. This attitude does not help; sooner or later you are going to have to argue it out. Where romance is concerned, keep a stiff upper lip until the relationship begins to improve.

10. TUESDAY. Profitable. Help with your finances could come from an unexpected quarter. This might be the beginning of a new era of cooperation with colleagues who know their way around the world of money. Developing new talents can improve your self-image a great deal. All you need is a bit of extra confidence and the world can become your oyster. Your home could be causing you problems at the moment. If structural repairs need to be done, there is nothing to be gained by putting them off even if the work turns out to be rather expensive. The result of a recent telephone call could be upsetting family members. Try to reassure them without revealing a secret.

11. WEDNESDAY. Lively. Go out of your way to understand what family members are currently worried about. They need some special support to get through a period of self-doubt. A contract should be carefully reviewed before signing. It is essential to go over all clauses thoroughly; make sure you are getting exactly what you want. An associate who has heard good things about you may offer you a higher-paying position. However, there are bound to be drawbacks, so delve into the proposition before giving your answer. Some useful research can bring a project to a successful and satisfying conclusion. There is a special opportunity at a distance.

12. THURSDAY. Useful. A mystery should be cleared up when a colleague confesses to some recent behavior that seems out of character. You may feel somewhat let down but not be inclined to take the matter further. A small legacy from a distant relative should finally come through, just in time to tide you over a difficult financial period. This might even prompt you to make your own will. Do not hesitate to make use of insider information to advance yourself at work. All is fair in love and war, and you know that your rivals would not hesitate if they were in your place. Get some fresh air this evening if you have been cooped up indoors all day.

13. FRIDAY. Fair. It can be hard not to feel a little anxiety when you see this date, even if you are not usually superstitious. However, edging into the day with a nervous attitude could actually attract bad luck, so think positive. You are reaching a crucial point of decision where joint finances are concerned. It is vital that you discuss fully with your mate or partner all available options for making the best use of your money. It should not be impossible to reach an agreement today. You may not be able to keep secrets from your colleagues for very long. Your honest and open Virgo nature makes it difficult to hide your true feelings. It would be best to admit any recent mistake rather than hope it goes unnoticed.

14. SATURDAY. Tricky. Although your romance appears to be going well, there is probably more happening just under the surface than you care to admit. If you have reasons to doubt the other person's motives, try to get to the truth of the matter. Money can slip through your fingers. There is a likelihood of squandering cash on items you do not really need or want, and also the danger of falling prey to a pickpocket unless you are vigilant. It would not be wise to attempt too much practical work.

This is an ideal evening to escape with a good video or book. If you decide to go out, avoid crowds.

15. SUNDAY. Unpredictable. It can be all too easy to get the wrong impression because loved ones are unlikely to express themselves very clearly. Make sure you have arrangements sorted out or there may be recriminations later on. Virgos trying to get in some quiet study are unlikely to do so without interruptions. Unfortunately the work you manage under such circumstances may not be up to your usual standards. To succeed, it will be necessary to be firm with intrusive family members. Some physical exercise can be beneficial; a long walk might appeal and also give you space to do some private thinking. Consider giving a home to a stray cat or dog.

16. MONDAY. Uncertain. The workweek may not begin in a very hopeful manner as the response to a recent application turns out to be disappointing. This can teach you not to pin your hopes on any one course of action; keep in mind that there are always alternative possibilities. A renewed interest in a serious subject that touches on the meaning of life should not be allowed to lapse. Visit your library or favorite web sites and search for meatier reading. An older relative's illness may make you want to do something to help. Certainly they will appreciate a visit and some flowers, or you might offer to do some housecleaning or yardwork.

17. TUESDAY. Opportune. Approach your work with a cheerful attitude and other people will be only too glad to give you their full support. This rule of life applies to all of your relationships. Remember that happiness is infectious. There is a risk that you may be tempted to dictate if you are given more responsibility than usual. Loved ones can be very useful in such situations, since they will soon tell you if you are getting pompous or overbearing. Getting your home fixed up exactly as you want it can cost a great deal of money. You must decide whether this is a priority or if there are other more urgent uses for your limited funds, such as a vacation or school tuition.

18. WEDNESDAY. Favorable. Turn your mind to making more money and see what ideas you come up with. As a Virgo you are certainly not afraid of hard work, which is a great help when extra funds are needed. A business matter that has been hanging fire should now be moving ahead once again. You have probably lost some momentum during the past few weeks and will need to work up enthusiasm in order to give it your best. At last a love affair that has been kept secret can be revealed to friends. This should make you feel much more secure about future prospects. Do not wait around hoping a loved one will call; take the initiative and get in touch without delay.

19. THURSDAY. Sensitive. Travel may be a problem. A trip planned for pleasure could turn out to be less than enjoyable. The best attitude to adopt is one of stoical acceptance; there is really no way you can hurry things along. Romance can get sidetracked for the silliest of reasons. It is vital that you let that special person in your life know what is on your mind. If you are disturbed they will sense it, and probably fear the worst. It would not be wise to splurge on an expensive vacation without first checking that it is really going to fulfill a dream. Otherwise disappointment is almost inevitable, and loved ones might blame you for building up their hopes and then letting them down.

20. FRIDAY. Good. Hobbies can become quite expensive when you get serious. If you are finding the cost of equipment a strain on your budget, it is time to consider how far you want to go. Ask yourself if it is essential to attain a professional standard, or would you be just as happy as an amateur? A small loan to a friend could become a source of embarrassment unless you make it absolutely plain just when and how you expect to be repaid. Taking a more serious interest in local politics can be rewarding. You should soon discover that it is possible to make positive changes, and this sense of personal power and responsibility can only boost your self-image as well as your reputation.

21. SATURDAY. Rewarding. It is fine to harbor a secret dream, but sooner or later you will have to let loved ones know about it if you are to begin your quest. Do not be afraid that they will mock you for being overly idealistic; they may well confide plans of their own in return. It could be time to revamp old but comfortable furniture; new covers would be a refreshing start. And the most well-worn wood will look all the better after some polishing. Find time to visit a relative who is ill, even if it cuts into your plans for the day. Put yourself in their shoes and you will realize how grateful they are that someone cares enough to make a little extra effort on their behalf.

22. SUNDAY. Spirited. Personal belongings have a way of disappearing at home, only to turn up somewhere you think you have searched several times. You have probably only mislaid an item that you fear is lost, so relax; it will reappear in its own good time. You may be romantically attracted to a newcomer to your social circle whose life is an unknown quantity. It would be intriguing to find out more about them. However, if they are overly secretive, warning bells should sound in your mind. Find an hour to go over finances with your mate or partner. There may be funds that had slipped your attention which would be extremely useful for a necessary purchase. Avoid using charge cards if possible.

23. MONDAY. Stressful. It may be difficult to even get through breakfast without angry words being spoken. Neither you nor your mate or partner are going to react very well to the beginning of the workweek. However, it is unfair to take out stress on each other, so try to contain yourself even under provocation. As a big project at work comes to a close, superiors could be looking for someone to blame in case the outcome is less than successful. Make sure you stay out of their sights or you might find yourself being held responsible for more than your fair share of involvement. Your Virgo gift of gab can get you out of a tight corner if you forget a promise or do not show up for an appointment.

24. TUESDAY. Lucky. Take the opportunity offered by a quiet start to this day to check out educational opportunities. Some diversifying could broaden your options for career development; see what is being offered. Dreams of long-distance travel may be fulfilled later in life, but at the moment a good book about exotic places might be enough to satisfy your wanderlust. A more businesslike image could be effective in promoting your own work. There is nothing like the appearance of success to impress potential customers. Resolve to leave the past behind you and cultivate a new, more optimistic and dynamic approach to all aspects of your life.

25. WEDNESDAY. Happy. You can get a new lease on life by incorporating alternative remedies into your health care. Take some expert advice and try aromatherapy or homeopathy; either can be gently effective. Daily chores may provide a quiet period during which you can mull over pressing concerns. It is surprising how much you can sort out in this way, almost without trying. Your romantic partner is likely to be doing wonders for your self-esteem. Having someone who genuinely appreciates your qualities and talents is very positive. Make sure you are equally as supportive of their strong points. A lottery or raffle ticket could be lucky for you.

26. THURSDAY. Misleading. Sometimes you just do not know where you stand when superiors give contradictory instructions. However, the problem may be that they do not know their own mind and are secretly hoping that you will make the right decision for them. Unfortunately you cannot rely on a friend's promise. In fact, you are probably aware that they have let down others before now, so it should not really be a surprise if the same thing happens to you. Unruly youngsters can be amused with any activity that occupies their lively minds, such as computer games. Dare to be different; buy an outfit that is more unusual than your normal taste.

27. FRIDAY. Demanding. A new structure of management at work may raise everyone's hopes of an improvement in working conditions. Unfortunately this only seems to be true for those at the top. If you want changes made at your level, you will have to start the ball rolling yourself. The temptation to splurge on large purchases for the home can be almost too much when you see furnishings that really appeal to you. However, it would not be wise to buy on impulse; first try to imagine just how the items would look once they are in position. Virgos who have been feeling blocked creatively can get off to a fresh start. Just do not fall into the trap of being overly ambitious.

28. SATURDAY. Challenging. Family relationships may not seem to be going at all smoothly at the moment. If jealousy has been aroused, it will be particularly challenging to make the peace between those involved. If you are entertaining at home, make sure the mix of guests is a safe one. Inviting friends who have problems getting along is just asking for trouble; you will not be able to rely on them behaving in a civilized fashion. A favorite piece of jewelry could be lost by sheer carelessness; check fastenings before you go out. Try to keep your temper with youngsters, even if they are more mischievous than usual. Trust your own instincts rather than advice from a so-called expert.

29. SUNDAY. Variable. A more assertive attitude can work wonders when it comes to sorting out problems with loved ones. As long as you know your own mind and state your opinions clearly, they should respond with respect. Be sure to get some exercise during the course of the day. Do not just talk about doing it; get out there and walk or jog. Plans for a weekend break may run into trouble when your ideas of a relaxing time do not match up with your your mate or partner's ideas. There is little point agreeing to do something that will only please one of you, so compromise is necessary. A quiet candlelit dinner for two can revive those old feelings of tenderness and romance.

30. MONDAY. Manageable. Either push yourself forward for promotion or you are apt to be overlooked; the choice is yours. It would be a pity to waste your talents when there is an opening just right for you to put them to full use. Virgos looking for romance may want to try a dating agency or personal ads in a magazine or newspaper. In this way you will get to meet a selection of possible partners, and they will be people who are not shy of commitment. Youngsters are likely to need a firm hand. Do not let them wear you down. Older relatives, especially parents, may be rather possessive at the moment, so you need to keep a cool head. Try to be objective with them, but point out that you are now an independent individual.

31. TUESDAY. Cautious. Pitting yourself against the combined forces of a loved one's family could be a waste of time. If they disagree with you, that will just have to be how it is. The most important thing is that you do not alienate the person you care for. A hasty action could result in a small accident. Be careful when working around the home, especially if you are using sharp tools. An old injury may flare up, causing you considerable inconvenience. It might be a good idea to visit the doctor to see if anything further can be done to alleviate the pain. Pets need especially gentle handling. Keep in mind that they depend on you totally.

NOVEMBER

1. WEDNESDAY. Exacting. There may be a strong temptation to get out of an awkward spot by being economical with the truth. However, honesty is definitely the best policy, if only because you are bound to be caught sooner or later if you are not truthful. You might have trouble with transportation over short distances. A problem could develop that makes you late for an appointment, only to disappear again mysteriously. Keep a stern eye on youngsters, who are apt to be in a more destructive mood than usual. It may be only natural curiosity that leads them to take things apart, but that is not much consolation when you are faced with a broken heirloom. Neither lend nor borrow anything of value.

2. THURSDAY. Excellent. Push ahead with current projects for self-development. Your Virgo determination to succeed is very strong. It is now possible to achieve more than usual, and every success will spur you on to ever greater heights. A romantic affair can advance to the next stage as you both begin to trust each other more. A deep connection gives you a profound sense of understanding without anything being said. Family events can help to renew relationships between relatives who have not met for some time. Blood is thicker than water, and even people with whom you do not have much in common can still become close simply because you are related. Accept any invitation you receive.

3. FRIDAY. Beneficial. Leisure pursuits will be more satisfying if you go into them in depth. It can benefit your self-image to push your talents as far as possible. A more creative approach to business may pay off. Applying some lateral thinking can help you get ahead of the opposition. You might have to spend more time than you realize trying to sort out details of written reports. There is a real danger of missing a vital deadline if you nitpick too much. The workday is likely to end on a rather unfocused note because no one seems able to concentrate. It might be smart to just call it a day and start the weekend early. Socializing this evening promises to be lighthearted and interesting.

4. SATURDAY. Fair. Sit back and take an overview of your current life. Review how far you have come this year toward achieving the goals you have set for yourself, and how much farther you would like to go in those directions. Household chores may seem less appealing than getting out into the wide world, so let them wait for once while you take a break. Close family members can be more understanding than you expect about the daily stresses of life. Everyone seems to have similar problems, and you can all support each other. Clearing out desk drawers may reveal letters waiting for an answer or bills that must be paid. Do not delay; begin making up for lost time. Entertaining at home should go well, so relax and enjoy the company.

5. SUNDAY. Variable. A cautious approach to the day would be wise. If you set out with high hopes of getting a lot done, you are bound to be disappointed. Caring for an older relative can be a demanding task. However, you owe them a debt, so try to fulfill your duties with good grace. A family day out will be more successful if you have a serious project in mind. It is easy to slip learning in by the back door so that youngsters find it enjoyable. Greater involvement in community affairs might seem a bit of a burden at first, but you will soon find it rewarding to improve conditions for yourself and your neighbors. You may even want to run for elective office.

6. MONDAY. Disappointing. There is no point claiming you can achieve more than is possible just because you want to impress someone. All that might happen is that you may fail and the person you are trying to impress will want nothing more to do with you. A legal case may not have the outcome that you expected, perhaps due to your unreasonably high expectations. There is nothing to do but swallow your disappointment and resolve not to make the same mistake again. Property negotiations could be causing some dissent between you and your mate or partner. Unless you are able to present a united front, you could be outsmarted at every turn.

7. TUESDAY. Expansive. Discussions with a friend or associate can be extremely profitable if they have some expertise you lack that would be essential to getting a project off the ground. If you are on the lookout for romance, enlarge your social circle and try meeting a different sort of person. Consider taking a leisure interest a step further by joining a club. Humor can be a vital ingredient in a close relationship; being able to laugh together can also get you through a tough period. Do not stonewall your mate or partner just to make the point that you are in a serious mood. It is safe to reveal your fondest hopes to one who loves you.

8. WEDNESDAY. Challenging. Gear up for a busy day. Mail is likely to be heavier than usual, and may contain some important items. It should be possible to get going on a work project that has been held up for some time. Essential information that you receive today should be the final piece of a jigsaw. Recent misunderstandings with loved ones can be cleared up if you have the humility to admit you were at least partly in the wrong. They are ready to forgive and forget. Out-of-town relatives could make a surprise visit, catching you on the run. They will not mind hospitality being rough and ready as long as you are genuinely pleased to see them.

9. THURSDAY. Uncertain. A loved one's confession could leave you feeling unsure about how to react. It is probably best to give yourself time to figure out exactly what the implications are. Be careful when using any electrical equipment; a faulty connection could cause a small shock. Try not to take any risks; if some electrical items are rather old, play safe and replace them. You can get to the bottom of a family mystery by asking those concerned a few pertinent questions. They might actually be glad to clear things up, allowing them to drop the emotional burden. Joint savings should be put into a sound, conservative investment, even if the returns are modest.

10. FRIDAY. Rewarding. Acting out of compassion is laudable, but it is foolish to do so if it hurts loved ones or yourself. Keep a sense of proportion so that you do not cause hardship for those close to you in favor of an idealistic cause. Resolve to give up an unhealthy habit that you no longer really enjoy. It could be something as simple as coffee, if you feel it is having a negative effect on your system. Where romance is concerned, all you should do right now is let events take their natural course. Do not begin to doubt that this relationship can be mutually satisfying on many levels. Travel requires some patience because delays and detours are likely.

11. SATURDAY. Stressful. A period of separation from a loved one could be wearing you down. The longer you are away from each other, the more you may worry about the relationship. Be assured, however, that once you are together again all will be well. Virgos considering a move need to decide whether to look around locally or in a wider area. There are many factors to take into account, but it is most important to find a house that seems comfortable from the first time you walk in the door. A close relationship could be threatened by a profound difference of opinion. Weigh whether other aspects of the involvement are strong enough to keep you together despite these differences.

12. SUNDAY. Sensitive. Allow self-doubt to creep in and the day can be ruined. You need to take the attitude that problems are there to be overcome, then believe that you can win over them. Dealing with parents or other older relatives requires a measure of patience when they stubbornly refuse to comply with your wishes. More tolerance on your part is also needed. Consult family members before making a decision that affects your everyday life. They will be just as involved as you in any change of routine. Consolidating plans for the future should help you feel a lot more secure. Check over your finances so that you have a clear idea of what you can reasonably buy without incurring overwhelming debt.

13. MONDAY. Exciting. A more creative period is about to begin for you. Do not be surprised if you wake up full of new ideas. Romance is favored because you are putting out the sort of vibrations that attract the opposite sex to you. Just remember to be a bit discriminating about who you get involved with; for once you can pick and choose. A chance for advancement in your job may come up; jump at it. Even an increase in responsibilities should be well within your scope. Work on your home is likely to be disruptive for some time, and tempers might fray in the uncomfortable conditions. The results, however, will be well worth the inconvenience, so be patient.

14. TUESDAY. Lively. Your input in a meeting may not seem to be appreciated as much as you think it should. In fact, there could be active opposition to your ideas, a sign that you may need to rethink them or at least tone them down. A close friendship may be developing along romantic lines, although neither of you admits it. Sooner or later you will be aware that you are emotionally involved, and then you can decide what to do about it. Public speaking is rarely a favorite occupation of Virgos, but as long as you have the strength of your convictions there is nothing to worry about. A night out on the town with friends should be stimulating.

15. WEDNESDAY. Confusing. It is natural to have an emotional rapport with a loved one that puts you on the same wavelength. Sometimes, however, it is also necessary to make your thoughts clear. Do not assume that you agree about issues you have never discussed; misunderstandings could heap up if you do so. The result of a competition might be somewhat disappointing, particularly if you were fairly convinced you would win. Chance plays a role in everything, and this time luck may have been against you. Friends can be almost bullying when they are eager to have your company. However, do not let them railroad you into going along with their plans if your heart is not in it.

16. THURSDAY. Buoyant. Put all your energy into pushing ahead with a personal goal and you stand every chance of a satisfying achievement. Being more extroverted than usual will convince other people of the seriousness of your intentions. It is important that any financial deal be absolutely ethical. If you are hoping to improve your security, do not be tempted to take any shortcuts. Work off excess energy in the health club or on a jogging trail. Otherwise you may find it difficult to settle down to tasks demanding concentrated effort this evening. You can make your voice heard in a local meeting. If you have a point to make, do not hesitate to speak up even in front of a hostile crowd.

17. FRIDAY. Fair. Recent problems you may have been experiencing in romance cannot all be blamed on your mate or partner. If you search your own heart, it should become clear that you must take a share of the blame. And you also need to take your share of responsibility to sort out the relationship. You will probably work best alone; distractions will be unwelcome. Make the most of the end of the workweek by completing unfinished business rather than starting anything new. Be very careful not to lean too much on the sympathy of a friend. This can stir up deeper emotions than you might be prepared to deal with, so moderate your demands. You are the perfect choice to lead a volunteer project.

18. SATURDAY. Changeable. Unless you make sure arrangements for the weekend are crystal clear, loved ones may blame you when things go wrong. Your own health or a youngster's may give you some anxious moments. Be sure to get sufficient rest. At this time of year it is especially important to eat well. You can also benefit from a daily vitamin supplement to your diet. A casual piece of gossip may throw doubts on your view of a current romantic relationship. You probably already know that the liaison is not perfect, but you must decide how much you are prepared to tolerate. Even though you might feel rather locked away from the world at home, a lengthy outing is unlikely to make you feel any more connected.

19. SUNDAY. Problematic. Loved ones may overrule you when it comes to deciding how to get the best out of the day. This is one time when you probably cannot get what you want, but at least you can please other people. Travel arrangements are apt to be delayed. Your plans might have to be revised as available time begins to dwindle. Keeping youngsters entertained will probably test all of your powers of patience and imagination. Where romance is concerned, it would be unwise to leave important words unsaid. The other person cannot guess your thoughts and could be waiting for reassurance. An attempt to organize paperwork is almost certain to fail; leave it for another time.

20. MONDAY. Reassuring. A new course of study could be just what is needed to fill your evenings. Find out what is available at local evening classes. A recent connection with a distant business concern may soon bring you some well-deserved praise. If you get the opportunity, build on this success; it can do your career a world of good. You can inspire friends and coworkers by a more personal touch. Sometimes it is appropriate to divulge information about yourself that can add an extra dimension to your relationships. Spending time at work chatting is not always a waste of time; you can learn a lot about each other's goals and dreams.

21. TUESDAY. Spirited. Inspiration may strike as you ponder how to increase your income by developing your natural talents.

It is unlikely that a money-making scheme will bring in much at first, but every little bit helps; there may be room for expansion later. Virgos looking for a new job may want to enlist the help of someone who is in a position of power. If they can pull a few strings on your behalf and mention your name, there is no telling where it might lead. Romance must not be one-sided. Do not put yourself out so much that your own needs and wishes go unnoticed. Unless relationships are based on give-and-take, equality is impossible.

22. WEDNESDAY. Chancy. You are heading for fireworks in a close relationship if you insist on maintaining your freedom at all costs. It is often not easy to get the balance right between intimacy and independence, but this should be your ideal. It would be unwise to play fast and loose with your personal finances right now. There may be the chance of making a fast buck, but the risk is apt to be unacceptably high. Leisure pursuits could be taking up so much of your time that you are beginning to neglect more serious concerns, such as getting paid work done. While your creativity must be nurtured, obligations must be fulfilled as well.

23. THURSDAY. Sensitive. Your Virgo critical faculty usually warns you when people are trying to pull the wool over your eyes. But on this holiday, as loved ones gather, there is a strong likelihood of your being taken in. A relative or friend may be trying to cover up a problem and buy time to patch it up, but this should not be allowed to go unnoticed. You are now more susceptible than usual to a sales pitch. Unless you have already decided to buy, try to restrain yourself. Otherwise you may end up spending your hard-earned cash on goods you do not really want or need. Pets may vanish for a while, but they are bound to be somewhere in the neighborhood so there is no need to panic.

24. FRIDAY. Good. If you are selling goods or property, make sure you get a price that is fair. It should not be difficult to do so because the buyer seems keen to finalize the deal. An emergency within the family might upset everyone briefly, but the situation is unlikely to amount to much. A positive outcome may be that you are drawn closer to relatives you do not often see. This is a good time to establish a secure plan for future savings. Even if you can only put away a small amount it is important that you make a start. Getting a written report finished should present no problems. In fact, if you approach the work with interest, it should actually be enjoyable.

25. SATURDAY. Demanding. Virgos caring for youngsters can expect to have a very busy time. They are likely to be real live wires, so do not plan any activity unless you will have sufficient time to give them your full attention. A radical reorganization of your environment could give you a fresh lease on life. Do not allow yourself to get stuck in a rut; go in search of some new impressions to stimulate your mind and your creative powers. Local shopping might be so lengthy and frustrating that you come home tired but without having found what you wanted. The most positive way of looking at this situation is to consider that you have at least saved some money.

26. SUNDAY. Smooth. Entertaining at home should be very successful. You do not need to worry about the details. Just let the get-together unfold in its own manner. Be sure to leave room for your guests' spontaneity. Romance may be just around the corner. Even if you have been without a partner for some time, take heart. A quite ordinary friendship could slowly mature into a close relationship that is all the stronger for having developed over time. Although you might wake up with big plans for what you want to do today, it would be wiser to be modest in your arrangements. In fact, more can probably be achieved in this way and with a greater sense of satisfaction.

27. MONDAY. Beneficial. Your health will receive a real boost from some extra exercise. Just keep in mind that moderation should be observed in all things. At the same time, do not be too lackadaisical. Home renovations should be going well; you are bound to be pleased to have more interesting surroundings. However, do not get too carried away or you will not be satisfied until the whole house is transformed. A more open attitude to achieving cooperation at work can be effective. Small groups might work together especially well, giving an almost family-like atmosphere of support. Stay at home tonight to recuperate after this busy day.

28. TUESDAY. Cautious. Be more careful than usual if you are driving. There is a tendency to consider yourself king of the road, but other drivers will not necessarily give way to you. You are unlikely to impress those in authority by being long-winded. Keep all reports and verbal statements short and to the point. Mulling over vacation plans for next summer can brighten a dark day, but there is little point being overly optimistic about what you can afford. In fact, browsing through expensive brochures might just induce a feeling of discontent. A romantic attachment may have to be played down until friends get used to the idea of your unlikely pairing with someone considerably older or younger.

29. WEDNESDAY. Tricky. Although recent spending on frivolous items has probably been pleasurable, the reckoning is inevitable. Just make sure you do not leave yourself short when it comes to buying essential items. It is true that money cannot buy love. Attempting to impress a romantic prospect by being overly generous is unlikely to be an effective ploy. In addition, you might always suspect that the other person was more interested in your money than in you. This is a favorable time for all social events. Do not be a hermit; go out and enjoy yourself. All work and no play makes a person dull, and as a Virgo you do tend to take life a little too seriously.

30. THURSDAY. Mixed. Your usual powers of organization may have failed you, making you unsure how to get some urgent work done on time. This is just where colleagues can step in and lend a helping hand. Your health is apt to be a little under par; you are now vulnerable to catching a cold. If you come down with a virus, take off enough time to recuperate properly or you will just become ill again. Youngsters should be doing well in their classes. You can do wonders in encouraging their sense of achievement. You may want to inspire them to take up an extracurricular activity through their school, such as sports or debating.

DECEMBER

1. FRIDAY. Challenging. Putting the final details of a plan into place might seem almost more than you can stand because you are so impatient to see the project as a whole. If you let the quality of your work drop, however, it could spoil the whole thing. It is time to give some serious thought to getting ahead in your career. Find out what options are open to you, and vow not to get stuck in a dead-end job. Youngsters are likely to come out with wisdom beyond their years. As well as being amusing, often their innocent remarks hit on truths you tend to avoid. The results of a recent diet or fitness drive should be satisfactory although you still have a way to go.

2. SATURDAY. Changeable. Shopping can be an interesting experience. Even if you go out looking for ordinary household items, you are likely to come back with unusual gifts for loved ones and even for yourself. This is a good day to buy or adopt a pet. You may decide to avoid run-of-the-mill animals; the family may get special pleasure from an exotic or pedigreed pet that is a real focus of interest. You may not seem able to find emotional equilibrium, noticing your mood changing from one minute to the next. It can be rather difficult for other people to have to cope with these swings, but with a little sustained effort you should be able to get some measure of control over them and get back on the right track.

3. SUNDAY. Erratic. There is every possibility of upsets because no one in the family is listening to anyone else. Instead of just talking past each other, allot a set time for everyone to have their say. Otherwise the day could dissolve into chaos. Getting household chores out of the way can be more challenging than usual, particularly with youngsters demanding your undivided attention. They may need everything explained to them, but teaching them in this way is more important than completing your tasks. Make time to get in touch with a brother, sister, or other relative you do not often talk to. It is too easy to slip out of contact. You will find plenty to discuss, including some surprises.

4. MONDAY. Tense. If you work from home, you could find yourself in legal trouble unless you get your paperwork sorted out. You cannot afford to make mistakes on accounts or other records; try to be more careful. Tension may be rumbling below the surface at work. Because a colleague's hidden resentment could effectively sabotage an important project, the matter needs to be cleared up as quickly as possible. Right now you cannot afford to take anything your mate or partner says for granted. They are in no mood to be brushed aside or ignored. Unless you give them your full and complete attention, there could be serious repercussions later in your relationship.

5. TUESDAY. Excellent. At last a romantic affair is beginning to crystallize into something more solid. You have probably waited a long time for this, so do not risk your happiness now by trying to rush things. Your creative powers are apt to be developing in the direction of more serious pursuits. Even a hobby needs to have a meaningful content to truly satisfy you. A recent attempt to put money aside should now enable you to spend a sizeable lump sum on pure pleasure. Indulging yourself will do you a world of good. Plan a getaway with your mate or partner; you will both benefit from escaping the strains of everyday life if only for a long weekend.

6. WEDNESDAY. Fortunate. Virgos who are looking for a new home may just find a dream house today. Whatever your luck, you are bound to see some unusual properties that broaden your ideas of what you would like to buy. Your nervous system can derive great benefit from a soothing sauna or massage. You need total relaxation and escape from the world. As one job ends, the opportunity for a less mainstream career may beckon. It is up to you whether you feel confident enough to step off the beaten track. If you have suffered recent heartache, you might find counseling helpful in expressing and coming to terms with your turbulent feelings.

7. THURSDAY. Difficult. Loved ones may not seem at all sure of what or how they are feeling at the moment. First they may say one thing and then another, leaving you unable to decide which is closer to the truth. A business project demands some bold thinking on your part. Although it is necessary to appear totally confident, do not be tempted to overextend yourself or you could crash in flames. If your mate or partner seems to be spending longer hours than usual at work, you are bound to feel somewhat neglected. However, right now this overtime is probably unavoidable, so summon up your reserves of sympathy when they come home tired and do not give them a hard time.

8. FRIDAY. Demanding. The result of an interview or test is not likely to please you very much. However, there is nothing to be done but learn a lesson from the experience and resolve to work harder next time. You may be required to travel quite far for work purposes, which could be inconvenient. However, if you do not go with good grace, there is little chance of coming home with success under your belt. Do not lose sight of the larger things in life as you daily struggle to get ahead. Unless you have long-term goals in view, what you are doing now may seem fairly pointless. A period of better relations at work is dawning, so make a point of socializing more with higher-ups as well as colleagues.

9. SATURDAY. Pleasurable. For once you can afford to loosen up and have some fun. Social events should be very pleasurable, and you should not even object to being the center of attention. A new acquaintance may turn out to have some influence in the sphere of your work. Do not pass up the chance to get to know them better; you never know when a word from them might come in handy. Even though you may feel like doing some serious study, it is apt to be quite difficult to find time to yourself. You could spend a more useful hour drawing up a timetable to get your free time better organized. An early night will do you a world of good.

10. SUNDAY. Promising. A new romance promises a more settled relationship than those you may be used to. You may feel the need to spice it up a little, but it would be very unwise to rock the boat in any way. This is a good time to plan ahead. Sit down with your mate or partner and discuss what you both have in mind for the future. Unless you have some firm aims, you will tend to drift from day to day without achieving anything very lasting. A trip to a romantic spot could put extra zest back in a close relationship. Pick somewhere with happy memories, and spring it as a surprise on your loved one. Try not to say anything controversial at a social event.

11. MONDAY. Fair. Life has come to the point when it is finally clear that you must find a way to balance career and family. Juggling the two means giving less than your best to both. Now you need to focus your energies. A new start bodes well for future self-development plans. You have gained an inner sense of authority which should enable you to take on ever more impressive projects. Money accumulated over the past few months can come

in handy for improvements to your home. Discuss with your mate
or partner what you both think is vital, then hire a professional
to do as good a job as possible. Do not take out your impatience
on children or pets.

12. TUESDAY. Misleading. Unless you say exactly what is on
your mind, loved ones will be left in the dark. There is nothing
to be gained by brooding in silence. What is needed is an open,
honest exchange of opinions. If you do not want to attend a family
occasion, do not let relatives persuade you against your will.
Sometimes it is important for family members to realize that you
have other commitments in your life that take precedence over
them. There could be some rather murky dealing going on as a
long series of negotiations is finally wrapped up. It might be better
to turn a blind eye if you do not have the power to intervene. It
is best not to get involved.

13. WEDNESDAY. Mixed. You could find the claims of an idealistic group beginning to encroach on your life. It is a good idea
to participate, but not to the point that you begin to resent the
time you spend on it. A social event may cause conflict with
friends, as small disagreements spoil otherwise enjoyable activities. If you are tempted to step in as peacemaker, be careful you
do not end up being blamed by both sides. Loved ones may encourage you to be more ambitious when it comes to honing your
Virgo talents. With their support behind you, it should be possible
to achieve more than you might think. Help out a friend who
needs a shoulder to cry on.

14. THURSDAY. Tricky. Someone who appears quite glamorous
to you may be putting on the charm deliberately. You may not
realize until too late that they are using you, so be very wary of
getting involved. It can be tempting to remember the past in a
sentimental light, but that may only make you dissatisfied with the
present. Memories are precious but can easily be distorted; it
would be a shame to rewrite your history. If you are feeling run-
down, make sure you are not burning the candle at both ends.
Fitting in both work and play can be demanding. Your body is
not designed to be pushed to its limits without time off for recu-
peration.

15. FRIDAY. Diverse. Daily routine tasks do not always have to
be done in the same way. Varying your habits can actually be very
liberating. Eventually you might even discover more efficient ways
of working. A workplace flirtation may depend more on mental
stimulation than physical attraction. It would be a good idea to
socialize and become friends, rather than pursuing a rather su-

perficial relationship. Do an elderly relative or neighbor a good turn, and the reward will be in their appreciation. Even small acts take on greater significance when they are done with true affection. Do not work yourself so hard that your nerves suffer; ease up a little.

16. SATURDAY. Easygoing. It can be rather difficult to focus on what you want to do because you are not really sure what would appeal most. For this reason let loved ones or friends do the choosing, and at least you will get pleasure from their enjoyment of the day. If you are trying to save money, shopping can be quite a challenge. You are likely to spend a lot without even being particularly extravagant, but you will want the best quality. It is not vital right now to have a strong sense of direction. More important is concentating on close relationships. Once you feel secure and loved, your creative potential will begin to flow and your self-assurance soar.

17. SUNDAY. Quiet. You are apt to feel quite tired, with any thought of exertion not at all pleasing. Leave heavy work to those who want to get some exercise. Pamper yourself on this traditional day of rest. Youngsters may be quieter than usual. If you try to find out what they are up to, they can be rather evasive. As long as they seem happily occupied, it is probably safe to leave them to their own devices. If you need to talk over issues with your parents or other relatives, it would be nice to do so over a meal. You will find agreement easier to reach if you all feel relaxed. A meeting at a friend's house could plunge you into the middle of a religious or political controversy.

18. MONDAY. Opportune. A financial transaction that has been hanging fire can be brought to a close at last. You should find that it has been worthwhile holding out to get the terms you want. It is not too soon to start thinking about finalizing plans for the end of the month. It would be a sound plan to have some small presents ready to exchange for surprise gifts that you receive. Try to work out a reasonable budget to cover all eventualities. A certain amount of tension may escalate if a loved one feels you are leaving them behind due to your efforts toward self-development. It is up to them to attempt to keep up with you; they should not hold you back.

19. TUESDAY. Beneficial. A romantic affair may begin to affect you more deeply as you discuss matters that are intimate and personal. Once you have overcome the first feelings of shyness, this profound sharing can be comforting and beneficial. Your health can be improved by eating less junk food. Try to avoid all harmful substances for a few days, and stick to a plain diet. The results should soon show in a clear skin, sparkling eyes, and renewed vigor. Your finances seem to be looking good right now. A habit of keeping detailed accounts enables you to keep a tight check on your everyday spending. If the current system works, you would be wise to stick to it.

20. WEDNESDAY. Good. Knowing more about your family background can give you a better sense of identity. It should be possible to find out about your predecessors from older relatives, who will probably be only too delighted to reminisce. If the opportunity arises to make some extra money, jump at it. Although your leisure time is precious, a temporary increase in your income will compensate for lost hours of relaxation. For once you should try to delegate some routine work to colleagues. You are not at your most organized, and will probably find it a challenge to remember appointments. Write down times and places for a meeting rather than trusting your memory.

21. THURSDAY. Spirited. It might be difficult to get much done today because the temptation to chat and gossip is strong. Other people will probably resent it if you try to cut short their conversations, so enter into the spirit. Try to fit in a shopping trip for household essentials so that you have one less task to occupy your mind over the coming days. A close relationship has become rather delicate; you may find it hard to say the right thing. Realize that the other person needs to be reassured about your affection, although they may not quite know how to tell you without making themselves vulnerable to your reaction.

22. FRIDAY. Bright. Gather yourself together and concentrate so that you can finish off outstanding work and leave everything shipshape for the holiday period. The reward for this will be a clear conscience and a feeling of satisfaction for work well done. Personal finances are in the spotlight. Look for ways to add to your savings. It would be ideal to find an investment that gives a steady return rather than something more risky. Youngsters are likely to be full of energy; it will take a considerable effort to keep them under control. Be prepared for heavy traffic to slow up a journey, although you should not have any urgent appointments. Allow extra time to board a train or plane.

23. SATURDAY. Manageable. The focus today is on last-minute shopping. It would be unwise to go far; look around locally and you should find everything you need. Just try to stay calm and in control. There may be some disagreements between family members as to arrangements for a gathering of the clan. Arrangements are never easy to sort out, and you will probably just waste valuable energy if you get involved. Recent high expenditure may have left you a bit short of cash at a crucial time. Loved ones, however, might be a little better off, and they should be able to give you a loan for the amount you need without inconveniencing themselves.

24. SUNDAY. Happy. Virgos who have been hoping for a romantic moment will probably not be disappointed. At last someone is going to pluck up enough courage to reveal their feelings toward you, then be on tenterhooks to know if you have the same feelings. A new health regime can do wonders for your sense of well-being. Every improvement in your health will give you additional zest for life. Keeping large presents hidden until the time is right to give them need not be a problem if you enlist the help of a neighbor. Avoid arguing with loved ones as much as possible; tension can strain the home atmosphere, but a dose of good humor should ease the situation.

25. MONDAY. Merry Christmas! The emphasis today is on relaxation. As long as you have done enough advance preparation, it should be possible to sit back and enjoy a pleasurable day. You will probably want friends and family around, and everyone is likely to be in a harmonious mood. Virgo romantics could be delighted with a surprise organized by a loved one to brighten the day. In fact, this can mark the beginning of a new phase in your relationship. Youngsters may be difficult to control and could get overly excited unless you exert a calming influence. Make a point of calling distant family members who cannot be with you on this special day.

26. TUESDAY. Calm. There is no need to make much effort today. This should be a time for winding down from the whole year. Ignore what you think you should be doing; for once you can put obligations and duties to one side and just concentrate on enjoying yourself. Youngsters will probably occupy themselves with a minimum of interference on your part. However, you might actually get pleasure from joining in their play and games. A romantic affair should be giving you a deep sense of satisfaction. Do not worry about how it is going to develop in the future. Just take it day by day, letting time take care of the rest.

27. WEDNESDAY. Favorable. This is an excellent day to do some serious reading. Take this opportunity to open a book you have been meaning to study for some time; it should be extremely rewarding. You and a loved one might want to brighten the dark winter hours by beginning to plan your next vacation. Make a resolution to start saving for it now so that you can treat yourselves to a dream trip somewhere you have always wanted to visit. Youngsters can show a surprising understanding of a subject you expect would be beyond them; all of your encouragement given now will bear fruit. There is no reason you cannot teach them things they do not learn in school.

28. THURSDAY. Unsettling. If you are feeling somewhat under the weather, adding more vitamins to your diet might be just the thing to buck you up. You need to eat well in order to boost your ability to fight off viruses; otherwise you may get one cold after another. It might be difficult to get organized. Normally simple tasks can take surprisingly long to complete. Your mind is apt to be elsewhere, mulling over a problem that might actually be beyond your capability to solve. Virgos who have been feeling unhappy on the job might find help at hand. It is unlikely that your good work has gone unnoticed; someone in authority is prepared to recommend you for a new opening.

29. FRIDAY. Challenging. A romantic liaison is in danger of coming to an end unless you can quickly settle your differences of opinion. It is up to you to decide if your principles are really more important than this relationship, and whether you are willing to hurt someone just to prove you are right. Money is apt to be somewhat tight after your recent expenditures. Now would be a good time to decide in what areas you can make savings. There may be several little luxuries that you would not really notice doing without for a while. Take care if you are doing practical tasks around the house. Proceed slowly should be your motto or there could be a small accident with a sharp instrument.

30. SATURDAY. Lively. Beware of trying to be too controlling of loved ones. They need freedom of choice just as much as you do, and will resent being swept along while you please yourself. Compromise is the essential factor in healing a rift with parents or other older relatives. You may simply have to bow to their wishes this once, even if it hurts your pride to do so. After the recent period of leisure, you may now have quite itchy feet and be eager to get on the move. A long drive would do you good, or a walk in the park; anything that gives you a change of scene and some fresh impressions unlocks your imagination. Conversations with your mate or partner can be particularly spirited and inspiring.

31. SUNDAY. Inspiring. As the year draws to a close, you have much to look back on and celebrate. Make a resolution to build during the coming months on the progress you have achieved in creative endeavors. This is a very fruitful path to pursue. Youngsters' education is likely to be on your mind. Any doubts or problems should be fully discussed with their teacher or school principal. You will probably find ways to improve prospects if you give it some serious thought. Recent tensions within the home may still be causing some trouble. If you allow this situation to continue, it could spoil an otherwise promising time. Try to sort out the problem without delay. Enjoy evening partying with the person who is most important to you.

VIRGO
NOVEMBER–DECEMBER 1999

November 1999

1. MONDAY. Calm. Someone who is working behind the scenes on your behalf is likely to do you a few favors. This is a useful day for catching up on neglected tasks which have been put aside for far too long. The atmosphere at work should seem warmer than usual, with people taking time to look out for each other. For Virgos who have been temporarily out of work, now is a good time to renew efforts to find another job. Get back in touch with an agency that helped you in the past. If you have moved, a potential employer may have no way of contacting you. Be sure to dress conservatively for an interview or meeting.

2. TUESDAY. Variable. This is another helpful day for completing neglected tasks so that you are ready for new starts. You may surprise yourself at the amount of work you are able to get through. Any matter which requires close cooperation with other people needs to be handled with care. Others are apt to be sensitive about your attitude. As a Virgo you have a tendency to sometimes be critical. Because of this, try hard not to allow this to show through in any conversation you have or any letters that you write. Discussions relating to property matters can be difficult. You may have to work hard to understand a banker's jargon and understand exactly what is at stake.

3. WEDNESDAY. Useful. If you have been feeling rather upset, today you should be able to find a way to perk yourself up. This is a good time for brightening your personal image. Treat yourself to a new outfit or a different hair style. If you are going for an interview or out to a business lunch, feeling good about your appearance can do much to boost your overall confidence. It should be easier to unleash your creativity on new work projects. The newness of what is taking place now is sure to stimulate you. Do not be afraid to push forward with your own ideas in the workplace. An influential figure is watching with interest and waiting to see what you can accomplish.

231

4. THURSDAY. Excellent. If you are still in the mood to improve your image, this is a propitious day to shop for new clothes. You have a good eye for color and style. Try to buy a complete outfit, including shoes and accessories. If you recently lost any property, it might be worth inquiring at all the stores and restaurants where you were and also putting an ad in the newspaper. It is possible that someone was honest enough to turn in the item. This is a good day for working up a new decorating scheme for your home. This evening you may end up feeling more positive about a get-together you have not had much enthusiasm about since accepting the invitation.

5. FRIDAY. Cautious. No matter how hard you try to be careful with your money, there are times when you end up going over the top. This is likely to be one of those days. If you do not really need to go out shopping, postpone the trip until another day so that you do not put temptation in your own path. You should be able to smooth over a relationship with someone you argued with lately. Sometimes it is through pure practical necessity that people cut through emotional red tape and take steps toward reconciliation. Do not worry about trying to anticipate what moves others may make; they are apt to catch you off guard.

6. SATURDAY. Difficult. Try to make this weekend easy on yourself. There are some individuals who will always rub you the wrong way because of a basic personality clash. Give such a person a wide berth. This is another day when the spending bug can bite you. If you go out shopping with your mate or with a friend, you may be inclined to spend less simply because the other person is there to witness what you do. For Virgo parents, children may be quite demanding today. You may need a break with purely adult company for a while. A neighbor may be prepared to do you a favor. Money due you from a friend may not be repaid as promised.

7. SUNDAY. Uncertain. You may not be in a position to make definite plans or commitments at the moment. Be honest about this rather than making any promise you may not be able to keep. If you are unattached, it can be difficult to get a new relationship off the ground. You may suddenly become tongue-tied in the presence of someone you find attractive, or when they call you on the phone. This is not the time to try to explain yourself. Instead, try not to worry too much about making a good impression. Just be yourself and act naturally. Chances are the other person is just as nervous as you and may be harboring the same doubts.

8. MONDAY. Sensitive. A new relationship may be slow to get off the ground, perhaps because both of you have work or family commitments. This is a favorable day to try to arrange to spend time together. It is possible that you will discover that you have more in common than you originally thought. In your business dealings it may be necessary to have more discussions than you anticipated, particularly in relation to beginning a new project. If you are not looking sufficiently to the future, others may have a curious way of reminding you to do so. Sometimes it is not a bad move to be a little impatient; let your feelings show.

9. TUESDAY. Satisfactory. As a Virgo you tend to function best when you are given clear guidance and then left to get on with the job. Today you may receive more of a free rein than usual. Do not hesitate to try out new working methods. Although what is tried-and-tested may be safe, you will not find other, perhaps better ways if you never give them a fair trial. For self-employed Virgos, this is a time to take a few well-calculated risks. There may be a very lucrative opportunity which requires a leap of faith in your own future. Do not be afraid to take that vital step. A family gathering should be very enjoyable this evening, especially if children are included.

10. WEDNESDAY. Challenging. If all is not rosy at home this morning, do not worry too much. Any small step which you take to try to smooth over the situation should achieve desired results. If someone close to you seems moody, the subtle approach is likely to be the best way to jolly them out of it. If you work for yourself, you may be thinking about acquiring property or merging with another business. You can afford to be innovative and consider unusual propositions. The time is ripe for expanding into new territory. If you work from home, consider sharing office space or hiring a professional telephone answering service.

11. THURSDAY. Buoyant. This is a day for thinking big in all respect. Self-employed Virgo people may now be in a position to afford to expand. If you have tended in the past to take on more work than you can comfortably manage, think carefully about how to organize in the future. There are a lot of options, and you need to be very selective this time around. It makes sense to opt for the higher earning option even if you are not totally convinced that it will be a success. New enterprises begun now are likely to prove more profitable than you expect. Keep tonight free of social engagements so you can get extra rest.

12. FRIDAY. Variable. The usual ideas you have for entertainment may seem too expensive, or maybe you want to treat yourself without going over a budget. In either case, consider what option will satisfy you while not breaking the bank. A friend may come up with some helpful ideas or even some practical support. If you are looking for a new place to live or for new office space and are concerned about the cost, it may be possible to juggle around your budget and find a way to afford what you want. This should be a satisfying end to the working week if you get together socially with colleagues this evening.

13. SATURDAY. Stressful. This can be quite a difficult day unless you stay in tight control. For Virgos who are in business, working relationships may be going through a more than usually demanding period. It may be a good idea to offer incentives, however small, in order to try to raise general morale. This is not the best time to bring up sensitive issues; you could end up creating further friction. In a close personal relationship you may not be able to resist saying what is on your mind. It could be important to discuss plans for the future no matter how wary you are of tackling the subject. Such a discussion could end up putting the relationship on a more stable footing.

14. SUNDAY. Unsettling. A romance which has had its ups and downs recently should be smoother today. It is likely that you will be able to talk you way through any problems or misunderstandings. Plans can be made for the future with relative ease. Arrangements relating to a long-distance trip that are upset at the last minute could be very annoying. It may actually benefit you to express how you feel in no uncertain terms. Others who are taking a lot for granted might end up taking you more seriously. Do not worry about a friendship that seems stressful just now. Keep in mind that no relationship is easygoing all of the time. If you have a sound basis, it will endure.

15. MONDAY. Fair. You can look forward to a productive start to the working week. You may need to work at a slower than usual rate, however, in order to ensure that mistakes are not made. This is a propitious day for starting a new project or even a job. You should have few problems getting along with colleagues. Be prepared to gradually learn a new technique or procedure. You are likely to achieve less by trying to race ahead or by pretending that you know it all. More experienced people, even those younger than you, are likely to be more than happy to fill you in on details relating to equipment or paperwork with which you are not familiar. Remind yourself that being professional does not have to mean being perfect.

16. TUESDAY. Productive. In your business dealings a more lighthearted attitude can work wonders. While you want to present a professional front, others can feel you are making too much of a casual situation by approaching it in deadly earnest. You can win other people's confidence by opening up a little. Although you may not like to admit to making mistakes or taking shortcuts, doing so can improve overall cooperation. After all, everyone is human with special talents and some flaws. And everyone makes mistakes. Anyone who pretends that they do not can seem a little too daunting for comfort or become a target for blame.

17. WEDNESDAY. Disconcerting. If relations with a loved one have been tense lately, do not put off a heart-to-heart talk any longer. Matters which have brewing below the surface are likely to come to a head of their own accord. As a Virgo you do not often lose your temper, but when you do you arc usually precise and forceful. This makes it crystal clear that you are not joking. If you feel that your recent emotional outburst was unjustified, it is up to you to apologize and try to make amends. However, if you feel you had every right to be angry, stand your ground. Only in that way will your feelings be respected.

18. THURSDAY. Pleasant. Relations with those you are close to should be a lot easier going today. If there have been eruptions in a partnership lately, the storm should calm now. It is likely that you will receive an apology from someone whose actions or words have been out of line. A letter in today's mail is likely to be heartening. Single Virgo men and women who recently met a potential partner may receive an encouraging communication from this new person. Tempting invitations are coming your way. If you are going out on a date this evening, expect it to be quite romantic.

19. FRIDAY. Good. An unusual partnership that you recently entered into has now passed the make-or-break stage. Review all of your relationships overall, including friendships. It may have lately become obvious to you that certain individuals are staying in your life only so long as you prove useful to them. This is a time to drop one particular individual who is doing too much leaning on you. There is little point continuing any relationship that is burdensome. If necessary, make the decision to cut loose. A new commitment relating to a business interest is likely to fill you with hope for the future. This is a starred time for a merger.

20. SATURDAY. Frustrating. It is necessary to get your finances in order this weekend. If you have a lot of debts to repay, you may have to spread your money around, paying a little here and there. You could need to renegotiate payment deadlines, especially if money due you has not come in as expected. Virgo people involved in a difficult relationship may no longer want to simply drift along in the hope that things will sort themselves out eventually. You will be best off taking more positive action. You may even decide to issue an ultimatum in order to find out if any real future commitment is possible.

21. SUNDAY. Rewarding. A joint partnership, whether relating to business or to your more private life, should be going from strength to strength. This is a favorable day for enjoying more of the good things in life. A raise in pay for you or for your mate may allow you to indulge in luxuries which you could not previously afford. You may feel an urge to get away together for a change of scene later in the day but not know where to go. Put your heads together and you are bound to come up with a good idea. Try not to set off too late; the traffic may be unpredictable and a restaurant or theater very crowded.

22. MONDAY. Disquieting. This is one of those days when you are likely to be very restless. If you are going on a long trip, the change of scene may do you good. However, there could be more delays to contend with than you expect. If you are driving, the trip could turn out to be especially tiring. It might be better to take public transportation if you have the option. There will be a number of routine matters to tie up before you can get out of town. You could spend a lot of time talking to people but elicit little information from them. You have to work hard to make your point in order to get the results that you want.

23. TUESDAY. Changeable. If you concentrate firmly on what you want to achieve, you should be able to make a dream come true. This is not one of your easier days, however. A work superior or other authority figure may not give you the approval or recommendation you seek. Do not give up at the first obstacle, however. Some people can be talked around to see things your way if you are prepared to humble yourself a little. Sometimes a formal request for help can get lost amid the bureaucracy. Be prepared to try a more personal approach, which should produce much more positive results. Use humor to ward off an argument.

24. WEDNESDAY. Lucky. If you have been thinking about trying to change track where career matters are concerned, this is a good day for taking the first step. Authority figures are likely to give you the support you need. If you are concerned about conditions at work which affect both you and fellow employees, this is a favorable time to speak up about them. You may be surprised at how effective you can be when you focus on resolving a problem rather than just complaining about it. News which comes your way concerning a property matter or proposed move is likely to be encouraging. People could be more agreeable than you expect.

25. THURSDAY. Enjoyable. Family matters are likely to be quite smooth on this Thanksgiving Day. If you recently asked a loved one for a special favor, you are likely to be feeling confident of the result. You may have enough time to get down to some basic fence mending among family members. Decide which problems can be put off for the near future and which should be ironed out immediately. This can lessen pressure on you personally. Conditions favor making plans for a get-together next month. You may discover what you need to know simply from noticing how different loved ones are responding to one another.

26. FRIDAY. Mixed. All of your relationships are likely to be quite easygoing and agreeable on the whole. It may be necessary, however, to take more time to show others that you care about them as individuals. Because doing so comes easily to you, do not rush through the preliminaries or someone may feel that you are talking down to them. This is a favorable time for working as part of a team. You should be able to make more progress by cooperative effort than you would through working solely on your own. A social event this evening should go well and could prove useful for linking up with new friends or potential clients.

27. SATURDAY. Variable. You may be inclined to dwell on the past. Something you see, hear, or smell could remind you quite vividly of a previous experience. If it was a negative experience, try not to dwell on it too much. Matters that make a strong impact cannot always be completely forgotten, but you do have the option to put negative thoughts out of mind. There is a chance now of bumping into someone you would rather not see, perhaps when you are out shopping. If there has been stress between you, be pleasant but not overly friendly. It may be better to pretend that you do not even remember the incident or problem.

28. SUNDAY. Pleasant. Neighbors and friends are likely to be particularly cordial. If you need a favor of some kind, now is a favorable time to ask. Generally try to take life at a slower pace. You may have to go on a trip, but do not make it hard on yourself. Allow enough time so that you arrive in good spirits. If you need a bit of cheering up at the moment, a shopping expedition could be the answer. So long as you can afford to splurge a little, doing so can perk up your spirits. If you are sometimes called in to work on weekends, this could be one of the days when you have to do so at short notice.

29. MONDAY. Confusing. You are likely to be happiest if you can make time to take care of neglected tasks. The earlier part of the day is best for this. You also may need to get personal telephone calls out of the way; if you work, you should be able to make some calls while the boss is out of the office. Your family may be more demanding on your time than usual. A burden you would rather not have, such as organizing Christmas activities, may fall on your shoulders. If you have not chosen to do this, at least put up a small fight. Keep in mind that people will only attempt to impose on you if you allow them to do so.

30. TUESDAY. Fair. If there have been underlying, difficult issues left undecided in your family, they could come to a head today. Do not hesitate to speak your mind. Sometimes you can be amazed at the depth of your own feelings. Others, too, may be taken aback if you suddenly blurt out exactly what you are thinking. However, it can sometimes be the one surefire way to clear the air and achieve something positive as a result. If your energy is ebbing due to an overload of work, a change of scene might help you pick up steam. Try going for a walk at lunchtime, for example; a breath of fresh air can also do a lot to restore your perspective.

December 1999

1. WEDNESDAY. Cautious. Money matters need careful handling if you are to avoid depleting your reserve funds. You are likely to put yourself in a stronger position by saying little rather than trying to explain the smaller details of a complex situation. In a close personal relationship, it is vital to respect the confidential nature of what you are told. A contract or agreement which you are about to sign may have hidden clauses which require further explanation. Question anything you do not fully understand. An associate with subtle and creative ideas is someone you can trust to turn a situation around in your favor.

2. THURSDAY. Satisfactory. This is a useful day to make a start on your holiday shopping. You can fulfill most of your shopping needs in one trip to a large mall. You may be able to negotiate a good deal if you are buying anything in bulk. Continue to keep a watchful eye on your spending; it can be all too easy to run up a large credit card bill in a short time. You may also find yourself more easily seduced by clever salespeople who are determined to sell the latest gadget or craze. Discussions with your family should prove rewarding even if you are hashing out a difficult problem or situation.

3. FRIDAY. Changeable. This is another day when you may be tempted more than you intend. Carry only a small amount of cash, or leave the credit card with the higher spending limit at home. This should make it a lot easier to avoid impulse buying. If you are negotiating a business deal at the moment, it is in your best interests to drive a hard bargain. As a Virgo it can be difficult for you to sell yourself or to take control, but this is what you should be doing. Otherwise you are apt to come out with a deal that will not make you satisfied for very long. Be prepared to blow your own horn and strut your stuff.

4. SATURDAY. Frustrating. The inability of other people to make up their minds and commit to specific arrangements can be infuriating at the moment. Although they may have genuine reasons for this, you may feel it is necessary to issue an ultimatum. This could be the only way that you can really plan effectively. Guard against making any promise that you may not be able to fulfill, especially when other people are issuing the invitation. It is possible that work colleagues may be in touch today, keeping you talking a long time about matters which have little to do with you. Try to cut the conversation short with a promise to continue the discussion on Monday.

5. SUNDAY. Variable. You are likely to have a choice of social activities. One may involve a long-distance trip, and therefore more effort, than the other, but that is the one that is apt to turn out to be the more interesting option. Self-employed Virgos need to sort out paperwork or contact people only available on the weekend. Expect one or two distractions which interrupt your concentration and tear you away from this. It is best to spread your time and energy around since you may find it difficult to concentrate for any length of time on anything that is detailed or in depth. Keep evening plans simple and relaxing; get to bed early.

6. MONDAY. Successful. This is a positive start to the working week. Casual conversations which occur early in the day could help you elicit information which you have been trying to get for some time. You can now bring together a number of plans which have been on the back burner. Be careful about the kinds of commitments you make today. Other people may take you strictly at your word although you may only be making loose promises. A friendly get-together this evening should be quite intimate and uplifting. Try to include a neighbor who is almost a part of your family circle.

7. TUESDAY. Useful. If you are at home for a part of the day, this can be a good time for decorating and for repairs which you have been putting off. If you are trying to get negotiations concluded, make specific appointments with the people involved. There could be a flurry of activity at work. You can finish up a tedious project if your put your mind to it. This evening you may want to opt out of a social meeting in favor of relaxing at home. It should also be a good time for impromptu entertaining, perhaps inviting some friends for coffee and dessert. Keep looking ahead; let go of the past.

8. WEDNESDAY. Confusing. If you are looking for a new home, check the local newspaper. You may find a lot more options than you expect. Real estate agents who know you are looking are likely to deluge you with property details. Be ruthless in deciding which properties you will view; it is unlikely that everything you see will be suitable. It is important to be more sensitive in dealing with neighbors and relatives. Because there may be some confusion over a matter which you want to discuss, be sure to make yourself crystal clear in your initial explanation. Avoid confusing a situation by going into too many details.

9. THURSDAY. Rewarding. This promises to be an easygoing yet rewarding day with numerous opportunities to go out and to be entertained. Certain people may be starting holiday celebrations early; join in enthusiastically. Whether Christmas festivities or other celebrations, you should find that your social life picks up now. If you have been thinking about trying a new sport or hobby, this is the perfect time. For unattached Virgos, a romantic opportunity may arise this evening through a local event. Do not hesitate to make the first move, keeping your conversation on the light side.

10. FRIDAY. Mixed. A romantic attachment is moving from strength to strength. Issues which have been a problem between you can now be quite easily cleared up. You may both be prepared to make a solid commitment for the future. In the workplace all may not be smooth. There could be an argument with a difficult associate who is seeing a situation from a broader perspective than you are. If you suspect that you may be suffering from tunnel vision, it is in your best interests to put yourself in the other person's shoes. Probably you both need to adjust your outlooks slightly and find common ground so that you can work together.

11. SATURDAY. Unsettling. You may be frustrated with the attitude of someone who is not willing to go along with your plans. If you are involved with a new partner or colleague, you may be starting to discover some prime differences of approach. However, just because you have a difference of opinion, do not assume that everything will be permanently wrong between you. One argument does not have to signify the end of the relationship. It is necessary to try to be somewhat flexible in your approach. As a Virgo you yearn to have everything worked out to the tiniest detail. Sometimes, however, it pays to go with the natural flow.

12. SUNDAY. Variable. You may not be in the mood for doing household chores. However, your sense of needing to have everything in good order could be the impetus to getting those tasks done and out of the way. You are sure to feel better after a general clearing out around your home. Getting your closet in order might turn out to be quite therapeutic, especially if there is something which you are trying to get out of your mind. A family get-together could be quite special. If you have been waiting for the right moment to discuss a private matter with someone close to you, this could provide the perfect opportunity.

13. MONDAY. Good. This is a highly positive start to the work-week. At work, aim to deal with one job at a time. You need to prioritize since there could be many demands on your time. Think about the future; this is the perfect day for making long-term plans. As a Virgo you sometimes find it difficult to concentrate on anything but the details of life. Today, however, you should find it easier to see life from a broader perspective. Make an effort to be more charitable toward work colleagues. Someone who does not seem to have their mind fully focused on the job may have private concerns that are distracting them. A shoulder to lean on may help.

14. TUESDAY. Difficult. This is not the best time for trying to mix the company of friends, neighbors, and family members. However, if you have such a social arrangement already planned, go ahead. If individuals do not get along, there is no need for you to take the blame personally. If you are contemplating an impromptu get-together, aim to keep it small and intimate. If you recently became involved with a new romantic partner, do not be in too much of a hurry to escalate the relationship. You need to get to know each other better before making definite mutual plans for the future.

15. WEDNESDAY. Disquieting. Unattached Virgos anxious to meet a new partner may be in luck. Early holiday gatherings at work or in your neighborhood may be your key to meeting that special person. You could find yourself in the middle of an awkward situation involving family members. If you are taking a new friend to meet your family, do not necessarily expect everyone to take an instant liking to each other. Although you naturally hope for this, someone is likely to say just the wrong thing at the wrong time. Your best bet is to be supportive and do whatever you can to smooth things over. Maintain a sense of humor no matter what develops.

16. THURSDAY. Mixed. The responsibilities of your home and family life may be weighing heavily on you. You may have to take time off from work to sort out a difficulty. Life in the workplace is apt to be quite busy; it is possible that you have to cover for an absent colleague. What you cannot do today is be in two places at the same time. If there is an opportunity to delegate some of your work to a colleague, do so. The up side of having to put in more time at work could be that you receive a bonus or overtime pay just when you need it most. Select the best of available options.

17. FRIDAY. Buoyant. You can make excellent progress with a joint venture. If you have been waiting for confirmation of an impending deal, it should come now. However, take nothing for granted. Things are likely to change by the hour or minute, but the basic arrangement or agreement should be set firmly in place today. It is unlikely that other parties will go back on their word no matter how the details get worked out in the end. You should find it easier to handle home-based responsibilities this evening, with family members available to share the tasks and make light work of them.

18. SATURDAY. Misleading. Although you should be cautious about chastising someone for their recent bad behavior, you need to find the courage to say something in order not to condone it. Sticking your head in the sand is unlikely to solve anything and will probably only prolong the inevitable confrontation. Important developments are likely in relation to a contract under negotiation. It may seem as though everything suddenly comes together. Home and family life should be especially rewarding this evening. Be careful, however, in discussing religion or politics. Someone's prejudice may turn out to be their driving force.

19. SUNDAY. Difficult. You may bump into someone you usually find hard to tolerate. Be prepared for an intellectual discussion which does not really interest you. Also avoid gossipy neighbors. Your best bet is to give these people a wide berth, or at least cut your conversation short. If you need to produce written work, you could find it hard just making a start. Once you can get over that, however, you should make good progress. It may be helpful to work in the library so that you are not distracted by visitors or telephone calls. Nothing should be taken for granted in a new friendship or romance. If you break a date, you may be seen as breaking off the relationship.

244 / VIRGO—DECEMBER 1999

20. MONDAY. Rewarding. You have good reason to pat yourself on the back and even boast a little about your current achievements. In addition, chances are that your results speak for themselves. There could be some kind of reward or acknowledgment coming your way. Today should be fairly easy, with much going your way. There may be an unexpected yet pleasant invitation. Someone could even be in the mood to throw a surprise party. Be confident that you will be able to tie up important outstanding work before the holiday celebrations are fully under way. Cooperation is yours for the asking.

21. TUESDAY. Disquieting. This can be a productive day in the workplace if you are willing to come to grips with a long-standing problem. With Christmas so near, you may not feel that you have the energy to devote to unraveling difficult problems. However, if you can muster a little enthusiasm, you should be able to put one huge problem behind you once and for all. Work superiors may apply extra pressure just when you need to take care of a personal matter. Try to keep cool and calm. If you deal with one issue at a time, you can do all that is expected of you and keep everyone happy.

22. WEDNESDAY. Variable. The pressures that kept you hopping yesterday are likely to lift today. The boss or another higher-up finally understands that you only have one pair of hands. Requests you made some time ago for updated equipment or extra assistance may now be granted. Even though Christmas is just around the corner and people are geared to festive activity, this is still a propitious day for a job interview or promotion discussion. As a result of the festive atmosphere, prospective employers may actually be more affable and easy to talk to. It is not smart to try to mix friendship and romance this evening.

23. THURSDAY. Happy. Any gathering involving friends is likely to be good fun. For Virgo professionals, this is an excellent day for entertaining valued clients. You may pick up more information in a restaurant than at all those previous boardroom discussions throughout the year. To make a special personal dream come true, you may have to travel farther afield than usual. A group night out is sure to be memorable. For Virgos who are romantically unattached, someone interesting may be a guest at a social gathering and make it a point to meet you.

24. FRIDAY. Satisfactory. On the whole this should be a satisfying end to the working week. Do not be too disappointed if you cannot tie up every single problem before the holiday. If you still need to purchase gifts, a last-minute shopping trip should be quite successful. Going out with friends or colleagues is the perfect way to celebrate. If you intend to drive, however, be careful about how much you drink. Enlist the help of family members to finish up gift wrapping or to help with some holiday cooking in advance. Be generous in giving a donation to a worthy charity on this joyful Christmas Eve.

25. SATURDAY. Merry Christmas! This may turn out to be a quieter Christmas than you expect. Relatives who would have a long way to travel to be with you may cancel out at the last minute. With fewer people around, there should be less for you to do. If you are feeling tired from having worked so hard to get tasks finished during the week, enjoy the chance for a day of rest. Close-knit family members are likely to be in touch if you are not spending the day with them. Catch up on all their news despite long-distance phone charges; consider the call a gift to yourself.

26. SUNDAY. Pleasant. Take a back seat today. Let other people do the entertaining. Your social activities should be pleasant, so long as you do not have to mix too much with colleagues. Put the working world well behind you this weekend. Neighbors who are intent on providing a good time may invite you to a noisy party. If it is really not your choice, you can use the excuse of tiredness and slip away quietly without anyone objecting too much or probably even noticing. You may have the sense of finally putting a chapter of your life behind you and being ready and willing for a new start.

27. MONDAY. Challenging. You should be feeling especially positive about all that is ahead of you. This is an ideal day for focusing on your main objectives for the future. If you go out socially, you are likely to be the center of a lot of attention. You are in the mood to enjoy the limelight now that you have had a few days of rest. For unattached Virgo men and women in particular, this could be the key day for meeting someone special. Try not to spend a lot of time at home. A walk should be invigorating. If you are working today, you should make excellent, fast progress and a lasting impression on higher-ups.

28. TUESDAY. Useful. Spend some time contemplating how you can achieve your dream in the future. Through joint efforts you may be able to make the greatest progress. You may instinctively feel that someone who comes into your life now is the right person to team up with. Trust your inner voice. If some criticism is being leveled at you, you may want to prove yourself to family members or colleagues. Try not to let what other people think matter too much to you. Now is the time to maintain your self-esteem and look to the future with renewed confidence. You have a lot to look forward to and a lot to offer.

29. WEDNESDAY. Fair. Do only what is necessary today. Money could be in short supply after the expensive holiday period. It could become obvious that you or another family member, perhaps a child, needs new clothing or shoes. You do not have to purchase everything all at once, however. It is a good idea to put together a long-term budget, which will help you spread the costs. It is also possible that you can pick up a few useful items in the sales which have already started. You may have to cover any significant expenses with your credit card, but try to pay it off in full as soon as possible.

30. THURSDAY. Manageable. If yesterday you were concerned and worried about money matters, today could give you a whole new perspective. There is likely to be a pleasant surprise or bonus affecting your finances. Or an investment made some time ago may finally begin to pay off even if you did not expect it to be a money-maker this year. If there is something important which you need to buy for your home, it might be possible to borrow it from a family member or trade for it with a friend or neighbor. If the item will benefit two of you, it is likely that you can arrange to share the expense.

31. FRIDAY. Tricky. With all the sales going on now, it can be tempting to spend beyond your means. Keep in mind that sales are intended to get you to spend, although the emphasis may appear to be on saving you money. Besides, buying at sales may cause you to make compromises that you might otherwise not be willing to make. It might be a lot more rewarding to set your sights on an item you really want to own, then come up with a long-term budget to pay for it. A friendly social gathering is the best way of bringing in the New Year. Consider staying overnight if you do not want to travel in the wee hours.

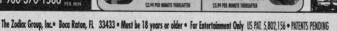

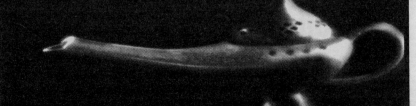